Recollecting from the Past

MUSIC / CULTURE

A series from Wesleyan University Press

Edited by George Lipsitz, Susan McClary, and Robert Walser

Published titles

RON EMOFF

Recollecting from the Past

MUSICAL PRACTICE AND SPIRIT

POSSESSION ON THE EAST COAST

OF MADAGASCAR

WESLEYAN UNIVERSITY PRESS

Middletown, Connecticut

Published by Wesleyan University Press, Middletown, CT 06459
© 2002 by Ron Emoff
Printed in the United States of America

5 4 3 2 1

Library of Congress Cataloging-in-Publication Data

Emoff, Ron.
  Recollecting from the past : musical practice and spirit possession on
the east coast of Madagascar / Ron Emoff.
    p.   cm.—(Music/culture)
  Includes bibliographical references (p.) and index.
  ISBN 0–8195–6499–0 (cloth : alk. paper)—ISBN 0–8195–6500–8 (paper : alk. paper)
  1. Folk music—Madagascar—Toamasina (Province)—History and criticism.
2. Betsimisaraka (Malagasy people)—Toamasina (Province)—Music. 3. Antandroy
(Malagasy people)—Toamasina (Province)—Music. 4. Betsimisaraka (Malagasy
people)—Toamasina (Province)—Rites and ceremonies. 5. Antandroy (Malagasy
people)—Toamasina (Province)—Rites and ceremonies. 6. Spirit possession—
Madagascar—Toamasina (Province) 7. Ancestor worship—Madagascar—
Toamasina (Province) 8. Toamasina (Madagascar: Province)—Religious life and
customs. I. Title. II. Series.
ML3760 .E47 2001
306'.09691—dc21   2001005368

For my father

Contents

∽

Illustrations

～

Acknowledgments

꜠

My fieldwork in Madagascar was facilitated at every stage by the kindness and generosity of Malagasy friends and acquaintances. In the first months innumerable people in the Tamatave region sheltered me, guided me to musicians and to *tromba* adherents, and patiently practiced speaking in Malagasy with me. For this last gift, I especially recall all the children in Tamatave who spent countless hours walking with me in the Indian Ocean surf or strolling through the *bazary be,* the large market, playfully talking and joking in Malagasy.

In Tamatave-ville, Velomaro, a powerful spiritualist, and his wife, Delphine, warmly welcomed me into their tromba community as well as into their daily lives. Rasoanirina Detty, Marie Yvonne, Honorine, and Andréa, all powerful Betsimisaraka *tromba* mediums there, also invited me into their spiritual practices and homes. Roger Jean Louis, soft-spoken caretaker of the president's residence in Tamatave, taught me to play Betsimisaraka ceremonial dance music, called *basesa,* on the accordion. Rather than explaining Betsimisaraka customs, Roger and his large family took me through them experientially over time. Jily, Thierry, Dina, and Tsiariagna, among many other musicians in the Tamatave countryside, helped me get into the groove of Betsimisaraka music. Dida, who owned a "quincaillerie" and small music studio in Tamatave-ville, introduced me into several music scenes there and nurtured an ongoing dialogue with me about musical performance and aesthetics, among other things.

One day early in my stay in Madagascar a young woman, Botomamo Kiki, called me over to the stall at which she was working at the *bazary* to chat. Kiki was fluent and articulate in French as well as in several Malagasy dialects and graciously offered to accompany me in these early days to speak for and with me before I was able to converse fluently in Malagasy. I thank Kiki for her patience, her devotion to my (our) research, and her open-mindedness, and for occasionally singing a Johnny Clegg or Bruce Springsteen song.

I fondly recollect all the late nights at the *bazary be* in Tamatave-ville selling cigarettes and peanuts with Velontsoa's wife, Mendoe, her small children asleep on my lap. Mendoe taught me a great deal about Antandroy ways and much more. She always showed immense generosity, diligence, and courage in the face of vast adversity. I will always warmly remember the early-morning piece of baguette (with coconut candy inside) and tea (hot water with sweetened condensed milk) she would prepare for me, things that would have been better suited for her own hungry children.

In the capital of Madagascar, Antananarivo, Mireille Rakotomalala, then a governmental deputy and Elie Rajaonarison, then secretary to the minister of culture, enthusiastically supported my project and offered critical suggestions, feedback, and invaluable procedural assistance.

Gerard Béhague, Steve Feld, Katie Stewart, and Robert Fernea sent encouragement, suggestions, and stories from back in the States, another world, which became more difficult to imagine the longer I was in Madagascar. I especially wish to thank Gerard Béhague (my dissertation supervisor), Steve Feld, Katie Stewart, and Veit Erlmann for their interactions with me over the years—their inspiration fuels each page of this writing. Michael Lambek and Jennifer Cole offered valuable suggestions on chapters of this book, in addition to sharing their own experiences of performing ethnographic work in Madagascar. I am grateful to my friends and partners in graduate school—Kathleen O'Connor, Eriko Kobayashi, David Henderson, Pete Kvetko—for all the laughs, Korean food, afternoons at the batting cages, and other diversions along the way. My mother, Selma Emoff, sent scores of cheerful letters to Madagascar. I especially thank my father, Al Emoff, who saw me through all these years of schooling and whose diligence and integrity have been a constant inspiration to me.

I gratefully acknowledge the Fulbright IIE and Wenner-Gren Foundation for anthropological research grants and the Wenner-Gren Richard Carley Hunt Fellowship, which have been invaluable to this research and writing. I also sincerely thank Ronald Crutcher and Michael Tusa, directors at different times of the School of Music, University of Texas at Austin, for granting me Visiting Scholar appointments while I was working on this book and greatly facilitating its writing.

In addition to all the Betsimisaraka and Antandroy with whom I lived and worked in the Tamatave region, I recall Vinelo, Velontsoa, Magnampy Soa, and Very Soa, four brilliant Antandroy musicians, devoted spiritualists, patient and generous teachers, and great friends, who in the face of immense daily adversity literally kept the faith, in part through their exquisite virtuosic musical/spiritual performance practices. *Ho an'ny havakô gasy–hipetraka foagna amin'ny fôko 'nareô jiaby.*

March 2001   R. E.

Some Preliminary Notes on Language and Pronunciation

∽

Distinctions between "dialects" of the Malagasy language rely largely upon variances in vowel or consonant enunciation and regional terminology. In the Merina dialect from the central Haut Plateau region, the letter "o" is pronounced like the "u" in "true." Among northern Betsimisaraka on the east coast, the letter "o" is sometimes pronounced as in the Merina dialect, but depending upon its position in a word or phrase, it also may be pronounced /ô/, as in the French word "non." The pronunciation of *tromba* is similar in both dialects, but that of *haiko* (haikô among Betsimisaraka) differs significantly.

Fairly universal vowel sounds in Madagascar are "e" like the French accent aigu /é/; "a" and "i" also resemble French pronunciations, as in "ch*a*t" and "fin*i*," respectively. Most often no "u" is written in Malagasy, nor are "c," "q," "w," or "x" used in writing. Depending on how quickly it is pronounced and the context in which it is used, /ai/ can either sound like "high" in English, or like the French /é/. In similar fashion, /ao/ can sound like "*ou*ch" or like "owe" in English. When preceded by a consonant in word final position, the letter "y" is for the most part elided, similar, for instance, to the more-felt-than-heard final "e" in the French word "livre." When in word final position, the vowels "a" and "o" (when not preceded by another vowel) are also generally elided. The word final "e" in Malagasy usually is not elided but retains its /é/ value, often slightly nasalized, as in *arab*e (road). In Antandroy speech, though, a word final "e" can be pronounced somewhere between the French vowels /é/ and /i/. There is much greater occurrence of the word final vowel "e" in Antandroy speech than in that of Merina or Betsimisaraka.

Throughout Madagascar, /tr/ is usually pronounced something like "tchr." Similarly, the pronunciation of /dr/ sounds like "dchr." Generally, /j/ is pronounced "dz," and /g/ is only hard, as in "green." When not preceded by a consonant, /r/ is usually rolled. In the Tamatave area in which I worked, the letter "n" has two possible values. Depending on its position in a word or phrase, it might be the velar nasal *eng*, as in "si*ng*er," or it can be pronounced as in "*n*ice" in English. I will use the symbol /gn/ to represent the *eng* phoneme (which in my experience did not occur in the Merina dialect of the Malagasy language). I've chosen this orthography because of the way this sound was written by Malagasy on the east coast; in some other literature on Madagascar, though, this velar nasal consonant has been represented as /ñ/.

The pronunciation of /s/ is more palatal than the alveolar fricative "s" in English but not as extreme as the alveo-palatal fricative "sh" in "ship." The palatal intensity of /s/ in Madagascar is more pronounced in the Merina dialect than in coastal ones.

Syllabic stress can change meaning. For instance, *làlana* means "road" or "path," while *lalàna* means "law." Plurality of object is not marked in Malagasy; thus, Malagasy terms in this writing can shift between referring to either the singular or plural.

"Malagasy" is an adjective that refers to the people of Madagascar, to their language, or to that which is associated with Madagascar. In the Malagasy language, this adjective becomes *gasy*, as in *olona gasy* (Malagasy person or people). Some Malagasy, usually Merina from the capital, found the French adjective *malgache* to be objectionable—they thought that it too closely sounded like *mal gâché* (*gâché* meaning spoiled or wasted). French acquaintances of mine in Madagascar did on frequent occasion criticize Malagasy for being childlike and irresponsible, incapable of properly taking care of themselves. Such a criticism voices current though historically contiguous European condescension, racism, and paternalism in Madagascar. It also echoes a more common colonialist impression that Africans in general are childlike and lazy (see, for one, Thomas 1994).

Recollecting from the Past

CHAPTER ONE

Introductions

᙮

This book is an attempt to move closer to a world of music and devotion in Madagascar, to begin to convey a performative aesthetics and a way of recollecting the past there. Throughout the east coast region of Tamatave—as well as the rest of Madagascar—Malagasy people practice *tromba* possession, in which powerful Malagasy ancestral spirits are (re)called into the present to heal illness, resolve disputes, offer advice, alleviate daily problems, and thus empower the present in various ways. In evoking distant personalities and pasts, *tromba* ceremonies are occasions for the emergence of collective as well as personal recollection. Malagasy dramatically interpret, critique, and alter varied pasts in recalling them in these ceremonies, often in order to make sense of the present. Telling histories—more precisely, dramatizing or enacting them—not only preserves and transmits the past in Tamatave, it provides a means of creatively incorporating the past into the present, or placing the present back into the past. Processes of incorporation themselves become aesthetic components in *tromba* ceremony.[1]

For spirits to become embodied in Tamatave, musical performance is most often required. Sound production breaks silence with spirits, alerting them that they are needed in the present. It appeases, entertains, and invigorates them feelingfully. Musical materials, genres, and performances themselves are also vital tools for narrating on varied pasts, for recalling and reorienting these pasts in *tromba* ceremony. One goal of this book is to transfer a feel for an east coast Malagasy aesthetics that guides both musical practice and ceremonial recollection from the past, the latter an inextricable facet of much performance practice in Tamatave. Thus, it will not do to simply describe, transcribe, replay, or analyze on paper musical and spiritual expression in Tamatave. This book represents an effort to translate into writing some musical and other performative tenets crucial to spirit practice and more in Tamatave. As translation, this book is intended not as copy but as *echo* of an original (Benjamin 1968; also Erlmann 1996: xvi). This writing is not only *about* Malagasy performance practices, it is in part an attempt to replicate expressive components of these practices, to take in and pass on some particular ways with which east coast Malagasy express themselves and recollect their pasts.

✒

The word *tromba* has several meanings. It sometimes denotes the royal ancestral spirit by which the medium is possessed, though it can also refer to an array of other non-royal spirits. *Tromba* refers as well to the possession ceremony itself. For instance, it is commonly said on the east coast, "Hisy *tromba* maraina," which means "there will be a *tromba* ceremony tomorrow." *Tromba* also can refer to the medium who is inhabited by the spirit. In a more general sense, *tromba* is used to denote the particular sacred belief system of spirit possession practitioners in Madagascar. For those Malagasy who neither revere nor practice *tromba* (many Christian Malagasy, for example), the term can have pejorative, even evil connotations.

✒

From overhead at 5 A.M. the Ivato airport on the outskirts of Antananarivo, the capital of Madagascar, glowed with the imprint of a swirling orange-red sky. This spectacular new hue of blazing orange played tricks with shadows lurking in the terminal's crevices. The building was being renovated at the time, yet in comparison to Roissy in Paris, it appeared barnlike and pleasantly simple, rising out of the nearby rice fields and zébu grazing grounds.

The last few days had been ones of insularity and close quarters—two full days of in-flight travel separated by a twenty-four-hour stopover in Paris. A small room in Montmartre afforded a last glimpse for a while of several familiar things—carpeting, full-length mirrors, porcelain, remote control. Upon landing in Madagascar, the brilliant sky, the terminal and runway resting in an expanse of terrain dotted with oxen, all engendered an opening up of space, a spilling out onto a Malagasy landscape beyond the spatial bounds delimited by airplane travel and the small Montmartre sleeping room. Complementing the sense of spatial ouverture at the Ivato airport was a sense of the compression or perhaps collapsing of time—somewhere in the last days of travel, nine hours of clock time had evaporated. These notable spatial and temporal experiences were as though portents, of different orderings of time and place, which would be so significant in Madagascar.

In the taxi approaching central Antananarivo the early morning air gave off an undefinable odor, learned later to be a mixture of the bittersweet smell of burning hardwood for cooking, exhaust from myriad leaded-gasoline-burning automobiles, and open sewers unable to contain the odor of decaying human waste. A morning earlier in Paris a trio of young musicians had been playing accordion, guitar, and bass in the street while people shopped at open-air stands or drank coffee in cafés. The combining odor of Antananarivo intensified feelings of (apparent) disjunction between this new Malagasy world and that of stylishly garbed Parisians taking in the sweet smell of fruitstands and the vapor of strong coffee steeping in Montmartre (coffee was brought to Madagascar by French colonials, along with a system of forced labor to farm it). And adding to this sense of disjunction, the recall of French shoppers overhearing "valses" played in the street on a diatonic accordion (an instrument that was brought to Madagascar by Europeans early in the twentieth century). Still fresh recollections of early-morning Paris transformed dauntingly into an inescapable mixture of subsistence, pollution, and putrefaction in the Antananarivo morning. This triad of urban process, subsistence/pollution/putrefaction, sadly was given shape in the dirty Antananarivo streets by equally dirty, sometimes deformed children in torn blackened rags, begging for change or for sakafo *(food). These children seemed like a breathing agglomeration of the Antananarivo landscape, a very embodiment of the fouled streets that seeped up to soil them and the acrid, unforgettable city scents that enshrouded and clung to them.*

꿍

This personal prelude is offered neither to exemplify nor advocate the expression of reflexive voice in the writing of ethnography. Rather, I have begun to muse upon Johannes Fabian's apprehension that ethnographies can be questionable representations unless they attempt to show their own genesis (1990: xiv). I have then combined with Fabian's caution a Malagasy fondness for *maresaka*, a complex sound, performative, interactional, and historical aesthetic in Madagascar. *Maresaka* means in part good talk; it is a component of the Malagasy practice of making introductions, of opening discursive encounters with long formulaic strands of friendly talk. These introductions, often implemented by the question "Inona ny maresaka?," (literally "What's new?") usually include information about one's relatives or where one has been recently, though these things would be expressed only after the proper response, "Tsy misy," or "Nothing's new." Some Malagasy on the east coast of the island even sometimes greet one another with "Talilio ka!" which asks in part what one remembers.

Malagasy ceremonies on the east coast themselves are usually introduced and opened with a formulaic past-invoking speech, a *kabary*. This is often a dialogic speech event performed between two groups of elders and addressed to both living participants and to the *razana,* the collective of ancestral spirits. Another daily greeting common on the east coast is "Akory kabaro?" which translates roughly as "What's the word?" *Kabary,* here in the form of a sort of argot, stands again essentially for good talk in everyday discourse, yet it also implies communicative contact with ancestral spirits—good talk among the living is also evocative of and of interest to these spirits. Thus daily as well as ceremonial introductions among Malagasy on the east coast of Madagascar commonly involve verbalizing about kinship and ancestral relationships. These introductions are imbued with a poetics of recollecting and voicing sometimes individual and sometimes collective pasts.

Tromba ceremony among east coast Malagasy draws upon a confluence of individual experience with *remembering that* something took place in the past (Casey 1987). Multitemporal recollections of Montmartre and Antananarivo presented above suggest such a confluence. The sound of an accordion in the Paris street sparks a memory of accordions being introduced colonially much earlier in Madagascar; the scent of coffee recalls a history of forced labor in Madagascar. Constructions of history in *tromba* ceremony also arise from combinations of varied modes of experiencing and recollecting. Physical sensations of the moment combine with one's own personal recall of certain events, as well as with collective remembering or imagining that certain distant pasts occurred, though in such remembering these past events themselves become embodied and real in *tromba* ceremony. For instance, hardwood incense, *emboka,* is burned to appeal to and lure ancestral spirits into the present, as well as to create a mood among ceremonial participants of reverence for and longing to commune with these spirits. The scent of burning *emboka* also evokes more individual recollections among *tromba-istes,* of other *tromba* ceremonies, of other people and places from their more recent pasts. Sometimes specific sensations thus act as referents that cross over or enmesh together distinct temporal realms. Personal recall also plays into *tromba* ceremony as mediums commonly become possessed by spirits that are modeled after their own individual experiences and pasts. Collectively remembering (or imagining) that certain pasts took place allows personalities of past royalty, colonial officials, and others to enter into a ceremonial event to empower and reorder the present. Such complex ceremonial recall, at once individual, collective, and imagined, is often cued by and encoded in musical performance. For example, certain musical instruments (accordions, for instance), materials, and rhythmic combinations used in *tromba* ceremony can infuse memory or imagination of the colonial era into this practice.

Depictions of my own still vivid recollections of arriving in Madagascar persist and return here as an introduction to another sort of discursive present, represented in and by this book. By recalling in words the lucid and sensual first feel of the space of Antananarivo, its scents, its moods, I attempt to approach or imitate in this written form some of the sensual and discursive elements of the Malagasy aesthetic of *maresaka*, as well as the introductory *kabary* vital to most Malagasy ceremonies. One means of beginning to bridge representational gaps between Selves and Others in writing might effectively arise from attempting to immerse one's own ethnographic writing in the very aesthetics and practices of other people, to allow ethnography to be sensitive to and even take on the shape of other principles of expressive articulation. Kathleen Stewart (1996), for one, effectively weaves local narrative practices into her own theoretical interpretations of such practices, not only illustrating an Other "cultural poetics" from the coal camps of West Virginia but creating a unique written cultural poetics, itself a combination of Self and Other. Critically questioning constructions of "marginality" involving Meratus Dayak people in South Kalimantan, Indonesia, Anna Lowenhaupt Tsing exclaims, "The theoretical edge . . . lies as much in how the story is told as it does in its conclusion" (1993: 32).

An endeavor to ethnographically emulate the unique performative practices and aesthetics of other people might well provide a means of "adopting a poetics of implication and entanglement against a poetics of purity and transcendence" (K. Stewart 1996: 23) of one's own. I should emphasize, however, that while this book is an attempt to voice some qualities of the Malagasy aesthetic of *maresaka*, the actual effectiveness of *maresaka* among Malagasy people is usually dependent upon the hearing or producing of sound, along with the experience of social interaction—one reason that my own written form here cannot create a complete *maresaka*.

Ethnographic texts, even reflexive ones, sometimes sound much like an omnipotent claim of possession over Other cultural truths. In a year or two's time a researcher supposedly has acquired ample cultural knowledge to compile an authoritative text on Others, who themselves have spent lifetimes or good portions of them acquiring whatever is passed on about them in ethnographies. Such author-ization occurs, for instance, in reductive statements about *the* Merina conducting oratory or *the* Antandroy dancing over their dead. Michael Herzfeld has recently observed that "scholars have certainly played an important role in the development of modern nationalism through their authoritative control over the conceptualization of culture. More than that, they have in a sense been the agents of the conversion of cultural data into natural truths" (1997: 68). With scholars mostly from and in "the West" conceptualizing prevalent cultural truths about distant people and places, what of the potential for neglecting to notice other modes of truth-making in these places? These other truths might even be more about unique *ways* of construing what is believable or valuable than about confirming cultural data.

As media for the construction of our own naturalizing truths, criticism and analysis, for instance, emerge in the West commonly as literary genres, distinct and distanced from the actual processes of practice or performance they might oversee. Modes of criticism and analysis in other parts of the world can be overshadowed or displaced, especially if reflection, interpretation, and analysis in other places are not emergent primarily in writing. These and other intellectual processes in distant places often are not separated conceptually from practice and performance, rather they are emergent through, integrated throughout, and inextricable from them. In terms at least of *how* they are expressed, Western academic cultural truths, conveyed in literature that would naturalize other people and places, can be conceptually removed from or lifted above the very other extraliterary modes of truth-expressing they try to capture.[2]

This book is not an edict by which one can now comprehend in a totalizing sense different Malagasy worlds somehow coeval or parallel with others. These are my own perceptions and experiences of a limited passage of research time and of the ever-fluid fields of experience, knowledge, and sentiment of specific Malagasy people. These fields themselves spanned and encompassed much more than the short time that I have been able to spend in Madagascar. When referring to specific events that occurred while I was there, I have written in the past tense. Ethnographic authority, of course, does not result simply from writing in the ethnographic present. I hope that use of the past tense will underscore that it is precisely the limited time period I spent in Madagascar that I am discussing. With use of the past tense I am also implicating the mutability of daily life on the east coast of Madagascar. Frequent serious difficulties such as cyclones, illness, economic instability and inequity, and much more, all sadly nullify any comfort in knowing that Malagasy friends are still carrying on in an ethnographic present as when I was with them. Letters I have received substantiate that the same people, now several years later, are not doing the same things in the same places. The past tense conveys as well, at least to me, my own dis-ease once back in the nervous system of the United States, at being separated from my Malagasy friends and from *tromba* practice.

I have struggled with how to go about giving agency and literary life to my Malagasy friends through this writing. The fact that these things need to be *given* seems immediately politicized and problematic. Long strands of translated Malagasy talk might complicate this difficulty in at least two ways: first, many musical matters were not discursively explained to me in great elaboration. Second, long translations might serve, erroneously, to make "them" seem or sound more like "us" (or even to make "me" seem more like "them"). When working with people in another language, unique modes of discursive style, poetics, and humor, among other things, clearly are difficult to transmit in translation. The problem is only intensified when attempting to write up musical performance. I certainly am not the first to ponder how or if one can effectively transfer sound experience into discourse. Without negating the value of attempting to create suitable poetically accurate translations, I am apprehensive nonetheless about the complex dynamics of "agentifying" distant others, and am wary that "by giving voice to those typically without 'agency,' we may find that our notion of agency is essentially and particularistically 'our own'—and often alien to the culture of subalternity we are attempting to study" (Dirks, Eley, and Ortner 1994: 38). Can one really equalize differentials of power and privilege in writing up encounters with Others—an equalization that might be misrepresentative or ephemeral? Should one simply own up to such differences?

I hardly mean to do away with reflexive ethnography or the importance of varied issues in the representation of real people. Rather I mean to assess these issues carefully and critically and to strive toward a method of representing Malagasy people in Tamatave, their practices and beliefs, in a manner close or similar to the ways in which these same people represent things. Foremost, I have tried to adhere in this writing to principles of *maresaka*, which call for combining fragments of different things into meaningful wholes, evoking and integrating varied pasts, as well as uncovering "the truth" sometimes only after much experience, interaction, and interpretation. I will return often throughout this book to *maresaka*, an aesthetic that greatly informs and imbues sound production and consumption on the east coast of Madagascar. *Maresaka* inevitably extends into a historicized sense of Malagasy-ness itself, dependent upon principles of fragmentation, combination, and incorporation.

Recalling the Past

Invoking revered ancestral spirits among Malagasy in Tamatave involves *recollecting*—in other words, reorganizing and extracting from varied pasts to construct *through enactment* meaningful presents. These pasts are not usually recollected in or as sequential temporal continuities but as combined fragments of varied time periods, places, and personalities. In regard to Sakalava people in the northwest of Madagascar, Michael Lambek has recently observed:

The spirits juxtapose distinct historical epochs. The juxtaposition is a part of their very constitution, for they emerge through contrasting signifiers of comportment, clothing, furniture, drink, dialect, and so on. What is still more significant, the space of performance enables the simultaneous display of successive temporalities. Sakalava history is thus additive in that, in principle, later generations do not displace earlier ones but perdure alongside them. (1998: 108)

In *tromba* ceremonies on the east coast as well, the spirit of an eighteenth-century Sakalava king (from the north), for instance, and the spirit of a Betsimisaraka (from the east coast) who died only several years earlier might both come into the same moment. Thus, (fragments of) different times and places could overlap concurrently, to frame a present moment while perhaps simultaneously engaging a distant past moment of action as well.

Musical performance not only engenders or empowers collective recollection among varied participants in a *tromba* ceremony, it transforms the past itself into something alive and palpable. Thus, for instance, the varied sounds of an accordion in ceremonial combination with other phenomena might bring into the present *tromba* ceremony elements of a colonial *bal,* or dance, opening up this (once) foreign performative genre as a source of power with which to appease and influence Malagasy ancestral spirits. Complex rhythmic, melodic, and harmonic textures, passionate interplay between instrumentalists, and an interconnective tripartite sense of rhythm, among other performative elements (explained in chap. 3) all add to temporal and spatial reorderings of the present among spirit mediums and other ceremonial participants. Musical performance facilitates the actual evanescence of temporal delimitations between past, present, and future during *tromba* ceremony, as it reorders the feel for the passing of present time in bringing up past times and events.

In *tromba* practice east coast Malagasy call upon their ancestors to heal and to advise them; to address and negotiate problems of everyday life, such as illness and other hardships; and to performatively make sense of a world often impeded by material poverty, illness, and environmental devastation. *Tromba* spirit possession ceremony is not only a devotional practice but also an active expressive event in which Malagasy comment dramatically, thus often metaphorically, upon their pasts. In these ceremonies, Malagasy also can celebrate their present, difficult as it often is.

Recollecting in *tromba* ceremony means refiguring and reconstructing with other modes of power. This is often played out musically through the alteration and incorporation of what had been varied foreign musical principles, instruments, forms, and even nonmusical materials into Malagasy spiritual practices. Musical performance in *tromba* ceremony itself provides a symbolic interpretive system with which to rework various pasts. Such musical refigurings of the past can implicate colonial presence and pressure upon Malagasy, as well as the ingenious ways in which Malagasy have not only coped with foreign intrusion but have turned things left over by colonialism into valuable components of their own practices. Malagasy reevaluations of foreign power in *tromba* ceremony led me inevitably to assess the efficacy or veridicality of conceptualizing a rigid structural dichotomy between "dominant colonizer" and "oppressed subject" in Madagascar. Such a dichotomy is often implicit in or overtly guiding interpretations of colonial and postcolonial situations. Rather, I favored becoming attuned to the room to maneuver that Malagasy create in between these endpoints (Chambers 1991). I was also led to question the authority of some resistance theories as they have been applied more broadly throughout Africa. These matters are taken up in chap. 7.

Doing as Knowing

Ka tsisy tromba ampitany any aminao? Mampalahelo izany . . . dia tsisy mosika tsara ampitany? (So there's no *tromba* where you're from? That's sad . . . then there's no good music there?) —Velontsoa, Malagasy friend, March 23, 1994

Daily experience became crucial to acquiring cultural knowledge in Tamatave. While this might seem to go without saying, experience was particularly vital on the east coast of Madagascar, in part since Malagasy there did not express their perspectives on some matters in direct or explicit verbal communications. Elinor Ochs Keenan has written of a general Malagasy discursive aesthetic of communicative indirectness and non-aggressiveness (1973, 1974). My own early encounters with people in the Tamatave region supported Keenan's observations on Malagasy discursive preferences. Speaking into a microphone seemed to make Malagasy uncomfortable. First attempts to ask direct questions in an interview-like setting were awkward and often sent the interviewee off on a storied tangent. The passing on of knowledge was usually more implicitly and interactionally encoded in performative settings, both within and outside ceremonial practice. For instance, I learned to play *valiha*, a Malagasy stringed instrument, from sitting night after night in one-room houses with Malagasy friends, simply listening to them play while feeling the music pass through bamboo slat floors, which were flexible and thus readily set into vibration.

Eventually, I was passed a *kaiamba* shaker and told only "Ao!" (There, do it!) Proper manipulation of the *kaiamba* was quite difficult and required much practical experience. These musicians knew that familiarity with the *kaiamba's* complex rhythm, often attuned to no particular "beat" of the *valiha,* came only from *feeling,* not knowing. Eventually, only after gaining some proficiency with *kaiamba,* the *valiha* was passed to me with the same instruction only, "Ao!"

This mode of teaching was not based upon an expectation that exact musical phrases and formulae be mimetically replicated, which might explain in part why *valiha* players each seemed to have such distinct performative styles. Rather, it was necessary for each musician to acquire the ability to perform certain recognizable formulaic *valiha* motives, though there was much room for creativity in one's own personal articulation of these often replicated phrases or melodies. Indeed, within these replicated structures, skilled melodic and rhythmic improvisations were crucial to the dénouement and meaningfulness of *tromba* ceremony. Musical learning thus was a transformational process, dependent upon imaginative musical interpretations and choices made by each musician. It seemed that I as well was expected to develop similar interpretive performance skills.

As the sense of Malagasy stories and histories in *tromba* practice most often rely upon enactment, engagement, and experience, these stories and histories usually are not texted in or by any one particular version. They, like musical compositions, are also actively interpretable and fluid. Among Malagasy on the east coast, oral tradition does not necessarily fix events, people, or occasions comfortably in a static mythic past. Rather these traditions often disrupt the past and the present into which it is brought. For example, sometimes even more recent, foreign personalities appear as *tromba* spirits. Appearances by such foreign personalities—even Malagasy ancestral spirits are in some sense foreign to east coast spirit mediums—bring ceremonial participants into contact with the goings-on of outside worlds, allowing Malagasy to position themselves within a global ecumene both past and present.

The significance of evoking the past on the east coast of Madagascar often is not lodged as much in the content of historical data itself as it is embodied in the *way* that pasts are remembered and enacted (see also Lambek 1998). Social and spiritual interaction themselves are often more important to many Malagasy than the reconstructing of incontrovertible accounts of past personalities and deeds. Significance is not simply symbolically emergent in performance, it is interpretable, negotiable, and reactive within it. As Edward Schieffelin suggests, for Kaluli in Papua New Guinea, meaning itself in Madagascar is a product of its own sociability:

. . . symbols are effective less because they communicate meaning (though this is also important) than because, through performance, meanings are formulated in a social rather than cognitive space, and the participants are engaged with the symbols in the interactional creation of a performance reality, rather than merely being informed by them as knowers. (Schieffelin 1985: 707)

My perceptions and interpretations of events on the east coast of Madagascar, then, relied largely upon performance, itself a historical and historicizing proceeding through which pasts could be experienced, sensed, and played with, beyond being simply known.[3] The transferring of Malagasy cultural "knowledge" to me, as illustrated above with an account of acquiring musical competence, occurred most often in performative transactions, both ceremonial and everyday.

Alluding to an epistemological component of performative process, Fabian asserts that while performance often reveals the nature of cultural knowledge, it can also conduct "the nature of knowledge of cultural knowledge" (1990: 19). Without suggesting some inflated self-importance, my participation in ceremonies in Madagascar in some sense became an occasional part of the nature of these particular performances. Overtly, once musically competent, I was performing some of the music in these ceremonies. More intrinsically, like foreign *tromba* spirits, I became a discussant, confidant, and humorist, among other things; in other words, an active discursive ceremonial participant. Thus, my presence was incorporated in the performative creation of ceremony-dependent *maresaka,* or in this instance, good talk.

Somewhat reciprocally, *tromba* ceremony left its performative imprint upon me as well as other ceremonial participants, in that *tromba* spirits usually verbalized for themselves directly to the living only during spirit possession ceremonies. After a ceremony they returned to their tombs or other places of disembodied rest. Thus, much had to be learned from and about these spirits in the very course of *tromba* ceremonies, for these were the only occasions in which one could encounter them in embodied form. The relationship between sound, spirit, and living medium had to be experienced ceremonially rather than explained as well because a medium later had no recollection of her or his own immediate moments of possession to pass on. Recollecting among the unpossessed ceremonial participants necessarily depended on moments of performative forgetting or, more accurately, never knowing experienced by the medium, whose own spirit became bodily displaced during possession.

In discussing ethnographic method, I have hesitated to invoke the notion of "participant observation." Michael Herzfeld has commented upon the oxymoronic nature of this concept (see also Dirks 1994: 499), which he critically suggests to be "an intervention in people's daily lives legitimized by claims of both a humanity that is shared and a sophistication that sets the observer apart." Herzfeld continues "[A]sking questions—a definitive facet of the observer-participant's role—is itself a status-related activity; the higher the questioner's status, the greater the range of available modes of interrogation" (1987: 16, 17; see also Fabian 1990). Malagasy people in some sense sidestepped this particular discursive imbalance by their very uncomfortableness with a question-and-reply mode of discourse. Situations in which I would be intervening, at least in this way, thus were for the most part circumvented. This is not to deny that other obvious imbalances in privilege and opportunity existed between myself and my Malagasy friends. I hope not to give the impression, no matter how fond I am of the Malagasy people represented here, that these inequities were somehow elided in my encounters. Indeed, such inequities have never strayed far from consciousness. Furthermore, I was always participating yet never a "normal" participant, sometimes observing while always being observed, and I occasionally felt as though I was simply taking in this new place, feeling few of the responsibilities implicit in observing, and possessing little competence for participating.

The Field and Ethnicity

I lived and worked on the east coast of Madagascar from 1993 through 1995 with two different groups of Malagasy people. Of these, Antandroy have regularly migrated to the east coast provincial capital of Tamatave from their ancestral homeland, Ambovombe, in the southern tip of the island. These migrations have usually been necessitated by widespread famine in Ambovombe, by the desire for wage labor found in the more economically active port town of Tamatave, and by the need to support elder family members who usually remain in the south. I also lived and worked among Betsimisaraka, historically the predominant Malagasy group in the Tamatave region. Most of the Antandroy and Betsimisaraka with whom I lived and worked had resisted, avoided, or simply not been interested in conversion to either Islam or Christianity, though they had sometimes been influenced by some factors attributable to these religious domains. These particular Malagasy still widely practiced *tromba* spirit possession, along with other ancestor-related customs.

Fieldwork is often framed by geographic, spatial, temporal, ethnic, and other categorizations or parameters that are commonly predestined by the researcher prior to entering a fieldwork environment. Before departing for Madagascar, I had designed my research to focus on "the" Betsimisaraka people, then the island's second largest group next to the Merina group in the central Haut Plateau region. In first conversations with Malagasy on the east coast, two assertions were repeatedly made. One was that "the" Betsimisaraka actually comprised two very different groups, Betsimisaraka *avaratra* (northern) and Betsimisaraka *atsimo* (southern). Each group was said to speak a dialect of Malagasy virtually unintelligible to the other.[4] Each group was also purported to perform different *fomba* (customs), and even to have dissimilar collective temperaments. Clear divisions between Betsimisaraka were also difficult to ordain because southern Betsimisaraka commonly relocated and were accepted into northern Betsimisaraka territory and practices. Jily, a Betsimisaraka woman from the south, for instance lived among northern Betsimisaraka and regularly played accordion for their *tromba* ceremonies. Members of either regionally defined group of Betsimisaraka also distinguished between northern and southern musical styles, forms, and repertoires.

Another frequent assertion made on the east coast was that current ethnic delineations were largely the result of geographic boundaries drawn by French colonials. Veit Erlmann has suggested, that for the African continent, "the central ambiguity in ethnicity . . . was the fact that it could be 'created' from above in an attempt to hamper unified political resistance against colonial subjugation" (1991: 69–70). According to Conrad Kottak, French colonials had employed and enforced ethnic boundaries that had already been established as provincial and territorial divisions through Merina expansion (1980: 4–5, 49). Kottak also asserts that Merina expansionism actually created a neighboring group of Malagasy to the south:

Betsileo have not always shared . . . consciousness of themselves as a distinct ethnic unit. Prior to their conquest by the Merina, there appear to have been no Betsileo. Rather, there were several statelets and chiefdoms located in different parts of what is now the Betsileo homeland. Their conquerors . . . created the Betsileo province of the Merina state . . . and, in so doing, provided a basis for Betsileo ethnic consciousness to develop through the present. (Ibid.: 4–5)

In addition, the group known as Mahafaly in the far south of Madagascar supposedly "do not presently form a social group. They claim no membership in a Mahafaly kingdom, tribe, or clan" (Eggert 1981: 151). The Malagasy government continues to verify the existence of a separate Mahafaly group, though Eggert claims there is no actual Mahafaly group identity expressed among the people of this region in southwest Madagascar (ibid.: 170). Although I cannot confirm this assertion about Mahafaly people, I did regularly hear in Madagascar that some geographic and ethnic divisions had been invented or influenced by Merina expansionism, European colonization, or a combination of the two. Additionally, the first colonial governor in Madagascar, Galliéni, had installed what was termed a *politique des races*, or tribal policy, which included the designation of local indigenous rulers for each group of Malagasy (Allen 1995: 112). This policy had been implemented under colonially conceived divisions of people and land in Madagascar.

How, then, to delimit ethnicity within specific complex contextual circumstances in the Tamatave region, and how to properly represent the unique local historical imaginations that had created and continue to maintain or transform such local groupings? Viably dividing up the fieldwork site into ethnic enclaves was also a delicate concern because land has had such important and specific meanings to Malagasy and because Malagasy ideas about temporal and spatial bounds often differ greatly from those prevalent for instance in the United States. Perhaps Malagasy made their own unique evaluations of how the Tamatave area was segmented or bounded.

To add to the complexity, Tamatave has historically been Madagascar's primary port to the outside world, so generations of Europeans, Indians, pirates, and Chinese, to name a few, have entered and settled there. "Betsimisaraka" could refer to people who looked very Chinese or Indian and who maintained beliefs and practiced customs quite distinct from other Betsimisaraka yet also knew and practiced Betsimisaraka customs. For example, in Fénérive-Est, a town approximately ninety-nine kilometres north of Tamatave-ville, there lived a woman whose father was Indian from Surat and whose mother was northern Betsimisaraka. This woman was a devout Muslim who dressed in traditional Islamic garb, including the conventional women's facial covering (*hejab* throughout the Middle East). She was also knowledgeable of and adept at Betsimisaraka customs and was accepted as Betsimisaraka by others in Fénérive-Est, even though her appearance and beliefs were unique. She identified herself ethnically as Betsimisaraka—she told me once, "Betsimisaraka voalohany izaho," "I'm before anything else Betsimisaraka." I could find only limited information on "ethnicity" or group diversity in the sparse literature about Betsimisaraka then available in Tamatave.[5]

In some ethnographic writing, ethnicity as ascribed cultural category is reduced to compilations and classifications of ritual terms, actions, behaviors, and traits. Such a mode of ethnography can fix people in a static world of externally imagined tradition, a world in which local peoples' histories and dialectical encounters with external worlds, for instance, might be subsumed into the ethnographic shadows.[6] Representations of ethnicity can take on a monolithic authority, inscribed as *the* characteristics of a group. Such an approach might overlook the likelihood that "identities" themselves are more realistically contingent, flexible, and imaginatively construed among a host of other situational qualities. An ethnographic voice that authoritatively freezes people in summations of cultural traits, while attempting to explain people, actually explains them away (see Taussig 1987: 10 on mythic subversion).

Group identity could be conceived differently throughout Madagascar. For instance, Rita Astuti (1995) writes that among Vezo, a group of Malagasy on the west coast, identity is an *activity,* defined largely through what one does. Vezo consider one such primary activity to be subsistence fishing. Astuti's observations among Vezo suggest in part that identities in Madagascar can extend beyond primordialist notions of ethnicity as an innate quality of human experience, beyond even instrumentalist claims that ethnicity is a socially determined condition, into universes of unique experiences in which self- or group consciousness emerges from *interaction* with a variety of phenomena (here including the environment). Indeed, much ethnographic literature overlooks the potential for identities to be combinations of intricate *processes* with which people negotiate their own sense of themselves in varying situations.

Nicholas Thomas also has noted the temporal as well as spatial separations that can occur in essentialist characterizations made of other peoples, specifically here in a well-known text written by Clifford Geertz:

The effect of *Negara,* in the end, is to abstract Balinese society as a picturesque, transhistorical essence, radically different from Western society. Despite the fact that the kinds and vocabularies of classification deployed in anthropological knowledge, and specific theoretical interests, have changed very considerably since the eighteenth century, there is an illusion of discontinuity in the sense that some form of essentialist partitioning has been crucial all along. (Thomas 1994: 94)

John and Jean Comaroff (1992) have opposed forms of ethnography that would objectify "contextualized savages" (p. 4). Rather, they advocate "a historical anthropology that is dedicated to exploring the processes that make and transform particular worlds—processes that reciprocally shape subjects and contexts, that allow certain things to be said and done" (p. 31). I emphasize throughout this book the significance of historical processes to Malagasy, especially as they variably construct Self and Other. Furthermore, bringing up histories specifically in *tromba* ceremony is not reducible solely to cognitive remembrance of past personalities and events. It involves the *experience* of interacting in replays of such historical processes and of participating in, commenting upon, playing with, and transforming such processes in the present.

I have thus chosen to focus upon varied ancestor-dependent musical practices that were co-occurring in the Tamatave region and upon the varying significance of these practices, rather than to try to establish specific ethnic designations that might arbitrarily divide this region. I even use the term "ethnic" guardedly, for recent usages such as "ethnic cleansing," "ethnic revitalization," "ethnic cuisine," "ethnic music," and the like have exploded this term into varied universes of significance (or beyond recognition; see Banks 1996: 166–71). In addition, in using this term there is an inherent danger of lapsing into older conceptual categories commonly based on "racial" or biological traits. In her opening to *In the Realm of the Diamond Queen*, Anna Lowenhaupt Tsing has given a sensitive appraisal of some misconceptions about ethnicity from the Philippines and Malaysia, stemming from "the poverty of an urban imagination which systematically has denied the possibilities of difference *within* the modern world and thus looked to relatively isolated people to represent its only adversary, its dying Other" (1994: x). In avoiding an approach that would attempt to define ethnicity or identity as an interpretive category, I hope to sidestep as much as possible a certain othering of Malagasy people and a use of categorizations that might be unfamiliar to them. While it will be necessary to distinguish between Antandroy and Betsimisaraka, I will not attempt to define Antandroy-ness or Betsimisaraka-ness. For one, subgroups of either of these peoples, based on a variety of criteria, also could be readily declared. Furthermore, being Antandroy in Tamatave-ville on the east coast often means something much different from being Antandroy in Ambovombe, in the south of the island.

Tromba practices and reverence for ancestral spirits ideologically, historically, and performatively bridge some gaps between Antandroy and Betsimisaraka living in the Tamatave region. In consideration of and respect for the importance that land, space, and particular places hold for both Antandroy and Betsimisaraka, I have allowed the parameters of the ethnographic site to be delimited by the Tamatave region itself and by the similar yet different beliefs that are held and practiced there. In addition, the ways in which Antandroy and Betsimisaraka evaluate or imagine each other within this shared space becomes an interpretive component later in this book.

Getting About

Musical instruments and replacement parts for them are scarce on the east coast of Madagascar, especially so in the villages. This region is very humid year-round, a climate not gentle on metal instrument parts or the cardboard bellows of accordions. Beyond these climatic difficulties most Malagasy on the east coast have little or no capital available to repair or replace instruments, especially accordions, which, whether new or used, are prohibitively expensive. I knew several former *valiha* players in the Tamatave countryside who had stopped performing altogether because they could not locate or afford to purchase strings for their instruments. Many people there told me that they used to play accordion but had forgotten how since they no longer had access to one. A gradual decline in the number of workable instruments in the villages of the northern Tamatave area explained in part a general diminution of *tromba* practice there in comparison to Tamatave-ville itself. In Tamatave-ville, supplies and parts of other things that could be worked into instrument parts were more abundant, especially near the large port there.

Widespread missionization and subsequent conversion to Christianity throughout the Tamatave countryside also have historically reduced the number of people who practice *tromba* there. Even most small villages throughout this part of Tamatave have at least one *fiangonana*, or church (usually a slightly larger version of a Malagasy hut built from bamboo or from *ravinala*, the leaf of a traveler's palm); many have two, one *katolika* and one *protestanta*. While there are also several churches and numerous Christian converts in Tamatave-ville, there are also many more corners there into which one could recede unfettered to practice *tromba*.

Tromba has on occasion been shunned and prohibited by European decree in Madagascar.[7] Jean–Marie Estrade, a French priest who in the early 1970s prepared a *thèse du troisième cycle* on *tromba* practice in Madagascar, described antispiritual policies imposed by the French colonial administration:

[D]ès 1923 le IIᵉ Congrès Psychiques à Varsovie émit le vœu que les pratiques occultes permettant de réveiller l'inconscient soient interdites par la loi, dans tous les pays, à cause des risques que cela représentait pour l'équilibre mental des sujets qui s'y livraient. (1985: 182)

The Second Congress on Psychic Matters at Varsovie, of 1923, sent out the edict that occult practices allowing the arousal of the unconscious be prohibited by law, in all countries, due to the risks that these practices represented to the mental equilibrium of the subjects who were succumbing to them.

French colonial prohibitions against *tromba* practice in Madagascar, with stiff penalties and even imprisonment imposed upon violators, continued until independence in 1960 (ibid.).

Unlike many of the villages throughout the Tamatave countryside, Tamatave-ville had numerous different thriving *tromba* communities, made up of either Antandroy or Betsimisaraka adherents. Several Betsimisaraka *tromba* musicians from the Tamatave countryside had even relocated in town because they could actually earn a (very meager) wage performing professionally for the varied local *tromba* communities there. Jily, the accordionist mentioned above, performed for approximately two *tromba* ceremonies per week in Tamatave-ville though she would also travel into the surrounding villages to perform for *tromba* if the villagers could afford to pay her.[8]

Most Antandroy musicians I knew in Tamatave-ville were less often concerned with local musical professionalism. Rather, they played frequently for the *tromba* ceremonies of their *havana* (their kin; for Antandroy this often indicated any other Antandroy) for little or no pay. I do not mean to generalize here about Antandroy or Betsimisaraka economic policies, for certainly some Betsimisaraka were less oriented to a system of capital exchange, and some Antandroy were more inclined economically in this way. Rather, I mean to attribute to the Tamatave area itself a particular economic history. Betsimisaraka have long been exposed to foreign contact in Tamatave and subsequently have been influenced by foreign modes of commerce. In contrast, due to often pervasive material poverty, as well as geographic isolation resulting in part from the difficulty of access to their southern homeland, Antandroy have been more removed throughout the past from European contact. Hence, they have commonly either avoided or resisted certain modes of exchange that have seemed foreign to them (Brown 1979: 110).

It seemed pertinent to me to become familiar with both the town of Tamatave-ville and the surrounding villages of northern Betsimisaraka territory. Indeed, people throughout this region sometimes expressed their own distinctions between customs in the town and those in the villages. Since *tromba* performance did not seem to be occurring consistently or regularly in many villages, I chose to divide my time between several Betsimisaraka villages and the port town of Tamatave (which I have been calling Tamatave-ville to distinguish it from the surrounding province also called Tamatave). In Tamatave-ville more numerous ongoing musical communities were thriving. I spent approximately half of my research time in Tamatave-ville, the other half traveling between several small villages or towns in the Tamatave region, including Betampona, approximately ten kilometres northwest of Fénérive-Est, Morondrano, on the Maningory River forty-five kilometres from Fénérive-Est, and Fénérive-Est itself.

Malagasy generally like to travel about and visit relatives in other parts of the island. My mode of perambulatory ethnography actually fit into a flow of movement already occurring in Tamatave. More broadly, anthropology and ethnography themselves have come about through histories of travel, exploration, and contact. Marcus and Fischer (1986) discuss attributes of "multi-locale ethnography." Marcus has since written that such ethnography "concerns itself with the complex relationships between settings of activity and addresses the key issue of unintended consequences in a much more elaborate, if not precise way than does the resistance and accommodation ethnography" (1998: 52). Clifford (1997) extensively takes up issues of travel and ethnography. He writes that fieldwork "'takes place' in worldly, contingent relations of travel, not in controlled sites of research" (68). Relatedly, Tsing (1993) details the movements of both her ethnographic subjects and herself.

Language Differences

The Malagasy language has been classified structurally as Malayo-Polynesian or Austronesian, and is thought to most closely resemble Maanjan, spoken in Borneo. Eighteen to twenty different regional variations or dialects of Malagasy are usually distinguished. The Merina dialect, spoken mainly in the capital, Antananarivo, and in much of the surrounding Haut Plateau region of central Madagascar, is often called *la langue nationale* by those Malagasy who speak both it and at least some French. Merina comprise the largest and often most powerful group in Madagascar, a group that, prior to French colonization (beginning officially in 1896), had conquered much of the island and thus subdued several non-Merina coastal groups. While I was there, Merina still often held a majority of social and political positions of control and privilege, even in Tamatave-ville.

Malagasy on the east coast who were not Merina usually referred to the Merina dialect as *teny Merina* (Merina speech) rather than as the national language. The choice of the phrase *teny Merina* over a Malagasy translation or variant of *la langue nationale* represents a particular mode of refusal by Malagasy *côtiers* to accept Merina hegemony. Malagasy on the east coast often casually warned, "Tandremo, fetsifetsy ny Merina!," which means that one should beware of Merina for they can be sly, manipulative, or deceptive. Such an evaluation derives largely from the purported verbal cunning of Merina. *Teny* Merina thus embodies not only phonemic and lexical difference to non-Merina speakers, but also distinctions in and even apprehensions toward particular speech modes. By rejecting *teny* Merina, Betsimisaraka were imbuing their own unique dialect of Malagasy with differential intensity; speaking *teny* Betsimisaraka often means in part not speaking *teny* Merina, and therefore not being sly or deceptive (*fetsifetsy*).[9]

Late-nineteenth-century evangelical sermons in Betsimisaraka territory were often given in the Merina dialect, much of which Betsimisaraka could comprehend though they did not speak this dialect on everyday occasions (Esoavelomandroso 1978: 30–33). Christianity and the language in which it was transmitted were purportedly received by these Betsimisaraka as affronts to their own devotional practices. In this instance *teny* Merina supposedly acted as referent of two modes of foreign power to Betsimisaraka:

one, the ideologic and territorial encroachment of Merina into the Tamatave region during this period; the other, the spread of Christian doctrine, which sometimes condemned or prohibited local ancestral customs.

Esoavelomandroso concluded that "l'évangélisation est donc perçue par les Betsimisaraka comme dangereuse" (1978: 33). In another sense, it is possible that Betsimisaraka might have reworked signs from within the imposing structures of Christian doctrine and thus perhaps creatively offset some of its "dangerousness." For example, when I was there, much public Christian discourse, especially Protestant discourse in Tamatave, vehemently railed against local spirit possession practices. Yet many people who practiced spirit possession believed in Jesus in varying ways, and some even regularly used his image in their own ceremonies.

Experientially, then, the Merina dialect is neither universally spoken throughout Madagascar nor does it engender a national identity that unifies different Malagasy peoples. It is important to recognize that individual dialects of the Malagasy language mirror unique practices, beliefs, and histories. Varied misconceptions about language within Madagascar are not uncommon. For instance, Merina acquaintances in Antananarivo commonly expressed the belief that there is little or no difference between their dialect and those spoken on the east coast. This belief echoes in part a condescension felt by some Merina toward coastal peoples—denying language differences in some sense denies the very existence of unique people on the east coast. Perhaps relatedly, Merina also sometimes spoke of the extreme laziness of *côtiers*.

Merina negation of linguistic difference is likely triggered in part by the usually limited experience they have when they travel east. Their visits are most often touristic or business-oriented and are usually restricted to the port town of Tamatave-ville or to vacation areas like Foulpointe, where one could readily encounter other Merina speakers. However, I observed local east coast dialects to be virtually incomprehensible to visiting Merina friends when they actually tried to interact with Betsimisaraka villagers— for instance, at the market in Tamatave-ville.

Antandroy and Betsimisaraka on the east coast each spoke very distinct dialects of the Malagasy language. The specific east coast Malagasy *tromba* practitioners with whom I worked though spoke neither French nor *teny* Merina.

Place

Anthropologist and Madagascar specialist Gillian Feeley-Harnik has referred to the significance of place among Sakalava in northwest and western Madagascar:

[P]eople are defined by their locations as commonly as by their genealogical or other relationships to one another. Toponymy is thus a subject of considerable interest throughout the island. . . . The reliquaries and tombs of Sakalava rulers in western Madagascar exemplify the association of places with memories of people. . . . In Madagascar, the importance of places in memorializing people seems to develop from ideas and practices tied to the ground, bodies, and the growth of bodies rooted in the ground. (1991a: 122)[10]

The Tamatave region itself is significant in different ways to Antandroy and to Betsimisaraka. For example, it contains Betsimisaraka ancestral burial grounds. The area also has been ground for varied struggles—over control of its resources dating back to early pirate activity there in the seventeenth century, to Merina expansionism throughout the past, to late-nineteenth-century French colonial takeover. More recently, Betsimisaraka ancestors fought and died over control of Tamatave in an anticolonial insurgence in 1947. Betsimisaraka territory has even more recently been the site of development and conservation organization efforts to preserve rapidly receding forestland there, to cordon off sometimes very large parcels of ancestral homeland to protect it from slash-and-burn rice agriculture. This has often meant keeping Betsimisaraka off their own land. One incentive for such territorial expropriation has been the preservation of forestlands for the study of local flora and fauna, such as lemurs, and even to set up ecotourist "theme" parks. The decimation of land from slash-and-burn agriculture continues to be a serious environmental problem throughout the east coast and sometimes is deployed in foreign conservation or development strategies that vilify Malagasy for their supposed ecological destructiveness. For instance, referring to such Malagasy forestlands, one author has stated, myopically, "In truth, this wonderful wilderness lacks status in the unromantic Malagasy imagination" (Allen 1995: 174). Certainly when one is perpetually hungry and constantly fending off varied illnesses, among a host of other serious problems faced daily by Malagasy, she or he cannot revel in what is unspecifically deemed to be romanticism in this citation. Furthermore, defenders of the Malagasy landscape seldom seem to have much grasp at all of what makes up the "Malagasy imagination," often depicting Malagasy simply as a collective of dull-witted environmental ravagers.

The land itself in the Tamatave region has long been and continues to be contested ground. Betsimisaraka sometimes expressed sentiments about the tenuous and contested current "nature" of their homeland. This sentiment would surface in critical comments made about local development projects. The directors of these projects commonly favored bringing Merina assistants and labor into Betsimisaraka territory over hiring local Betsimisaraka. They also commonly seemed indifferent to the actual problem of slash-and-burn agriculture *among* Betsimisaraka and to local needs and desires. I was told numerous times by Betsimisaraka in the villages that they would happily change their agricultural practices if they were simply shown a more productive, less environmentally destructive method by which to grow their rice crops.

Feeley-Harnik's words, above, take on a particular significance in Tamatave: "the importance of places in memorializing people seems to develop from ideas and practices tied to the ground, bodies, and the growth of bodies rooted in the ground." This image of *growing* bodies rooted in the ground resounds metaphorically with the character of Betsimisaraka and other east coast Malagasy ancestors—spirits not fixed in death but acquiring through it a vivacity, mobility, and even heightened authority. Such extended authority emerges in Betsimisaraka *tromba* ceremony specifically when spirits of Sakalava royalty come to inhabit Betsimisaraka mediums. These are spirits of kings who had presided in their lifetimes over northern and western Sakalava kingdoms but who had had no immediate control over Betsimisaraka or the Tamatave region on the east coast when they were in power. These Sakalava spirits, rooted in another ground on the opposite side of the island, come to Tamatave to take temporary control, to (re)empower people there, perhaps to transfer the power rooted in the ground of their royal tombs from which they emerge into Tamatave itself, a region without an illustrious history of kingdoms and royal power of its own.

For Antandroy in Tamatave-ville, the Tamatave area is often meaningful for what it is not, for the fissures it creates between them and their ancestral homeland, Ambovombe. This distancing from ancestral homeland and kin, painfully inescapable among Antandroy, has become part of a daily poetics of loss and dislocation. One such expression of loss is a commonly sung recollection of an imagined woman named Belina. Belina represents a collective (men's) longing for lost love. The singer would begin by lamenting several times, "Aia Belina e?" (Where is Belina?) and would go on to elaborate upon this image of an ethereal Antandroy woman lost or left behind. Although Belina is also sung about in Ambovombe, recollection of this mythical figure in Tamatave-ville particularly intensifies sentiments of dislocation for Antandroy, who are already missing so much about their homeland. Another example of such a poetics of dislocation is a lament commonly voiced by Antandroy when they are reminiscing about Ambovombe or extolling the difficulties of daily life in Tamatave: "Tsisy havako aty." This phrase (literally, "Our kin are not here") expresses as well a sense of emptiness that accompanies being separated from Antandroy family members and ancestral places in Ambovombe.

Tamatave-ville, though, offers migrating Antandroy the means to procure enough capital to support their elder relatives yet in Ambovombe and to make offerings to their ancestral spirits, largely by purchasing and eventually slaughtering cattle in honor of these spirits. Antandroy thus can creatively manipulate the exchange value with which the local area has historically been endowed, so as to nurture their own ancestral customs. Antandroy men can usually find work as guardians (*gardiens* in French, *mpiandry* in Antandroy speech) for Tamatave store owners; Antandroy woman often sell wares or food items at the market. For Antandroy this is an ambivalent existence, torn between a beloved homeland that cannot support them and these borrowed spaces in Tamatave-ville, which just barely can. Tsiately, an aging Antandroy *ombiasa* (healer, seer, advisor, among other things) who had lived for the past eleven years in Tamatave-ville, reminisced about the foreignness of wage labor to him and the transformative, displacing effect it had had on young migrating Antandroy: "Tsy mitovy ny asa agny Ambovombe izany sy ny asa eto Toamasigna. Be, be tokoa io vokatra ny hitako taty. Nisy karama! Izay tsy ny lalagna nody" (The work in Ambovombe was not the same as that in Toamasigna. The pay-off that I saw for the work here [in Toamasigna] was indeed big— there was salary! The allure of earning a salary in Tamatave has not made it easy for us Antandroy to get back home).

Both Antandroy and Betsimisaraka contend with disconnection from sacred places at another level: whereas the spirits, or *fagnahy,* of one's direct ancestors rest in tombs in one's own homeland, it is the northern and northwestern regions of the island that house the tombs of powerful Sakalava royal ancestors. These royal tombs are still maintained and cared for by those northerners and westerners engaged in what had earlier been known as *fanompoana* or royal service (see Campbell 1988 and Feeley-Harnik 1988, 1991). Some Antandroy and Betsimisaraka *tromba-istes* in the Tamatave region consider themselves yet to be engaged in *fanompoana,* since they are in the service of royal *tromba* spirits even though they live far from the royal tombs of their *tromba. Tromba-istes* in Tamatave thus have to practice a modern, territorially distant mode of *fanompoana.* Both Antandroy and Betsimisaraka can feel varied degrees of either connectedness with or disconnectedness from sacred ancestral places.

⤥

In *tromba* practice, east coast Malagasy revalue and remaster their pasts, while also reorienting their present worlds of experience. Yet such historicizing reevaluations are not made specifically, for instance, to enact challenge or resistance toward dominant forces from the past or toward more recent counterparts of such forces in Tamatave. *Tromba-istes* often revalue signs of foreign intrusion to *take back,* aesthetically, from inequitable situations both past and present, in accordance with principles of their own performative aesthetic, *maresaka.* It is vital to recall throughout this book that history in Tamatave does not necessarily exist simply as a body of incontrovertible knowledge, as fixed accounts of past facts, data, or events. Rather, histories are often encountered in imaginatively fluid events imbued with the emotional, musical, familial, and spiritual vivacity of socially and often politically charged interaction. History here is not simply emergent in or through ceremony or ritual—ceremonial proceedings *are* the historical. Among Malagasy in Tamatave, to recollect ceremonially means to embody and express in the present an expanse of historicized consciousness, interpretation, experience, imagination, and critique.

Emphasis is placed throughout this book on the magnitude of the variegated concept of *maresaka* among east coast Malagasy. Through this aesthetic, performative practices based upon fragmenting, combining, incorporating, reevaluating, interpreting, and sounding all come together to resemble what Steve Feld has called an acoustemology (acoustics plus epistemology), a sound sense of daily and ceremonial life. Through varied powers inherent in sound production, Malagasy in the Tamatave region thread together in action and interaction a confluence of the historical, the cultural, the spiritual, the memorable.

CHAPTER TWO

Some Background on Tamatave

✍

This chapter introduces some specific histories in the Tamatave region pertinent to musical and spiritual practices there. It is by no means meant to be an exhaustive engagement with published, archival, or voiced historical sources. As a way of recalling the past, this brief and segmented history contrasts with Malagasy ceremonial recollection, which draws not from texts to be read or remembered but from dramatically interpretive events of social immersion and interaction. Yet in its method of fragmenting, extracting, and reassembling from specific historical moments, this chapter does in some sense resemble historical process in *tromba* ceremony. Later in this book, specific colonial and missionary accounts of Malagasy practices return as double-edged discourses that likely have become entangled in the very development of these local practices.[1]

While exact histories of the populating of Madagascar have been elusively difficult to pinpoint, the island's earliest inhabitants are believed to have arrived there from Southeast Asia between fifteen hundred and two thousand years ago. Waves of Indonesians or Malaysians, specifically, along with Bantu-speaking peoples from southeastern Africa supposedly followed.

By the twelfth century, Islamic Indian merchants were exerting a marked influence in southern parts of Madagascar (Gueunier 1994). Recollection of distant and more recent Islamic influence often becomes a central component in some *tromba* practice in Tamatave. Portuguese, reported to be the first Europeans to arrive in Madagascar, in 1500, withdrew quickly, due largely to their widespread susceptibility to local disease. By late-seventeenth century, numerous European pirates had settled on the east coast of Madagascar, from Foulpointe, forty-five kilometers south of Fénérive-Est, and Ile Sainte Marie, some fifty kilometers northeast of Fénérive-Est (in the Indian Ocean), northward to Diégo Suarez (see fig. 1).

Diégo Suarez

Mahajanga

Fénérive-Est

TAMATAVE

Tamatave-ville

Antananarivo

Morondava

0   km   100

Toliara

Fort-Dauphin

Ambovombe

Fig. 1. Map of Madagascar. Tamatave, Fénérive-Est, Fort Dauphin, Diégo Suarez are colonial names still commonly used among Malagasy people.

These pirates were often primarily motivated by material gain, commonly accomplished through the use of force. Some pirates were purported to be particularly ruthless, attacking all ships indiscriminately, even those of their own country (Brown 1979: 75).

There have also been waves of missionaries, other merchants (Chinese, for instance), and of course French colonials to settle in Madagascar. The east coast port of Tamatave-ville has specifically been the point of entry for many of these visitors throughout the past. Toamasina is Tamatave's Malagasy name, pronounced "Toamasi*gn*a" in east coast dialects.

One account of pirates who had settled on the east coast of Madagascar noted that

ils ne vivaient pas ensemble, ayant chacun leur domaine . . . ils étaient riche en or, en argent, et en d'autres objets précieux, mais ils manquaient de ce qui était nécessaire à l'éxistence de chaque jour, habillements, vin, eau-de-vie, etc. (Quoted in Grandidier 1959: 27)

they did not live together, each having their own property . . . they were rich in gold, silver, and in other valuables, but they were lacking that which was necessary to everyday existence, proper clothing, wine, brandy, etc.

Early pirate-settlers are portrayed here as individualistic and wealthy yet idle in European everyday matters—proper clothing, wine, and brandy—all things generally valued by Europeans, though perhaps not by European pirates living in Madagascar. European wine and brandy might not have been readily available to pirate-settlers in the Tamatave region, though *betsabetsa,* a mildly alcoholic drink made from fermented sugarcane, and *toaka gasy,* a strong locally made rum, likely were abundant. This account of pirate-settlers in Tamatave underscores the dire absence of European alcoholic intoxicants there—"ce qui était *nécessaire* à l'éxistence de chaque jour." Consumption of wine and brandy—drinking in European fashion—thus was deemed essential to daily life among pirate-settlers (stereotypic representations of the rum-drunk pirate aside).

In colonial evaluations of Betsimisaraka, overconsumption of *betsabetsa* and *toaka gasy* was commonly painted as a deleterious human flaw, even as a marker of east coast "ethnicity." For example, a colonial era account of Betsimisaraka in the northern Tamatave region portrayed them as "timides, doux, très malléables, mais d'une nature apathique; ils sont d'autre part, de funestes habitudes d'ivrognerie" (Aujas 1905–6: 87), "timid, pleasant, quite easily manipulated, but of an apathetic nature; they otherwise are of the most fatal habits of severe drunkenness." Late in the colonial era the following observation was made: "Les Betsimisaraka sont assez nonchalants et travaillent pour satisfaire médiocrement leurs besoins immédiats" (Arisivim-Pirenena [anon.] 1958), "the Betsimisaraka are rather indifferent and work to take care of, only in a mediocre fashion, their immediate needs." An earlier document, written in 1884 by a British missionary, described Betsimisaraka as "a happy people, full of good nature and high spirits, and [they] seem to take a very cheerful view of things—they cannot be silent, and they seem to have a collection of inspiriting and mirth-provoking songs, which they are never tired of repeating" (Little 1970 [1884]: 32–33). Betsimisaraka were often described by colonials as naive, easily manipulated, apathetic drunkards, happy natives, or even unimaginative musicians (never tiring of repetition).

Any Betsimisaraka agency in matters of contact with foreigners is significantly neglected in these early accounts. Betsimisaraka "apathy," for instance, perhaps resounded with or mimicked pirate-settler behaviors, such as their languid disregard for European convention. Welcoming and honoring visitors has a long history throughout Madagascar's varied regions–perhaps Betsimisaraka were actually attempting to liken themselves to their European "guests." Indeed, in current *tromba* practice among Betsimisaraka, welcoming foreign personalities into the present and taking on their characteristics play an ineluctable role.

European observers commonly overlooked the role that a mimetic faculty might have played in early contact between Europeans and Malagasy. Walter Benjamin begins his brief essay *On the Mimetic Faculty:*

Nature creates similarities. One need only think of mimicry. The highest capacity for producing similarities, however, is man's. His gift of seeing resemblances is nothing other than a rudiment of the powerful compulsion in former times to become and behave like something else. Perhaps there is none of his higher functions in which his mimetic faculty does not play a decisive role. (1978: 333)

Taking into consideration as well Taussig's (1993) speculations on the dynamics and significance of first contacts, in which he asks "Who is mimicking whom, the sailor or the savage?" (p. 76–77), perhaps Betsimisaraka were interpreting the pirate-settlers' behavior through mimicry, eventually even taking on some foreign characteristics as their own. Conversely, the pirate-settlers' disregard for daily European necessities might have reflected not simply a scorn for European conventions but might have implied as well a fondness for those of Betsimisaraka. Subsequent chapters take up the varying significance of mimesis and accommodation in Tamatave.

Perhaps "nonchalance" or "apathy" were deployed by Betsimisaraka as means of refusing to cooperate with early British missionaries or French colonials. Gillian Feeley-Harnik has written that "French administrators distinguished Malagasy groups according to their capacities for work, and thus 'progress' along Western lines" (1989: 82). It is not known whether Betsimisaraka were aware of such colonial strategies, but if so, perhaps they realized that they could better recede from colonial contact and control by appearing to be less "capable." Edward Said suggests that "laziness" was not simply an inherent characteristic among Southeast Asians during the colonial era. Rather, it was used by them as a method of recalcitrance, to sidestep cooperation with colonials:

When they travelled through India in 1912, Beatrice and Sidney Webb noted the difficulty British employers were having with Indian laborers working for the Raj, either because laziness was a form of resistance (very common elsewhere in Asia as S. H. Alatas—*The Myth of the Lazy Native: A Study of the Image of the Malays, Filipinos, and Javanese from the Sixteenth to the Twentieth Century and Its Function in the Ideology of Colonial Capitalism*—has shown) or because of the so-called 'draining theory' of Dadabhai Naoroji who had argued to the satisfaction of nationalist parties that India's wealth was being drained off by the British. (1994: 203)

Similarly, James Scott notes "the ordinary weapons of relatively powerless groups: foot dragging, dissimulation, false compliance, pilfering, feigned ignorance, slander, arson, sabotage, and so forth" (1985: 29). Elsewhere he writes of other maneuvers that serve to furtively disavow authority:

[F]or many peasants, activities such as poaching, pilfering, clandestine tax evasion, and intentionally shabby work for landlords are part and parcel of the hidden transcript. For dominant elites, hidden-transcript practices might include clandestine luxury and privilege, surreptitious use of hired thugs, bribery, and tampering with land titles. These practices, in each case, contravene the public transcript of the party in question and are, if at all possible, kept offstage and unavowed. (1990: 14)

Among Betsimisaraka, "laziness" likely worked as a hidden transcript of non-compliance with colonials. Discourse involving the laziness of the local "savage" among colonials themselves likely fueled an underlying disavowal or subversion of the very power of Betsimisaraka not to comply.

꩜

Contestation and violence sometimes clouded other past events in Tamatave, though a unification of varied factions eventually came about among Malagasy people in this region. At the beginning of the eighteenth century, some of the different clans within the Tamatave area unified under the command of a local ruler named Ramanano, calling themselves *Tsikoa*, "qu'on ne renverse pas" (Grandidier 1959: 29), "those who are steadfast." Ramanano established a viable armed force in Vohimasina, two kilometers southwest of Fénérive-Est, itself initially a European pirate settlement. Ramanano, however, revealed himself to be cruel and often violent, burning crops to intimidate neighboring peoples, selling women and children into slavery, and desecrating ancestral tombs. Under the command of Ratsimilaho, who was the son of British pirate Tom Tew and a Malagasy princess, other clan members mounted an offensive against Ramanano and the Tsikoa and eventually secured the areas surrounding Fénérive-Est, Foulpointe, and Tamatave-ville. Ratsimilaho gave his partisans the name Betsimisaraka, "'les inséparables,' car ayant tous les mêmes intérêts, ils s'étaient juré de rester unis jusqu'à la mort" (ibid.: 31–32), "'the unseparables,' because all having the same interests, they were sworn to remain united until death." Ratsimilaho's own distinctiveness as half European suggests that, even early in the eighteenth century, being Betsimisaraka — of "the many who do not separate"—was effectively more about belonging to a federation of diverse peoples than it was about homogeneity.

Ratsimilaho later took the name Ramaromanompo and was called by other Malagasy, though not disrespectfully, *zana-malata,* or mulatto child. Although Ramaromanompo held much influence and power in the Tamatave region, Betsimisaraka still purportedly remained "a confederation of small groups rather than a united kingdom" (Brown 1979: 101). Ramaromanompo, seeking in part to strengthen his power, asked for and received a woman from the leader of the *Zafimbolamena* (grandchildren of gold) group of Sakalava people, who occupied a large western region of the island. Sakalava kingdoms had attained powerful status in Madagascar by this time, due in part to a notable rapport between Sakalava and Europeans. Ramaromanompo named his son Zanahary (a name now used in Madagascar to refer to a supreme being, who, among other things, oversees activity in the spirit world).

Disintegration rather than unification among Betsimisaraka continued under the rule of Zanahary, who unleashed a violent campaign upon his subjects and was eventually assassinated in 1767. Zanahary's successor, his oldest son, Iavy, was detested by his subjects for complying with the French slave trade and for warring with neighboring Malagasy. Iavy's son Zakavolo succeeded his father in 1791. He came to be hated by Europeans for his incessant demands for gifts from them and for his often insulting response to their refusals to meet his demands. He was deposed in 1803 by his own subjects with the assistance of the French gouverneur général des iles, Magallon. Zakavolo was eventually assassinated.

By the last decades of the eighteenth century, French colonials had already established control of Ile Sainte Marie off the coast of Tamatave, and they had constructed trading posts up and down the east coast of Madagascar. By 1810 Zakavolo's uncle, Tsihala, had become "chef" of Tamatave, though only after much dispute between another uncle and Zakavola's two sons. This dispute fomented anarchy among other Betsimisaraka. The French colonial administration, represented by commercial agent Sylvain

Roux in Tamatave, was actually in economic control of the Tamatave region around this time period.

Jean René, another *zana-malata,* took control of Tamatave in 1811, and he ruled "avec justice et intelligence, à l'égard aussi bien des Européens que des autochtones" (Grandidier 1959: 51), "with justice and intelligence toward Europeans as well as natives." In 1817, Merina king Radama I, intent on conquering the rest of the island, arrived in Tamatave from Antananarivo with twenty-five thousand men and with no forewarning to nor compliance from Jean René.[2] Radama had an affable accord with Europeans, especially British, and under his rule, numerous teachers and others from the London Missionary Society were welcomed into Madagascar.

In 1825, Betsimisaraka, who had hoped for but never received support nor aid from France to protect them from Merina expansionism, mounted a revolt against Radama and his forces in Tamatave, but this insurgence failed to drive Merina out of Betsimisaraka territory. Radama's expansionist campaigns were unsuccessful in gaining control over southern regions of the island, therefore, Antandroy were not subjected to his domination in their own homeland.

Radama's successor in the Merina aristocracy, Queen Ranavalona I, was vociferously anti-European. She even outlawed Christianity in Madagascar. According to one report, "toute la musique d'avant était abandonée à cause de la reine Ranavalona I" (Rason 1933: 59–60), "all earlier music [in other words, European music] was abandoned because of Queen Ranavalona I." Jean Laborde, one European who did gain Ranavalona's favor, was known to have industrialized the island to some degree. Using forced labor, he had a gun factory built for Ranavalona in Merina territory. Ranavalona died in 1861 and was succeeded by her son, known as Radama II. He restored relations with Europe and proclaimed freedom of religion for Christians while disassociating himself from his own Malagasy royal rituals. A prohibitive law reflecting Radama II's displeasure with Malagasy customs was enacted in 1862 (see Bloch 1986: 145). Many of Radama II's subjects, who were overtly anti-European as well as anti-Christian, began to engage in a popular wave of possession by ancestral spirits, called *ramanenjana.* This en masse possession event has often been interpreted as an oppositional reaction to a perceived state-sanctioned dilution of traditional Malagasy culture (*ramanenjana* is discussed in chap. 10).

During Radama II's reign, newly arriving Merina and Europeans to whom Radama II had granted unimpeded trading rights were forcing fierce competition for the available local resources in the Tamatave region. As one result, Betsimisaraka were often forced, in their own homeland, to labor under Merina or Europeans. In some cases, desperate Betsimisaraka became indebted to Merina moneylenders; Merina expansion into Tamatave also clearly disturbed ancestral organization of the land. Some Betsimisaraka resisted these foreign intruders, for instance, refusing to grow surplus rice only so that Merina could profit from it. Some Betsimisaraka even took refuge in the forest to escape Merina and European oppression (Ellis 1985: 42).

Resentment toward Merina intrusion into and appropriation of the Tamatave region commonly surfaced in remarks made among east coast Malagasy while I was there. For many non-Merina, it is commonly *fady* (taboo, *interdit*) to wed a Merina, an interdiction that reflects in part an older mistrust of Merina. On several occasions I saw distressed non-Merina parents seek the intervention of an *ombiasa* (healer, herbalist, seer, advisor, manipulator of fate, and often spirit medium) to deal with a child who was determined to wed a Merina. The ombiasa often would call upon her or his connection with ancestral spirits to prevent such a marriage. The explanation given by east coast people for this apprehension toward Merina always referred to histories of Merina exploitation on the east coast, as well as to the common sentiment there that Merina had been and still are *fetsifetsy,* or deceptive and dangerous.

In 1895, French colonials subdued the Merina kingdom, which freed the east coast in many respects from Merina control. Merina often remained there, however, retaining privileged social, economic, and political positions. With Madagascar officially a French colony in 1896, Galliéni, the first French colonial governor there, aggressively sought to break the remaining power of the Merina aristocracy in Antananarivo and to extinguish pre-existing British influence, in part by installing French as the official language. Paul Rabinow has noted two stages in Galliéni's "pacification" policy for Merina territory in central Madagascar: first, abolition of slavery and of the existing feudal regime of landholding among Merina; second, "the physical and intellectual development of the conquered people, amelioration of their social state, and the economic exploitation of the country through native labor" (1989: 159).

Remarking upon the preexisting state of Merina hegemony on the east coast, Galliéni himself observed:

Hors du plateau central, en pays Betsimisaraka, l'état social était des plus primitifs; l' hégémonie "hova" avait nivelé les situations; les chef locaux avaient perdu tout pouvoir; d'ailleurs, en raison du genre de vie des indigènes, de la nature du pays, offrant, par ses ressources naturelles, à peu près tout ce qui est nécessaire à leur existence matérielle, les privilèges auxquels les populations du haut plateau attachaient un grand prix, étaient pour les Betsimisaraka dénués d'importance. (Galliéni 1896–1905)

Outside the central plateau in Betsimisaraka territory the social conditions were some of the most primitive; the *hova* [usually denotes aristocratic status among Merina] hegemony had leveled the local order; the local chiefs had lost all power; moreover, because of the type of life led by the locals, of the nature of the countryside, offering, by its natural resources, roughly all that was necessary for their material existence, Betsimisaraka took for granted material things that the people of the haut plateau greatly valued.

Galliéni recognized the socially and politically debilitating effects that the encroaching Merina aristocracy had had in Betsimisaraka territory. He also restated an essentializing assessment of Betsimisaraka as apathetic and in this case unappreciative of the wealth their territory offered them—a variation of the "lazy native" myth.

East coast Malagasy commonly expressed to me that they or their ancestors had sometimes even welcomed French colonials as vanquishers of intruding Merina forces. One early observer, de St. Andre, wrote that Antanosy, a southeastern group of Malagasy, also had sided with the French in the late eighteenth century because they detested Merina hegemony (1886: 38). Ironically, once French colonials discovered a sentiment among Betsimisaraka that French control was preferable to Merina domination, they enlisted Betsimisaraka support to subdue Merina control in Madagascar. Once under the aegis of French colonials, Betsimisaraka received no special favors, in fact, they were commonly forced to cede their ancestral land to these new masters and to work cash crops such as coffee.

European colonization forced many Malagasy to contend with two distinct governing systems: one of their own ancestors, another of modern Europeans (Bloch 1971). Tensions between *fomba vazaha* (customs of white outsiders) and *fomba gasy* (Malagasy customs) reportedly surfaced. Recitation of politically charged oral histories, for instance, evoked apprehension. A whole generation of Malagasy were hesitant to perform such recitation for fear that their local versions might disagree with newly inscribed official histories and thus would be seen as subversive (Ellis 1985: 156). Might Malagasy, though, have been able to creatively transform or encode their verbal art so that it would meet some of their needs, even within the social and political strictures of the time?

Fomented by social and political tensions, a rebellion was staged against the French colonial administration in 1896 by a Malagasy resistance group known as Menalamba, "the red shawl." The French colonialist regime was much too powerful to be expelled by Menalamba activists. Although they sustained few casualties from the Menalamba insurrection itself, over six thousand French colonials in Madagascar had been killed by the end of 1896 by disease, largely from fever attributed to malaria (Brown 1979: 250).

Among *tromba-istes* and even Christian Malagasy, illness is frequently believed (or feared among Christians) to be caused by *tromba* spirits who are demanding any number of things from the living.

A resistance organization known as the VVS (*Vy*–[iron], *Vato*–[stone], *Sakelika*–[network]) was led, in part from France, by Jean Ralaimongo, who had roomed there briefly with Ho Chi Minh (Brown 1979: 260). The VVS continued to oppose French colonial presence in Madagascar into the twentieth century. With the support of an organization known as Mouvement Démocratique de la Rénovation Malgache (MDRM), Malagasy eventually mounted a rebellion against the French colonial regime in 1947. Betsimisaraka villagers in particular suffered severe losses at the hands of French forces, which included Senegalese soldiers enlisted to fight for France. A story circulates frequently on the east coast that waves of disease were wrought upon French soldiers during 1947 by *tromba* angered at French disregard for Malagasy ancestral customs. Another story has it that, after battles, bodiless uniforms of French and Senegalese soldiers would be found strewn across the battlefield, another sign of ancestral intervention in this conflict.

The French colonial administration in Madagascar swiftly crushed the 1947 rebellion and then continued on a campaign of retribution. The following account graphically illustrates French brutality upon Malagasy in the Tamatave region during and after 1947:

des prisonniers auraient été chargés en avion, puis lâchés vivants au-dessus de certains villages passés à l'insurrection. Des expéditions punitives, suivies d'exécutions sommaires, sont renouvelées plusieurs fois, contre certains villages aussitôt incendiés et rasés. . . . Plusieurs témoignages concordants affirment que, pour effrayer les populations, les patrouilles revenaient du combat en exhibant des lobes d'oreilles. (Tronchon 1982: 79)

prisoners would have been loaded into an airplane, then ejected, still alive, over certain villages loyal to the rebellion. Punitive expeditions, followed by summary executions, were reinstated several times, against certain villages which were immediately set afire and razed. . . . Several corroborating testimonies affirm that, to frighten villagers, colonial patrols returned from combat displaying severed Malagasy earlobes.

In his memoirs, Jacques Rabemananjara, leader in the MDRM, described his torture by French colonials and their attempts to force him to implicate his confrères in the 1947 rebellion:

Ma première connaissance avec la torture. Dans une petite salle attenante au bureau du chef de la Sûreté, M. Baron, avant de m'y faire conduire, remet un nerf de bœuf au Sénégalais Jean–Marie, chargé de l'opération, et sort de son bureau. Pendant ce temps, la dame secrétaire de Baron murmure quelques mots à l'oreille du Sénégalais. Celui-ci me dit, une fois dans la salle de torture: "Madame ne veut pas moi te frapper. Si moi te frapper, toi mort comme le petit." Il me fait agenouiller sur la pierre nue et mouillée. A cheval sur mon dos, me tenant par la nuque, il me plonge la tête jusqu'au cou dans un bidon d'eau sale qui sent le pipi et le pétrole. Il me retire quand je vais être asphyxié, me replonge après quelques secondes de respiration.

Une demi-heure de ce supplice, nouvel interrogatoire. (Rabemananjara 1947, quoted in Tronchon 1982: 285)

My first acquaintance with torture. In a small room adjoining the office of the Chief of Security, M. Baron, having forced me to go there, gave back a whip to the Senegalese Jean-Marie in charge of the operation, and left his office. During this time, Baron's secretary murmured some words in the ear of the Senegalese. He said to me, once in the torture room: "She no want me hit you. If me hit you, you dead like a dog." He forced me to kneel over the bare, wet stone. Straddling my back, taking me by the nape of the neck, he thrust my head to the neck into an oil drum of fouled water that smelled of urine and kerosene. He pulled me up just as I was about to be asphyxiated, then rethrust my head after some seconds of respiration. Half an hour of this punishment, a new interrogation.

Horrifying images—for one, the consignment of colonial savagery to Senegalese agents. While ordained by French administrators, better that other Black savages carry out such atrocities! A strategy—unleashing one savage upon another in an arena of primitive Otherness, to keep colonial hands clean. Taussig has written, "It is not the victim as animal that gratifies the torturer, but the fact that the victim is human, thus enabling the torturer to become the savage" (1992: 152). And Rabemananjara, highly educated and compassionate, having his head forced into a pot of fetid urine. Indeed, Rabemananjara's own civility rings through this account. In the midst of his own suffering, he reveals neither malice nor contempt for his Senegalese torturer or the French colonials in charge. Strangely, Europeans, noncognizant of their own brutality, have commonly condemned Malagasy ceremonial practices as senseless savagery, as hysterical, pathologic, or demonic.[3]

France granted Madagascar independence in 1960, and Philibert Tsiranana became president of the Malagasy "première république." He sustained a close alliance with (more aptly political and economic dependence upon) France and French advisors. In 1975, after three years of student strikes and political unrest, Didier Ratsiraka installed his socialist government in Madagascar. Ratsiraka had and still has numerous staunch supporters in Betsimisaraka territory, due in part to his claims to being Betsimisaraka.[4] Ratsiraka has been able to instill a somewhat unified sentiment of political allegiance among Betsimisaraka, though this has not viably represented a nationalist identity in the Tamatave region. Indeed, varied Malagasy senses of self and community on the east coast are much more affected by territorial and ancestral connections than by state-elicited ones.

These histories in the Tamatave region intone acts of dissension, betrayal, oppression, and misappropriation. Both Betsimisaraka and Antandroy in Tamatave though have creatively extracted from these frequently turbulent pasts whatever they could use to embellish their unique practices and to honor their own ancestors in the present, as will be illustrated in the following chapters. A mimetic faculty has been differentiated and regulated among *tromba-istes* on the east coast of Madagascar. Here, only desirable qualities of foreign presence are recollected and extracted, while colonialism's savageness remains in its past.

CHAPTER THREE

Spirit Practices on the East Coast

⌒

Numerous distinct *tromba* communities were thriving in the town of Tamatave-ville when I was there between 1993 and 1995. I participated in both Antandroy and Betsimisaraka practices. Antandroy exclusively participated in Antandroy ceremonies, whereas Betsimisaraka ceremonies might include participants from some of the other Malagasy groups who had re-settled in Tamatave, attesting to one incorporative property of Betsimisaraka ritual practice. Betsimisaraka and Antandroy *tromba-istes* did not attend each other's *tromba* ceremonies, except in the rare instance in which a Betsimisaraka might seek the assistance of an Antandroy healer (chap. 11). Knowledge that I moved freely between different *tromba* communities did not seem to trouble any of the *tromba-istes* I knew in Tamatave.

I was usually able to frequent at least one *tromba* event per week when in Tamatave. In any one village in the northern Tamatave region, *tromba* ceremony was less frequent than in Tamatave-ville, so I often traveled between three different villages, Betampona, Morondrano, and Fénérive-Est (a town, though much smaller than Tamatave-ville) when word arrived of an upcoming ceremony. I also attended and participated in numerous other ceremonies throughout the Tamatave countryside, such as *tsaboraha,* sacrificial ceremonies meant in part to please and honor ancestral spirits. Much "non-ceremonial" time was spent in the villages, for instance, in the rice fields; trekking into Fénérive-Est with fruit, coffee, and wares to sell at the market there; chatting or playing music in more informal settings. Nonceremonial time in Tamatave-ville would often be spent with vendors or guardians at the market, chatting with *tromba-istes* in their homes or on long walks through town, and playing music informally.

While most Malagasy in the Tamatave region believe in one way or another in ancestral spirits, and they might perform ceremonies that evoke connections to these spirits (such as *tsaboraha*), I would estimate that less than half of the Malagasy throughout this region actively practice *tromba* spirit possession. The following are introductory scenarios of some spirit practices in Tamatave-ville. I spent a great deal of both ceremonial and everyday time with the particular people represented here.

Velomaro and Delphine

The first Betsimisaraka *tromba* practitioners with whom I established a rapport in Tamatave-ville were Velomaro and his wife, Delphine, both approximately seventy years of age and both Betsileo, one of the eighteen to twenty different groups in Madagascar (from the south central part of the island). Velomaro and Delphine had been living in Tamatave since their youth. They both spoke Betsimisaraka (northern) and were essentially considered to be Betsimisaraka by other Malagasy in Tamatave, another indication of a pervasive incorporativeness among Betsimisaraka. Velomaro was one of the most respected mediums and healers in the area. When not practicing *tromba,* Velomaro often practiced his *sikidy* divination or tended to his few cattle; Delphine spent most of her time cooking, washing clothes, or going to the market.[1]

Neither Velomaro nor Delphine spoke French, and during this early period in my research I did not yet speak Malagasy fluently. Our first encounters were mediated by Kiki (a nickname for Jacqueline), a Betsimisaraka woman I had met one day at the market. During my first several months in Madagascar, Kiki accompanied me as mediator and translator, communicating for me with musicians and *tromba* practitioners who did not speak French. Kiki and I would visit Velomaro and Delphine, simply getting to know them, conversing, joking, and trying to explain to them what I was doing in Madagascar. Velomaro and Delphine seemed to become very fond of Kiki and me—a sentiment very much reciprocated. They always offered us advice, shelter, food, good humor, and access to their ceremonial practices, and they asked nothing in return.

Velomaro seemed uncomfortable trying to answer direct questions that I posed through Kiki, though he always tried to accommodate my inquiries. I remembered again Elinor Keenan's observations on communicative indirectness.[2] Guided by this same discursive aesthetic of indirectness, Kiki had been reluctant at first even to alert me of its immediacy in my interactions with Velomaro and Delphine. Velomaro simply suggested on his own that I attend his next *tromba* ceremony, the following week, to see things for myself. He also told us: "Tsy magninona fa manao sary anareô," "It's no problem for you two to take pictures." Kiki explained to Velomaro that we had a videorecorder, and he agreed as well to let us videotape the cere-

Photograph 1. Velomaro at *tromba* ceremony in Tamatave-ville, possessed by Andriamaro.

mony. Velomaro, of course, knew of the local video houses that showed foreign, mostly *Rambo*-like films, but he was not acquainted with portable equipment such as mine (I was using a very compact Sony Hi–8 videorecorder). This machine allows one to view immediately afterward what has been recorded. Postceremonial viewings through the videocamera became very popular with Velomaro and other *tromba-istes* at his ceremonies.

Photograph 2. Delphine posing just after *tromba* ceremony in Tamatave-ville.

Although it might seem a naive realization, it struck me then how much Velomaro and I were conditioned by different senses of what is "natural." "Nature" is sometimes thought to refer to a realm or to conditions independent of, beyond, or above culture. I mean to implicate the social constructedness of nature here. *Tromba* was natural to Velomaro—it worked for him, it had worked for his ancestors, and he had no need to question its workings. Indeed, *tromba* spirits and their powers, although constructed or resurrected in *tromba* ceremony, were natural to Velomaro. It was also unnatural to Velomaro to be interviewed or to be put on the spot by me to remember specific things.

On the other hand, *tromba* was new, fascinating, and perhaps even a bit intimidating to me at first. After several years of graduate school it was natural for me to want to search for information, to ask questions. Pondering natural differences between Velomaro and myself—in other words, cultural differences—I recalled Katie Stewart's distinction between decontaminated and contaminated theory:

> "Constructive" social-scientific theorizing sees its object from a decontaminated distance while "contaminated" deconstructive theorizing disrupts the distance between observing subject and the "real" world of objects; it mixes with its object and includes itself as an object of its own analysis. (1991: 395)

In these early encounters with Velomaro, I was realizing my own "contamination," *by* as well as *of* his world, and how much I would need to be an object of my own analysis.

The ceremony was to begin in the early afternoon. When Kiki and I arrived at Velomaro's house, Velomaro and Delphine were sitting on mats outside, casually chatting with other family members and *tromba-istes*. Both Velomaro and Delphine delighted in joking and making small talk, *miresadresaka*. Among other things, they were talking about the young wife of Tatasy, the accordion player for this day's ceremony. Tatasy was perhaps forty-five years old, and his wife was eighteen.[3] Velomaro and Delphine were playfully discussing the likelihood that Tatasy's wife would not stay with nor remain faithful to her older spouse. In fact, six months later Tatasy's young wife did leave him to return to her village in the countryside.

ᔐ

Tombo Daniel has a job at Port Toamasina—long physical hours, very little pay. Marcelline, his wife, makes me a bit nervous—she primarily wants money from me, often eyeing me with a glint of desire. They have performed together in France, and Ben Mandelson included two tracks of them on his Globe Style recording from the 1980s of Malagasy musics. Tombo Daniel is well known as a *valiha* player throughout Tamatave-ville though none of the tromba-*istes* with whom I've so far become acquainted employ his services. There seems to be some apprehension among them about Tombo Daniel's and Marcelline's apparently extraordinary preoccupation with obtaining large sums of money, which most tromba-*istes* don't have. Indeed, "tombo" translates as "profit." Perhaps a sense that they have in some way "sold out"? Tombo Daniel has been friendly and seems to enjoy talking with me; he seems to want to assist with my research. He invites me to accompany him to a tromba ceremony next week *en brousse,* prodding jokingly that it will be a daylong trip in a *lakana* (canoe) and would I be up to it? Marcelline objects passionately, saying that I'd have to pay them 50,000 FMg to be able to attend; she then rather suddenly becomes sullen and withdrawn. Tombo Daniel whispers to me, with what seems to me embarrassment, that I won't have to pay them this sum, though one should offer rum, cigarettes, and a small amount of money to tromba at the ceremony. After some whispering between Tombo Daniel and Marcelline, she seems to have an abrupt change of heart, and Tombo Daniel then instructs me to set up my recording equipment. Tombo Daniel (on *valiha*), Marcelline (on *kaiamba*), and his children (who sing and dance) proceed to perform tromba music for several hours, a personal show for me to record. Tombo Daniel winks and grins several times at me throughout.

Everyone needs money and things here. But play-for-pay or contrived sessions are of limited use. Can I reconcile my privileged presence here, my intrusion into people's personal lives and sacred practices?

(From my notes, November 28, 1993)

෴

In the course of our preceremony chatting, Delphine mentioned that there were distinct *tromba* communities in Tamatave-ville, some of them rather exclusive. She explained to Kiki and me that Tombo Daniel performed the music for one such exclusive group of *tromba-istes.* Velomaro, Delphine, and the rest of their *tromba* community did not practice or even socialize with this other group. Yet Delphine defended Tombo Daniel's character and his musicianship. She implied that Marcelline was a selfish woman who was plagued by malevolent spirits from farther north. Northern Betsimisaraka territory in particular is often thought to shelter a large number of *mpamôsavy,* or spell casters. Delphine suggested that we avoid Tombo Daniel and Marcelline, that they would try to profit from us. Kiki made a point of telling me that Delphine's way of telling this story was very drawn out, even somewhat evasive, that Delphine seemed not to want to say anything directly negative. Velomaro had remained silent; he even seemed to be wincing throughout this story. I gathered that he did not approve of such critical talk about his neighbors. Indeed, the more I became acquainted with Delphine, the more I learned that she very rarely criticized other people or things.

After perhaps an hour more of talking, Velomaro led us inside the house, which consisted of one small room with bamboo slat walls and corrugated sheet metal roof. Velomaro, Delphine, their son Charles (and later Charles's wife and infant) all lived together in this one room. Inside, Delphine began to tend to a small tray of burning *emboka,* an aromatic wood in the Tamatave region that is set smoldering to appeal to *tromba* and to alert them that they are being requested to appear at the present ceremony.[4] While the scent of burning *emboka* lures ancestral spirits into the present, it also sensually affects *tromba-istes* themselves. Its sweet odor can evoke the goings-on and moods of other *tromba* ceremonies, thus sometimes placing *tromba-istes* into other occasions or bringing those occasions into the experiential present. For instance, one older woman who was a spirit medium at this ceremony later told me that the smell of *emboka* brings up for her strongly emotive and detailed recollections of being a child in her father's house and of his own *tromba* ceremonies when she was a child.

It is important to note that possession among the *tromba-istes* with whom I worked in Tamatave was not a spontaneous phenomenon, but that *tromba* spirits had to be formally invited, stimulated, and appeased before they would appear (the case of *bilo* affliction among Antandroy, discussed later, is differentiated because these spirit forces are not literally considered to be *tromba*). Jean Rouch found that when he showed Haouka mediums in Ghana a film of themselves possessed, this viewing itself caused mediums to go into spontaneous possession, an effect he called "a kind of electroshock" (Rouch 1988: 232, quoted in Taussig 1993).[5] Bourguignon has described some Haitian *vodun* possession as the spontaneous result of "stress situations . . . without the ritual situation" (1976: 17). Such spontaneous possession did not occur among the *tromba-istes* with whom I worked—much preparation and performance was required to call *tromba* spirits. Musical performance, though, was *not* needed by all mediums throughout the island, nor even throughout Tamatave, to invoke possession. The authenticity of these extramusical possessions was sometimes questioned by Antandroy and Betsimisaraka in Tamatave, who did insist upon the primacy of music for possession.

Delphine also prepared a bowl of sacralizing water, into which she placed *tany malandy,* a white kaolin-like mineral used as a curative and purifying agent. She added some silver coins and a small piece of branch from a bush freshly taken from the yard. On the ground in front of the *emboka* altar a man in his thirties knelt, shrouded in a red *lamba hoany,* a large cotton wrap decorated with a pastoral scene of Madagascar and a short proverb. *Lamba hoany* (usually called simply *lamba*) are worn nonceremonially as well by both men and women, especially in the villages. Special ceremonial *lamba* are reserved solely for *tromba* ceremony. Red *lamba* are particularly favored and demanded by several very powerful Sakalava and Merina royal *tromba* (recall the late-nineteenth-century Malagasy resistance group called Mena*lamba,* "red *lamba*").

Once the alter was in order, Velomaro began to give a lengthy *kabary,* addressing both the present living participants and the ancestral spirits. This oration consisted largely of formulaic welcomes, requests for good health, and praise for these spirits, the *razana.* The speaking of ancestral names brings these ancestral personalities vividly into ceremonial consciousness, as preparation for bringing them more fully in embodied form into the present. Behind Velomaro were approximately ten women, most of them thirty to forty years old, and the accordionist, Tatasy, who began to play immediately at the close of Velomaro's *kabary.* Four or five of the women sitting on the ground, who later would go in and then out of being possessed by different *tromba,* were accompanying Tatasy's accordion by playing insecticide-can *kaiamba* shakers or by clapping in varied rhythms. Most of these women were established *tromba* mediums, who would usually become possessed by lesser spirits so as to provide company for the more powerful primary *tromba* to be called that day. Betsimisaraka *tromba-istes* insist that ancestral spirits prefer to have many other *tromba* present so that they can *midôla,* or play together. Such play, manifest in combinations of dancing, joking, drinking, smoking, sound density, and other actions is a primary interactional component of the performative aesthetic, *maresaka.*

[I]lay mosika izany, endrika amin'ny falifaliagna, ilay zavatra atao mba mpiravoravo ilay vahoaka. (Roger Jean Louis, Betsimisaraka accordionist in Tamatave-ville January 24, 1994)

This music is the image form of joyousness, that which brings happiness to Malagasy people.

Sound production not only notifies ancestral spirits that they are needed in the present, it contributes greatly to the actual embodiment of spirit into medium. These spirits are in essence controlled and directed in the present as musical and other acoustic waveforms play upon, against, and into body and psyche. The ceremonial body itself becomes a medium within which spirit and physical soundwave intermingle. For instance, enraptured *tromba* among Antandroy *tromba-istes* sometimes lay their borrowed head or body upon an accordion or *valiha* to bring body and spirit into sentient unity with sound. Joyousness in these ceremonial circumstances ensues as living ceremonial participants and revered ancestral spirits thus commune, to drink, dance, talk, and otherwise socialize together; thus, Roger Jean Louis's synaesthetic evaluation of music as "the image form of joyousness"—music that can take on its own visual shape, in the joyous social and spiritual interaction it facilitates.[6]

Delphine administered moistened *tany malandy* to the forehead and then the arms of the man in the red *lamba,* leaving white streaks across these areas. *Tromba* enter through a medium's head. *Tany malandy* purifies this point of entry as well as other parts of the body. The man in the red *lamba* had arranged this ceremony because he had been having persistent troubling dreams in which his wife, recently deceased, was making demands upon him and plaguing him with unkind taunts. Velomaro had consulted his *sikidy* divination seeds in an earlier meeting with this man and determined that the spirit of the man's wife wanted to possess him. The present ceremony was intended to invite the deceased wife's spirit into her husband's body and in so doing release the man from the tormentuous dreams in which his wife appeared.

The first communication between a *tromba* and its intended medium is commonly through dreams. In the case of royal *tromba,* a powerful man dressed in red, for instance, might make varied demands upon the dreaming person. Illness, difficult dreams, or other problems are often diagnosed by *ombiasa* as signs from *tromba* that they want to inhabit a particular person. Unless they are invited into the present with an elaborate ceremony, such as this one, *tromba* could plague that person with illness and bad fortune and might perhaps even cause her or his death. Some illnesses are determined by *ombiasa* to be non-*tromba*-related, in which case the patient might be advised to go to a *dokotera* (doctor). Colds or flus usually result in this sort of diagnosis, though most Malagasy in Tamatave cannot afford to go to a European-trained doctor. Intestinal ailments and inexplicable body pains are usually interpreted to be caused by *tromba* wanting to inhabit the afflicted person.

Velomaro had become possessed by Andriamaro, a powerful king who came regularly to him. His temperament had become very solemn, distant, even cautious. This transformation had been facilitated by Tatasy, who had played one of Andriamaro's favorite accordion tunes. Andriamaro thanked me for being there and for the cigarettes and "limonade" (a bottled soft drink) I had brought. He gently took my hand and after a brief moment of reflection said with a grin, "Tegna matanjaka 'anao!" (You certainly are strong!) Yet I had taken his hand rather timidly, not forcefully at all. Furthermore, I could not yet speak Malagasy well, I could not comprehend processually what I was experiencing, and my role in this particular ceremony was marginal. In actuality I was a quite disempowered guest.

A Malagasy king, an ultimate sign of Malagasy power, in the body of Velomaro, an influential and powerful person in Tamatave, was making a joke with a representative of foreign power, myself (with my entanglement of recording devices, cords, and notebooks). This was the substance of Andriamaro's clever comment: even with all my technological equipment, I was still subordinate at this ceremony to Malagasy and their royal ancestors.

Indeed, one royal spirit in the body of a woman medium told me that if he so desired he could erase all that I had recorded with a wink of his eye (to the delight and laughter of other *tromba-istes* present). However, he good-naturedly assured me that he would not interfere with my record-ings—after all, he wanted to view them himself on another occasion. In spite of my mass of electronic equipment, the *tromba-istes* present recog-nized that I was not so strong there. For one thing, *tromba* spirits could ef-fortlessly disempower any of my equipment. Later, more familiar with Velomaro's own clever sense of humor, I was certain that he had been playing upon the irony of differentials in empowerment at that moment in his *tromba* ceremony.

By then in Velomaro's ceremony, I had become an object of interest to the various *tromba* who were possessing Delphine and the several women in front of the altar. Much joking was going on about me, the *garamaso* (literally, the man with the transparent eyes). It was unusual for *tromba* spirits to encounter a *vazaha* (who wasn't a *tromba*) at such a ceremony, though they were quite pleasant and receptive, reservedly engaging me in discourse and testing my humor. One male spirit, embodied in an older woman medium, became quite frightened of me. Only after much assu-rance from Kiki that I had come as a friend and that I was *not* French, did this spirit become more relaxed, even friendly toward me. Kiki told me that this spirit's person had been killed at a young age by a colonial soldier dur-ing the 1947 anti-colonial insurgence in Madagascar.

A spirit entering the body usually causes the medium to emit rapid, force-ful voiced exhalations, a repeated "hooey" coming from deep in the dia-phragm, along with rapid hyperventilating. Some mediums' heads would snap around, sometimes dangerously it seemed to me, or their bodies would convulse uncontrollably and rapidly. Several times, upon observing the bod-ily signals of the arrival of a *tromba,* Tatasy and some of the *kaiamba* players or those participants who were clapping hands would hasten to the side of the medium about to be possessed. They would play and clap forcefully to-ward the medium's ears and head, driving tactile sound waves into and onto the body as enticement to a *tromba* to enter that body. Indeed, the penetra-tion of sound waves into the body or its force upon it seemed to parallel the infusion of spirit into that body. On other occasions, Betsimisaraka musi-cians asserted the power inherent in sound when they assured me that if they were to direct enough of their music at me, *tromba* would then come possess me as well. The sounds of the *kaiamba* seemed particularly effective for enticing *tromba* to enter the body at Velomaro's ceremony.

Dressing and redressing in the proper garb desired by particular *tromba* as they arrive are crucial processes in Betsimisaraka *tromba* ceremonies. Betsimisaraka mediums bring plastic satchels with the wardrobes of their various *tromba* to each ceremony. There was one elderly woman at this particular ceremony, not a *tromba* medium, whose duty it was to assist mediums in changing costumes as different *tromba* came to them. One or more such dressing attendants are commonly present at Betsimisaraka *tromba* ceremonies. Some *tromba* demand privacy for dressing, so a white *lamba* has to be held up by the attendant(s) as partition from the rest of the participants.

Redressing is also a ritual process in Merina *famadihana,* a ceremony involving the rewrapping and reburial of ancestral remains. In fact, Gillian Feeley-Harnik (1989) draws a connection between rewrapping the dead in *famadihana* and redressing the ancestral spirit as possessed medium in Sakalava *tromba*. In both Merina and Betsimisaraka territories there has historically been considerable contact with colonials and other Europeans. Among Antandroy, who generally have retained an insularity from foreign contact, elaborate recostuming in *tromba* ceremony in Tamatave is not practiced, nor does the role of dressing attendant exist. Thus, I gathered there might be some symbolic significance to the redressing process that perhaps implicates varying degrees of European or perhaps Islamic contact (a connection supported by Michael Lambek, who recently told me that, in northwestern Madagascar, Islamic presence has indeed influenced clothing style among Sakalava [personal communication, 1999]).

By that time in Velomaro's ceremony several *tromba* were drinking rum and smoking cigarettes. In accounts of possession or trance states, specific substances or actions are sometimes thought to be primary agents in bringing on alterations of consciousness. For instance, in the Putumayo area of Colombia, hallucinogenic *yagé* induces shamanic curing visions (Taussig 1987). Shona in Zimbabwe purportedly drink millet beer and dance as inducement to becoming possessed (Berliner 1981). Gilbert Rouget has also attributed dance with "a cathartic role" in "the realization of the state of enthusiasm" (1980: 118). In Tamatave, rum is consumed heavily only by particular *tromba*, usually after a medium becomes possessed. Little if any consumption of alcohol occurs prior to possession (perhaps a small amount as part of a *tsodrano,* or benediction). Some *tromba* spirits even prohibit their mediums from ever drinking rum. Dancing also would occur in a ceremony only after possession. Thus alcohol or other chemical substances would not seem to contribute to the actual inducement of possession in *tromba*. Nor does dancing contribute in its physiologic effects upon body and psyche, such as in its capacity to induce endorphin production.[7]

After approximately six hours of constant accordion and *kaiamba* playing, sporadic outbursts of dancing among the possessed women, and much discursive interaction among everyone present, the man in the red *lamba* was still sitting solemnly in front of the altar. He had not yet been visited by his deceased wife's spirit, even though other *tromba* had been devoting themselves to ministering to the invited spirit. This was done largely, as mentioned, by playing *kaiamba* as well as speaking directly into the ears of the man, applying perfume (*rano magnitra*, "sweet water") under his nose, blowing cigarette smoke into his face and ears, anointing his head with water from the bowl of *tany malandy*, silver coins, and herbs, as well as gently caressing and patting his body. All of these corporeal and sensual tactics were intended to stimulate the medium's body in various ways, or, more precisely, to stimulate the *tromba* spirit itself to convene with the medium's body. The ceremony continued for several more hours, but the spirit of the man's deceased wife refused to come. Tatasy, trying to appeal to this reluctant *tromba*, eventually tried several different tunes on the accordion, including a polka and some compositions in 4/4 meter. The *kaiamba* shakers dropped out for these compositions. Tatasy later explained that, since this woman had died only recently, he thought that her spirit might be enticed by newer musics, ones other than the usual Betsimisaraka ceremonial genre, called *basesa*. However, the desired spirit never did appear in the course of this ceremony, even though many other spirits made an appearance.

The various *tromba* of Delphine, Velomaro, and the other women in front of the altar eventually departed to a composition played by Tatasy, which he explained later as a "returning home tune" (*hira andeha hody*). Velomaro and the others helped the man in the red *lamba* to his feet. He had great difficulty standing, for he had been kneeling before the altar without changing position for several uninterrupted hours. He painfully walked off the aftereffects. He seemed exhausted and perhaps a bit depressed.

The next day, Velomaro and Delphine explained that the spirit of this man's wife had not come because the man had unwittingly ignored Velomaro's order to take several purifying baths. *Tromba* usually demand cleanliness of their human mediums, often imposing strict though varying *fady*, or taboos, on, for example, the consumption of pork, crab, and chicken. Each of these is often believed to be *maloto* (dirty). Some of these *tromba* prohibitions are similar to those commonly imposed by Islam. While these particular *tromba-istes* did not voice a connection in regard to food restrictions, they did enact other recollections of Islamic influence in Madagascar (chap. 8). Velomaro added that this had still been a successful and efficacious ceremony: "Les *tromba* étaient contents de cette cérémonie. Ils réglaient le procédé et ils sont venus même que le *tromba* de la femme morte n'est pas venu" (Kiki's translation from Malagasy into French). In English, "The *tromba* were content with this ceremony. They presided over the proceedings, and they came into the present even though the *tromba* of the dead woman did not come."

Tompezolo and Famboara

Antandroy *tromba* ceremonies in Tamatave-ville are characteristically much smaller and more consistently solemn than those of Betsimisaraka, which are often quite boisterous in character.[8] In my experience only one *tromba* spirit at a time would come into the present in an Antandroy ceremony, thus interaction between this presiding *tromba* and the nonpossessed participants would be focal. Betsimisaraka ceremonies would rely more upon direct engagement *between* numerous powerful Others. The unique character of either Antandroy or Betsimisaraka *tromba* practices corresponds to distinct recollections of differing pasts, which is taken up in subsequent chapters.

Tompezolo, an Antandroy woman in her late twenties, and her husband, Famboara, had left Ambovombe for Tamatave-ville one year earlier, intending to acquire some capital there for their elder family members still in Ambovombe. They had a one-room house in one of the Antandroy quarters on the edge of Tamatave-ville. Tompezolo and Famboara performed *tromba* perhaps once a week, often by request from another Antandroy with a specific problem. And they often performed *tromba* for themselves and other Antandroy as devotional practice, distinct from any particular need to heal, advise, or resolve disputes. Many of the Antandroy in Tamatave-ville are younger, like Tompezolo and Famboara. It is often these younger, more able-bodied Antandroy who leave Ambovombe to search for wage labor or other capital gain in Tamatave-ville. When not practicing *tromba*, Tompezolo and Famboara spent much time selling fruit and vegetables from a stand at the market in their quartier. They were often boiling root vegetables, corn, or *antaka*, a small, hard bean from the south, for sale at their stand. Famboara was also adept at *sikidy* divination, and he was visited regularly by other Antandroy needing his assistance.

When Tompezolo was a teenager, she suddenly began to have severe recurring pains in her right forearm, along with troubling dreams in which an elderly non-Antandroy Malagasy man would make demands upon her. An Antandroy *ombiasa* in Ambovombe diagnosed these symptoms to be signs that a *tromba* spirit was interested in her. Thus, she would need to perform an initiative ceremony to formally instate herself as a spirit medium. This ceremony included the sacrifice of a young goat and musical performance, both needed to sacralize the event, and to coax the particular spirit interested in Tompezolo into arriving in her body for the first time. Since these first dreams, Tompezolo had been a devout *tromba*-iste. Most of the interactions I had with Tompezolo and Famboara were permeated with talk of ancestral spirits.

Tompezolo's *tromba* altar consisted of a bricolage of seemingly disjunct things. She always had *emboka* burning, a bowl of sacred water, and a fragment of *tany malandy* in the altar space. Tompezolo's altar commonly also included a playing card–size picture of Jesosy (Jesus), a small statue of the Virgin Mary, a handkerchief with red, green, and white sections (a miniature copy of the flag of Madagascar), a small hand mirror, plastic sunglasses, a few French francs, and an Antandroy *vangovango,* a silver bracelet that in part engendered connections to the specific lineage of Sakalava ancestors called Zafimbolafotsy, or grandchildren of silver (more on Tompezolo's altar appears in chap. 6).

An hour or so of musical performance might occur before one of Tompezolo's *tromba* would come to her. The music during these early moments—usually on *valiha* at most of Tompezolo's ceremonies, though also performed on accordion—would be heated, incredibly fast, complex. Musicians did not become possessed by *tromba* while performing, though they might become spirit mediums in other contexts in which they were not performing music. While waiting for a *tromba*'s arrival, Tompezolo would sit solemnly in front of her altar, chain smoking (Tompezolo did not usually smoke), gazing intently yet, seemingly, at nothing in particular, or perhaps oiling her braided hair. It was inconceivable to Tompezolo and her friends that one might try to call *tromba* without musical performance—the spirits simply would not respond. Indeed, ancestral spirits at Antandroy ceremonies in Tamatave-ville always arrived only after a considerable amount of musical and other energy had been expended.

Nofy Soa ("good dream," a nickname), another young Antandroy, was a frequent participant in Tompezolo's ceremonies. He was particularly adept at verbal discourse with the ancestral spirits, often making *tsodrano,* or benedictions to them. He often offered a continuous running narrative to, about, and for the *razana,* the collective of ancestral spirits, during the course of a ceremony. He also would provide continuous *kaiamba* shaker accompaniment with the *valiha* player. Nofy Soa himself was not a *tromba* medium.

Once a *tromba* arrived, Tompezolo's body would begin to spasm and quiver with an extremely rapid frequency. Her facial expressions and bodily posture would change drastically and convincingly. She would often speak in a dialect then unrecognizable to me—this was the Sakalava dialect, spoken by her *tromba.* Famboara had become adept in Sakalava so that he could mediate between Tompezolo's spirits and the other Antandrory *tromba-istes* who did not speak this dialect.

Interestingly, in consideration of the importance of varied modes of communication between ancestral spirits and the living, Tompezolo would sometimes become possessed by one particular *tromba* spirit named Moany. This spirit was incapable of speaking (*moana* means mute or unable to

Photograph 3. Tompezolo, Tamatave-ville.

speak). When Moany arrived, Tompezolo became reserved, distant, introspective. Famboara explained that Moany was part *vazaha,* or White outsider. I wondered if Moany's character perhaps reflected well-circulated
knowledge and experience of *vazaha* condescension toward or exclusion of
Malagasy people.

During an Antandroy *tromba* ceremony the *valiha* (often called *maro
tady* or *maro vany* [many strings] by Antandroy in Tamatave-ville) was
commonly passed from person to person, for there were numerous accomplished Antandroy *valiha* players in town. I never witnessed such communality of musical performance in Betsimisaraka *tromba* ceremonies, in

which one musician on either *valiha* or accordion was hired to perform for the length of the entire ceremony. Again, Betsimisaraka, long accustomed to foreign contact in Tamatave, may have sometimes been more influenced by individualist ideas and practices arising from such contact; however, individualist behavior or sentiment might not necessarily evolve simply from having had contact with foreigners. Differing ideas about performance practice—here its communality or individuality—perhaps trace and reflect different amounts and kinds of influence from outside worlds.

Once possessed, Tompezolo and other Antandroy mediums often positioned themselves eventually in front of the performing musician and laid their body upon the *valiha* or their head upon the *gorodora* (accordion), swaying, quivering, or shaking in synch with the music. Musician, medium, and *tromba* spirit thus became conjoined in sentient union. Music and the physical compression of sound waves effectively engendered the tactile unification of past and present, royal and everyday, self and other, musician and nonmusician in the body of the possessed and in the space of the *tromba* house.

When possessed by *tromba*, Tompezolo and other mediums, both Antandroy and Betsimisaraka, take on the specialized skills and knowledge of their particular spirits. This often includes extensive knowledge of varied herbs and tree barks used for healing, the ability to see into the future and back into varied pasts, and the wisdom to advise and to settle problems. At my first *tromba* ceremony with Tompezolo, a young Antandroy man had come complaining of severe shoulder pain. One of Tompezolo's *tromba* revealed that he himself had caused the pain, because he wanted this man to become his medium. Tompezolo's spirit mixed a complex combination of herbs and shaved tree barks and instructed the man to mix it with water and to drink it. The spirit then told the man that he would need to buy some *lamba* and rum, bring in musicians, and perform a *tromba* ceremony to formally become his medium. The afflicted Antandroy man seemed pleased with this result—that he would become a *tromba* medium.

On one occasion, I accompanied Marie-Yvonne, a Betsimisaraka *tromba-iste*, to see Tompezolo. Marie-Yvonne had been having some severe back pain, which had persisted even through several visits to Betsimisaraka healers. Antandroy are often known, sometimes even feared, throughout Madagascar as the most adept in spiritual and healing matters. A myth of Antandroy wildness and savageness commonly circulates through some circles in Tamatave (chap. 11).

Once the final *tromba* of the day left Tompezolo's body, to a "going home" composition performed by the musicians, she would return to her shy, smiling, reserved demeanor. With her posture relaxed and her hair

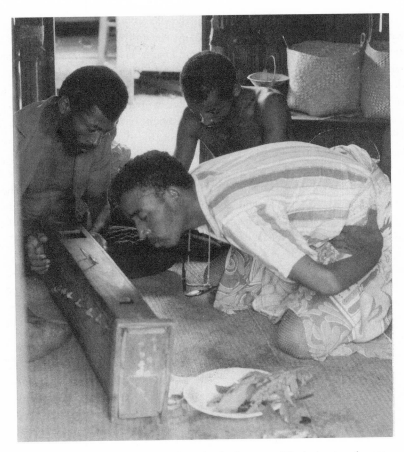

Photograph 4. Zoma Velo, possessed, putting body onto *valiha* during *tromba* ceremony; Velontsoa on *valiha*.

⌇

down, she would ask Famboara and the rest of us to detail what had happened while she was possessed. The mood in the *tromba* house relaxed, often to include much joking and perhaps a meal of rice with beans.

⌇

Today commemorates the 1947 Malagasy insurrection against colonial domination. This rebellion was greatly fueled by participation from villagers in the Tamatave region. Tamatave-ville though is strangely quiet and non-commemorative in appearance today—no parades or public events, seemingly little individual recognition of this day as a special one. Are people perhaps weary of remembering?

I've just returned from about a month in the villages—anxious to see Magnampy Soa, Velontsoa, Tompezolo, Vinelo, my Antandroy friends in Tamatave-ville. Antandroy at the market, some of whom I barely know, are grabbing me, embracing me emotionally, all inexplicably, until one Antandroy woman I do know informs me that a story has been circulating about a vazaha being killed *ambani-volo,* or out in the countryside. It was feared here in town that I had been the victim. I headed for Velontsoa's. My arrival didn't agitate him emotionally as it had the others. He told me that he had been consulting his sikidy, thus he knew I was okay. In fact, he knew that I would arrive on this very day, he was expecting me. We had better go immediately to Tompezolo's though, he told me whisking me off in her direction. Tompezolo at first seemed stunned to see me, then she leapt to her feet and grabbed me, erupting with delight. She had feared that Velontsoa's sikidy might not be accurate in vazaha matters and she had given in to the rumors that I was dead. Famboara told me that she had been refusing to eat, that she had been deeply upset. After much verbal tsodrano to the razana and relieved talking with me, Tompezolo went into a small box of things, pulled out a single silver Antandroy *kavina,* earring, and gave it to me. "Ho'anahy izay?" (Is this for me?) I asked reservedly. Tompezolo said cheerfully "Iah, fa tsisy fagnomezana io kavina io— fahatsiarovana izay" (Yeah, though it's not a gift, but something to always remember me by.

(From my notes, March 29, 1994)

࿇

Velontsoa

࿇

First meeting with Antandroy musicians in Tamatave-ville, set up by Dida, a Merina entrepreneur in Tamatave-ville. A prearranged recording session. The sun has set. I can smell and hear the Indian Ocean close by. There is one *valiha* player, Velontsoa, one *kaiamba* player, Mandimby Soa, and two women, Toronasy and Vatsambinee, all who are sitting barefoot in the sand in the courtyard of Dida's small music studio, a weather-worn colonial-style house. The scene feels awkward, as though these Antandroy musicians are not quite comfortable with Dida or me. Or perhaps Dida is not comfortable in their presence.

Velontsoa and Mandimby Soa are completely entranced and absorbed when they play. Velontsoa leans his upper body nearly horizontal over and very close to the *valiha,* which he is straddling in the sand. The sound escaping from the two sound holes appears to prop him up in an acoustic weightlessness—exquisite sounds. Rivulets of perspiration roll off his face onto his bare chest. Mandimby Soa speaks/chants much and heatedly while playing *kaiamba,* apparently to no one in particular. Velontsoa is performing masterfully, a complex music that is ecstatically new to me, upon an instrument that appears to be constructed of salvaged parts of other things and well-worn planks of wood. Velontsoa is playing so rapidly, accurately, and beautifully that it is almost disturbing—as though this is more music than one person could make and articulate so well through such a worn-looking instrument.

Dida tells me in French that Velontsoa says there's no *tromba* without music—music communicates with or invokes ancestral spirits. Dida also informs me that Mandimby Soa has asked if he can have my shoes.

(From my notes, October 10, 1993)

ᥬᵔ

Tompezolo preferred Velontsoa as *valiha* player for her *tromba* ceremonies. Velontsoa was a consummate musician, using every available moment in the day to play the *maro tady,* as he would often call the *valiha.* Velontsoa was extraordinarily gifted as a musical improviser. He was constantly adding new and reworking old musical material. Such improvisatory skill was a crucial factor in the creation of ceremonial *maresaka.* He would play for hours on end, both during *tromba* ceremony and on everyday occasions. When playing *valiha,* Velontsoa seemed unmoved by the passage of time or by occurrences around him. He did not seem to become worn down by wear on the body—for instance, from sitting in a cramped space or from plucking thick, taut metal wire strings, which can carve away at the flesh on one's fingers.

Velontsoa was employed as a guardian at a small automobile garage across town from the large market in Tamatave-ville. He was allowed to live there with his wife, Mendoe, and their four children in a one-room bamboo dwelling that they had to share with shelves of used grease-black car parts stored there by the Merina boss. Their cramped auto-part-fouled space was intruded upon regularly by the Merina garage workers, who entered irreverently without knocking or checking to see what might be happening inside. Velontsoa was often performing *sikidy* for other Antandroy, who would come to his small shared house for assistance with various problems. About *sikidy,* Velontsoa told me that the *razana* could communicate with the living through formations of *voafagne* (seeds), flat round grains from the seed pod of a tree held to be sacred by Antandroy. While the performance of *sikidy* is not dependent upon music, it is frequently young Antandroy musicians who are adept at this practice in Tamatave-ville. Thus, there seemed an implicit connection between musical acuity and other forms of spiritual communicativeness among Antandroy.

Mendoe would spend all day cooking, cleaning, washing clothes, and tending to her children. After dark she would leave for the market, with her young children, to sell cigarettes and peanuts throughout the night, mostly to prostitutes, drunken Malagasy military men with old Soviet-issue automatic rifles dangling haphazardly from their shoulders, and operators of *pousse-pousse,* a rickshaw-like vehicle (from the French *pousser*).

Velontsoa agonized inwardly over the scant possibility that he would ever be able to ameliorate his situation, that he and his family might ever escape material poverty, frequent illness, and social discrimination. Velontsoa's anguish was intensified by the fact that he could not capitalize on his extensive musical skills, though he was aware that some Malagasy popular musicians, such as Rossy, were able to do so. Velontsoa found relief from his torment in his intense spiritual devotion. He also drank rum heavily, and once returned from a drinking session with other Antandroy beaten nearly to death, apparently for having turned his frustration on others.

Velontsoa was always very kind, generous, patient with, and even protective of me. We spent countless hours in his small, motor-oil-fouled house, lit by one small kerosene lamp, playing *kaiamba* and *valiha* together. Often I would begin by playing *kaiamba;* then Velontsoa would pass me his *valiha* and would patiently and encouragingly accompany my first slow and wobbly steps on the instruments. When I could play well enough, Velontsoa gave me his instrument to keep, one coveted for its exquisite tone by other Antandroy *valiha* players in Tamatave-ville. Velontsoa's reputation as musician, instrument builder, and *sikidy* performer was unsurpassed.

Magnampy Soa and Very Soa

Magnampy Soa was playing his accordion again today in the street. He was barefoot and wearing torn and soiled rags—his accordion is equally worn and street-soiled. He manipulated the instrument imperiously, exploiting a great variety of sonorities and timbres. Sometimes he delicately coaxed soft tones from the instrument, pushing and pulling the bellows slowly and softly. Then he would shift to overworking the bellows in a maniacal fervor. [I noticed that the left-hand buttons of his accordion are tuned differently than on my own accordion, though I could not ascertain from this session exactly how the tunings vary.] He sometimes twisted the bellows on his push in and draw out of the accordion to effect a raucous-sounding slap that seemed to serve as accentuation of varied rhythmic pulses. He whistled and hissed, cigarette dangling from the corner of his mouth, all in synch with his accordion playing. His powerful body bounced, jerked, throbbed, slapped the pavement, also in synch with his playing. An overwhelming scene to overhear—left me choking back sobs of intensity.

I bought Magnampy Soa a pack of cigarettes and drank a *toaka gasy*, a rum, with him—hardly adequate compensation for such spectacular musical skills. Neither of us seemed to know what to make of the other.

(From my notes, October 15, 1993)

Whole families of Antandroy lived in roadside encampments throughout the large central market in Tamatave-ville, barely shielded from the nearly constant passing of trucks, autos, small motorcycles, and shoppers. These Antandroy shelters were pieced together from fragments of sheet plastic, cardboard, and bits of rusting old roofing sheet metal *(tôle),* all tented between deteriorated colonial-style cement buildings and the sidewalk below. In the daytime, Antandroy sold fruit, cigarettes, peanuts, and bread on makeshift stands from their places on the side of this busy road. Throughout the evening, Antandroy men were employed by Merina or Indian merchants whose shops often provided the only vertical wall of their encampments. Indian shopowners in particular are often called *Karana* in Malagasy, a term likely derived from Koran that sometimes carries a derogatory inflection. Antandroy were paid only minimally by these bosses to sit from sundown to sunrise as guardians of their shops. Some Antandroy had small houses in one of the Antandroy quartiers of Tamatave-ville, but the nature of their constant day-into-night work usually kept them at the market most of the time.

Antandroy often evoke apprehension, even terror among some other Malagasy. For one thing, they are said to unrestrainedly kill anyone who steals from them. Thus, Antandroy presence itself is enough to deter any notion of thievery. Antandroy men, barefoot and clothed in garments soiled and torn from this constant street existence, would commonly be found at night sitting calmly on the ground in their encampments, contemplative, with silver-tipped spears poised against their bodies.

I came to spend a great deal of time in Tamatave-ville with two Antandroy twin brothers, Magnampy Soa and Very Soa, who had migrated from the south to seek wage labor. Magnampy Soa and Very Soa were both extraordinary accordionists. They lived with their large families in two separate Antandroy encampments on the main road that forms one perimeter of the market in Tamatave-ville. Both brothers, their wives, their numerous children, and extended family members all slept on meager beds on the concrete sidewalk within these shelters. Several times a year the local gendarmes in Tamatave-ville forced Magnampy Soa and Very Soa, as well as other Antandroy, to tear down their shelters and move off the street. A covert "tax" was usually collected by the gendarmes from Antandroy, who then eventually reclaimed their sites and rebuilt their encampments.

Photograph 5. Very Soa, playing accordion from his fruitstand at the large central market, the *bazary be,* in Tamatave-ville.

While Magnampy Soa and Very Soa did not receive any share of the capital gain accrued in the shops they guarded (only their inadequately small guardian wage), they each creatively exploited and empowered the space in front of their Karana shops for its potential as a store of their own from which to sell fruit, cigarettes, and bread. Thus, they were able to extend into the street the system of capital exchange that governed inside the shops. Magnampy Soa and Very Soa did not practice *tromba* ceremony

with the frequency or regularity of Velontsoa and Tompezolo. Their time was consumed with their fruitstands and guardian responsibilities, with providing for their very large extended families living with them. Velontsoa and Mendoe had four children; Tompezolo and Fanboura had none—they had comparatively fewer immediate people to care for. Yet even with greater familial responsibilities, Magnampy Soa and Very Soa spent every available moment playing accordion. As spiritualists they were just as intent as those who practiced *tromba* more regularly.

Once when coming to visit Magnampy Soa, I was led by one of his young children to an old colonial-style cement building a few blocks away. Inside, several Antandroy men, including Magnampy Soa, were sitting on boxes or wooden pallets. The room was dark and damp, usually uninhabited. A tape recording was playing a single voice, an Antandroy man singing lamentfully. Magnampy Soa signaled to me not to speak. I took a seat with the men and listened to the tape. Later Magnampy Soa explained that an elder Antandroy man had died the day before in one of the Antandroy quartiers on the edge of town. The tape was of a man yet living in Ambovombe who was known for his exceptional voice—he was singing for the dead on this recording. This event was implicit with a doubled sense of loss. These Antandroy men were lamenting the loss of a friend and family member, but there appeared to be another mode of separation here, signaled by the need to play a recording in the absence in Tamatave of a singer skilled in this particular mode of song.

∽

Antandroy can invoke fear in Tamatave-ville, partly because of their well-known, unusually strong connection with ancestral spirits (chap. 11). From their corners of the market, they are frequently playing music easily audible to other Malagasy who often neither like nor comprehend what they hear. There are acoustically demarcated, marginalized Antandroy zones on the streets around and through this large market. Other Malagasy usually venture into these zones only long enough to purchase a *voatsabo* (watermelon) or some *akondro* (bananas), for Antandroy are commonly believed to have the best fruit for sale.

Later in the evenings, Magnampy Soa, Very Soa, and other Antandroy guardians could abandon somewhat the system of capital exchange with which they were often so preoccupied during the daytime. They would use much of their guarding time to perform spiritual musics throughout the night. From these spaces Antandroy created a musical *maresaka* that was above all communication to and with revered ancestral spirits, a *maresaka* quite distinct from that created by Betsimisaraka and other Malagasy.

CHAPTER FOUR

Maresaka

～

When Malagasy on the east coast exclaim "*maresaka* izay!" or "*maresaka* e!"—"in the groove" might be homologous—they are usually making an aesthetic evaluation, often of a performative moment that is particularly pleasing or masterful. *Maresaka* calls for the combination and integration of a density of varied sonorities, visual elements, and bodily movement. It involves not only sound production among the living but also the resultant sound, motion, emotion, and often commotion of ancestral spirits interacting and celebrating joyously in the present with the living.

Maresaka created by the living can then also call upon ancestral spirits to dance, drink, joke, and converse with one another as well. These spirits consequently create their own interactive mode of *maresaka*. Feeley-Harnik has noted the potency of discursive power among Sakalava: "Silence is what buries people, but only talk can bring ancestors back out of the dead" (1991b: 45). Among Malagasy on the east coast, it is not only talk that empowers ancestors (and subsequently the living), but an imbrication of sounds—varied rhythms, timbres, textures, volumes—along with the combined sounds of handclapping, dancing, laughing, joking, singing, and chanting.

Bruce Kapferer describes some effects of the combined immediacy of sound and movement in Sri Lanka:

In the Sinhalese system, dance fills out the time-structure of music and makes visible its movement and passage. An essential property of the time-structure of music and dance is that it constitutes a continuous present. Musical time is movement and passage filled out in its existential immediacy. Because of these aspects, members of the ritual gathering who are engaged within the musical context of the patient can share the same vivid and continuous present, which is an experiential possibility of music. Musical time is reversible, and it is in this reversibility that the structure of music and dance finds its essential coherence. The time-structure of music and dance tends both forward and back in the very moment of its presentation to the senses. (Kapferer 1986: 198)

In Malagasy ceremonial performance, music and dance create an immediacy of shared experience between ceremonial participants and ancestral spirits, in part complicating temporal boundaries and order in the present moment (as well as the past, since the present is reciprocally projected into it). In *tromba* ceremony musical time is combinative as well as reversible (Lambek uses the term "additive" [1998: 108]), as it brings present and past into one other. An eighteenth-century Sakalava king, for instance, could interact in his own court with the spirit of a Malagasy prostitute who had died only in the past year. Moments later, or even at the same moment, a French colonial administrator might enter into the present to give advice to and joke with an American (myself), all in a dramatic imbrication of differences.

The makeup and intensity of *maresaka* is often complemented by visual elements. In terms of a general visual aesthetic, highly ornate material crafts are not conventionally produced in Tamatave. Both Antandroy and Betsimisaraka there commonly remark upon material beauty in a *tanty* (sisal basket) that holds rice well, is tightly woven, has strong handles, or is the proper size (for carrying chickens, for example); or in an Antandroy *vangovango* (silver bracelet) that is not ornate on European terms yet is an item imbued with the Antandroy power inherent in silver itself. Malagasy on the east coast find things to be visually beautiful that are structurally sound, handmade, have a tight weave or a good fit, and work well. This is a material aesthetic of interiorization, of seeing inherent values and meanings in things, of embedding and finding style on the inside (Sontag 1990: 17). Musically, this aesthetic of interiorized beauty transfers into the complexities and subtleties of a performative weave between musical time and historical time. It is also emergent when Malagasy extract dormant acoustic value along with unique historical and spiritual significance from apparently disparate nonmusical materials, such as industrial cabling and roofing sheet metal, or when they structurally rework from within once colonial instruments.

Imbrication, recycling, recirculating, and combining are visually embodied in Tamatave in everyday practices: houses held together with disparate reused materials; clothing patched together from fragments of other clothing and nonclothing, such as remnants of burlap sacks; musical instruments pieced together from salvaged parts of other nonmusical things (or instruments otherwise altered). While material poverty has been pervasive on the east coast for some time, it is often admittedly difficult to separate exigency from aesthetic. Yet these practices do not simply reflect necessity arising from extreme material poverty throughout this region. They are inherent with an aesthetic choice as well. The term *fifangaro,* which translates as "intermixing," itself is often used in reference to cooking, instrument construction, musical performance, house building, making clothing, and more.[1]

The production of *maresaka* also is often reliant upon elements of the infusion into Malagasy practices of what is felt to have come from distant places.[2] In *tromba* spirit possession ceremonies the music that is essential to calling and communicating with ancestral spirits is performed upon co-lonially introduced accordions or on *valiha* with unraveled industrial cable strands for strings. The body of the *valiha* is sometimes constructed from thin, corrugated roofing sheet metal called *tôle*. East coast Malagasy commonly value these once foreign things as mediums for the embellish-ment and intensification of *maresaka*. Tombo Daniel explained to me that metal strings and metal-body *valiha* produce more *maresaka* than older versions of this instrument constructed of bamboo. He said that the voice of the newer instrument projects better over the often loud panorama of sound created by the crowd at a ceremony. Tombo Daniel also said that, historically, if one lived in the villages, she or he most often could not af-ford to own an accordion, so the *valiha* had been prevalent there. He in-sisted that the *valiha* represented to him an original, pure *basesa* (genre of Betsimisaraka music and dance), while the accordion had had more trans-formative effect upon Betsimisaraka practices. (Tombo Daniel said liter-ally, "Tegna 'original' *basesa* ilay valiha . . . tsy maintsy fa tegna pira *basesa* mihitsy" [the *valiha* is the truly original *basesa* . . . it is necessarily the real, true *basesa*].)

In *tromba* ceremony in Tamatave, there occurs an indexical linkage between bringing what had been foreign materials, ideas, and even expres-sive forms into sacred Malagasy ceremony—indeed, depending on these things—and in bringing ancestral spirits into the ceremonial body. These spirits are always already in some sense foreign to the mediums on the east coast who invite them into the present. The most powerful spirits in *tromba* ceremony are usually Sakalava royalty from the northwestern re-gions of Madagascar or Merina royalty from the central Haut Plateau re-gion. Both of these other groups of Malagasy are distinct—linguistically and ancestrally, for instance—from Betsimisaraka and Antandroy on the east coast. Thus, a majority of *tromba* spirits in essence are foreigners when on the east coast. In addition, some *tromba* spirits, such as Georges Klint-sky and Sadam Hoseny, are personalities who come from outside Madagas-car to enter into a Malagasy present to interact within it. Appearances by such foreign spirits also attest to a component of *maresaka* that relies upon incorporating outer into inner, of making things more locally potent by in-corporating the dissimilar or distant into local practices.

The manipulating of musical time is another important component in the musical aesthetic *maresaka*. Temporal reordering in and by musical performance encompasses both taking control over time and a giving into it, a constant reworking of musical time concurrent with a surrendering to historical times. *Tromba* possession means, in part, stepping beyond the spatial and temporal coordinates of the present moment, yet it is the acoustic intensification of this moment that brings the past into it and projects the present back into the past. *Maresaka* does not freeze time in *tromba* spirit possession ceremony; it conflates varied times into an interactional past/present. The musical performance itself actualizes the temporal structures of such empowering timelessness: the long duration over which one composition is drawn out, the shifting in and then out of phase between *kaiamba* shaker and *valiha* or accordion, as well as the cross-rhythmic capacities of the *valiha* and accordion themselves, the essential improvisation that takes place inside more defined replicated phrase structures, and a complex tripartite rhythm that is a vital component of most Malagasy ceremonial music. Historical time thus is brought into synch with everyday time through manipulations of musical time.

Foreignness as Always Already Familiar

A collective sense of a particular past of *métissage,* or intermixing, is sometimes expressed on the east coast.[3] *Métissage* can be a lived-in style of remembering that emanates in part from a self-awareness among east coast Malagasy of varying combinations of Southeast Asian or Austronesian, African, Indian, European, Chinese, and Islamic ancestry. One such recollection involves the first inhabitants of the island, called *vazimba*. Malagasy commonly describe *vazimba* as composite beings, in which disembodied spirit characteristics combine with human ones. This particular consciousness of a combining past is mirrored as well in beliefs about the present. Many Malagasy express sentiments that their own spirit and living worlds are intimately interwoven or inseparable from one another, each different yet interdependent. *Vazimba* sometimes are recollected in combinations of Southeast Asian and African characteristics. Histories in Madagascar thus can thrive on a Malagasy consciousness that always already embodies an imbrication of varied origins. In addition, the heterogeneous makeup of Betsimisaraka has already been discussed. This ethnic marker itself has often indicated, throughout the past and into the present, a federation of diverse peoples *defined* in part by their incorporative diversity.

Malagasy could thus in varied ways feel themselves to be mediums in the present for the confluence of different historical times and personalities.

While it has been widely acknowledged that colonialism in Africa has been a forceful and constant background against which other, subsequent cultural change must be evaluated (Erlmann 1983, for one, has expressed this), it is vital to consider that, in Madagascar and likely throughout Africa, unique local ways of imagining, constructing, and recalling varied pasts can provide a powerful background, perhaps even a foreground, to changes evoked later by colonialism and other global phenomena.

Bricolage

Specific aesthetic dimensions of *maresaka* can vary among different Malagasy people in Tamatave. Yet similar principles of fragmenting, incorporating, recirculating, and reassessing guide the variable shape of this aesthetic. Among both Antandroy and Betsimisaraka, *maresaka* takes on some qualities of what Levi-Strauss (1966) has termed bricolage, in which people make do "with whatever is on hand." One should keep in mind that performative choices made in Tamatave involve both selection and rejection of certain materials and ideas on hand. Antandroy and Betsimisaraka are not so compelled as *bricoleurs* that unique senses of value and meaning are subsumed. Indeed each finds value in different combinations of things, and each (re)assigns value to things differently. For instance, the Betsimisaraka accordionists I knew all had repertoires of French-inspired *valses*. Antandroy, while not unfamiliar with foreign musical genres, did not play *valses* at all. The significance or negation of *valse* performance in Tamatave is taken up in chap. 7. Betsimisaraka also preferred a particular make and model of accordion, which they played essentially as it came from the factory. Antandroy insisted on a different model of accordion, which they would vastly rebuild, altering harmonic and timbral order, for instance, before they could perform on it.

The "bricoleur" is adept at using signs, at reassessing and reassigning value, at constructing new, meaningful wholes from fragments. Signs, in Peirce's terminology, necessarily "address somebody." Levi-Strauss's recall of Peirce's phrase is useful here, in that Antandroy and Betsimisaraka choose and manipulate their own distinct musical signs, or signing systems, in particular to address their ancestral spirits. Subsequent chapters in this book evoke subtle ways in which Antandroy and Betsimisaraka also address each other and in which they each might have addressed (or refused to address) colonialism and other modes of foreign contact from their respective pasts. In some situations, capacities to create bricolage themselves might serve in part as "communications" about domination, heralding the resilience and creativity of the dominated.

Among urban Yoruba musicians in Nigeria, Chris Waterman (1990a) has described a "modernist bricolage," in which traditional values are expressed and even enhanced through technologized musical means of production:

> I was fascinated by the melding of "deep" Yoruba praise singing and drumming, guitar techniques from soul music, Latin American dance rhythms, church hymns and country-and-western melodies, pedal steel guitar licks and Indian film music themes, and by the fact that this modernist bricolage could so effectively evoke traditional values. One jùjú bandleader made the point neatly: "You know, our Yoruba tradition is a very modern tradition." (P. 2)

On the east coast of Madagascar, bricolage and imbrication themselves are and have long been "traditional" values. Composite making is part of a historical consciousness in Tamatave that precedes experiences and recollections of contact with certain other worlds. Bricolage here extends beyond a modernism (or postmodernism) that might produce an effusion of materials and signs that become disjoined from an initial or inherent significance or value. In Tamatave, bricolage amounts to a unique way of recollecting, with its own history.

A taste for bricolage furthermore is not confined to distant places fragmented by colonialism. Placing worlds of experience closer together and perhaps de-exoticizing the notion of bricolage, Steven Feld draws a likeness between Levi-Strauss's *bricoleur* and the ethnographer, each "a combined inventor, scientist, artist, technician, jack-of-all-trades. In ethnography, *bricolage* is the sorting through of 'facts,' impressions, remarks, texts, and recordings of many viewpoints in order to assemble the bits and pieces of substance whose collage properly illuminates the cultural construction of actions and events" (1990: 15).

Sound Structure of/from/into the Past

The following illustrations of some brief segments of two Antandroy compositions demonstrate graphically some of the musical manipulations that contribute to the ordering together of past and present in *tromba* ceremony. Specifically, these illustrations evoke a subtle alternating in- and then out-of-phase rhythmic orientation between *valiha* and *kaiamba* that commonly imbues ceremonial musics in Tamatave. In fig. 2, *kaiamba* pulses align rhythmically with the phrases played on the *valiha*. Each one-measure *valiha* phrase occurs with and is synchronized by two *kaiamba* pulses. *Valiha* phrases, however, do not necessarily remain aligned with *kaiamba* pulses this way throughout this composition, known as *midegana*. The *valiha* can shift independently of the *kaiamba* to move in and out of phase with its pulse.

Fig. 2. Segment of *midegana* performed on *valiha* by Velontsoa, in which *kaiamba* pulses align symmetrically with *valiha* phrases.

In contrast, in fig. 3, *valiha* phrases and *kaiamba* pulses are out of phase. The *kaiamba* pulse aligns with an upbeat leading into the *valiha* phrase. An apparent triple meter in the *valiha* is countered by a compound out-of-phase quadruple meter in the *kaiamba*. While the occurrence and frequency of *kaiamba* pulses remain consistent, metric and rhythmic elements of *valiha* phrases shift frequently throughout this composition known as *mira feo,* which is commonly part of the same performance as *midegana*.

I must add that east coast Malagasy did not conceptualize bar lines, metric groupings, or beats as I have shown here, nor did they write down their music in any sort of notation. These figures are meant simply to illustrate specific rhythmic features of this performance practice. These transcriptions admittedly are not intended to address concerns about how to accurately represent on paper peoples' musics, speech modes, or other expressive forms. In fact, that one would attempt to capture and analyze simply a phrase of two of *tromba* musics would likely be antithetical to Betsimisaraka and Antandroy concepts of how music works and flows. These musics are not so much ordered by time, which a transcription might suggest, as they *reorder* time. These illustrations are offered here only to help visualize certain elements of phrase structure and of rhythmic and melodic move-

Fig. 3. Segment of *mira feo* performed on *valiha* by Velontsoa, in which *kaiamba* pulses do not align symmetrically with *valiha* phrases.

ment and to show how different performative components might fit together musically. They are by no means meant to actualize music sound, sentiment, or performance so that these can be lifted somehow off the page.

As these illustrations suggest, Antandroy music can rely upon frequent alterations in rhythmic emphasis as instruments shift in and then out of phase with one another. I found that during moments in which *valiha* and *kaiamba* seemed not to be in phase, I had an awareness of two distinct metrical beats or time frames, though I was usually unable to hear acutely or focus fully upon either one. There was a sense of being lost in or absorbed between the "beats." A valence is attained by contrasting and imbricating varying phase relationships. Playing upon musical differences, emergent as well in crucial musical improvisations, is a subtle aural facet of the aesthetic *maresaka*.

I must also note here that Malagasy did not express any sense that components of their musics were out of synch with one another. I have been using "out of phase" here to refer specifically to the physical disalignment of waveforms or musical pulses, not to suggest a sense of rhythmic discordance or abnormality.

The very rhythmic essence of temporal and spatial shifts between *kaiamba* shaker and *valiha* or accordion is based upon another mode of combining, here of a polyrhythmic sense that integrates, in varying combinations, metrical groupings of 6, 3, and 2 pulses. This multipart rhythm informs most Malagasy ceremonial musics. Figure 4 illustrates three distinct senses of rhythm which Malagasy often express in hand-clapping during a *tromba* performance. What appears in the transcriptions as essentially a 6/8 meter in the *kaiamba* is really heard by Malagasy as a pastiche and interaction of several rhythms. Indeed, at a micro-level, even each "pulse" of the *kaiamba* represented here is actually composed of a density of pulses, as countless seeds or pebbles strike the inside of the resonant chamber of the instrument.

In some musicological writings, a gestalt of hearing has been proposed to explain the effect of African musics, especially of African rhythms. For example, writing recently about a combinative rhythmic sense among Tumbuka-speaking people in northern Malawi, Steven Friedson refers to "multistable" or mutually exclusive gestalt illustrations, such as Rubin's goblet, in which one sees either a goblet or a pair of human profiles facing each other; the image not focused upon serves as background. This illustration purportedly "parallels in visual terms the creative (read artistic) activity taking place in *vimbuza* drumming. Metrical shifting, which is characteristic of all the *vimbuza* modes and which in essence binds them together into a coherent system, is the acoustical *and motional* equivalent of multistable

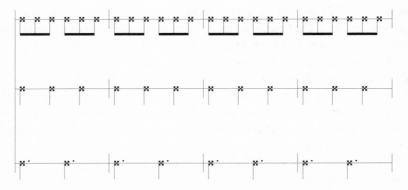

Fig. 4. Three rhythms inherent in most Malagasy ceremonial music. When clapping these rhythms, ceremonial participants may employ any one of these rhythms by itself or any or all of them in combination.

visual illusions" (1996: 140–41). In Tumbuka drumming this property of shifting between foreground and background thus becomes an auditory experience. Friedson continues later in the same chapter:

In *vimbuza,* dancer and spirit, drummer and singer encounter each other within a field of shifting rhythmic figures. Here, musical structure itself is conducive to the blurring of distinctions between subject and object—and between inner and outer time. *Vimbuza* drumming is seductive in this way, and it is structured to be so through its shifting rhythmic perspectives. Spirit and Tumbuka meet in the music of *vimbuza,* and both are transformed as a result. (Ibid.: 158)

Referring also to Rubin's goblet, Cornelia Fales suggests that "the illusion provoked" by Burundi *inanga chuchotée* performance "is the *exact auditory analog* of the figure-ground illusion in vision" (1998: 180). Both Fales and Friedson contend that with special training one can become adept at shifting between seeing or hearing either pattern in such gestalts, rather than perceiving only one or the other. Thus, some Africans apparently shift performatively between perceiving and hearing different foregrounds or backgrounds in their musics, shifts that then can reorient temporal frames or otherwise enhance or even define ritual experience for them.

While attempting to explain the local efficacy and power of rhythmic or other musical combinations, one consideration seems to be missing from these gestalt-informed theories. Specific rhythmic or timbral combinations themselves certainly might be meaningful and effective as auditory corporeal cues. They also might work because of subtle referential associations inherent in and invoked by them. Thus, it is possible that compound rhythms, such as in Tumbuka drumming or complex timbral interrelationships between instrument and voice in *inanga chuchotée* performance, are not only meaningful themselves, in their immediate causative acoustic agency upon psyche, body, or spirit; perhaps such musical combinations also work as acoustically potent metaphoric referents that in subtle fashion direct one's musical experience or consciousness to other places, times, and events. The tripartite ceremonial rhythm, for instance—what might be described as hemiola—works (though differently) among either Antandroy or Betsimisaraka as a combination of physiological effect and acoustically historical referent (chap. 7).[4] And as part of the accordion's evocative power as a once colonial instrument, current Malagasy modes of ceremonial performance on this instrument are inextricably linked to some elements of the French *valse*, overheard during and subsequent to the period of European colonization in Madagascar. Certain sounds and sound combinations produced on the accordion, for example, affect east coast Malagasy and the process of spirit possession itself in part because of the specific recollections these sounds can evoke and embody.

Genres of Musical Maresaka

Betsimisaraka practice a music and dance genre called *basesa,* which is defined in part by the tripartite rhythm described previously. Betsimisaraka *basesa* is distinctively performed at a tempo much slower than that of Antandroy music. "Popular" *basesa* compositions are also played by electric guitar and drum kit bands, though the accompanying dance is often more globally influenced, by current *soukous* dance styles such as *kwassa kwassa,* and *sega* dance music from Ile de la Réunion, for instance. Ceremonial *basesa,* on the other hand, is a heavy-footed dance performed with arms hanging down at one's side. A more subtle distinctive feature of *basesa* is linguistic, for performing this genre often means singing in Betsimisaraka rather than some other dialect. Another important genre of Betsimisaraka music is the *valse,* which is *not* performed for *tromba* ceremony.

Betsimisaraka also make finer distinctions in ceremonial accordion *basesa* performance. There are accordion compositions, called *morceaux* by Betsimisaraka, which are specifically for *tromba* possession; other *morceaux* which are for different ceremonies, such as *tsaboraha.* In these sacrificial ceremonies ancestral spirits are engaged more collectively in varied levels of communication with the living; however, possession by spirits usually does not occur. This generic distinction is especially important in *tromba* practice because particular spirits have specific favorite *tromba morceaux* to which they respond. Spirits might not arrive in the present at all if the proper compositions are not performed for them. Some Betsimisaraka refer to nontromba *basesa* as *osika,* which derives from the general Malagasy term for music, *mosika.* A translation of *osika* would be something akin to folk song. An important variance between *osika* and *basesa* for *tromba* ceremony is in ways of improvising within either genre.

Antandroy do not use the term *morceau* when speaking about their musics. Indeed, French words rarely occur in Antandroy speech in Tamatave-ville (and only occasionally in that of Betsimisaraka). Furthermore, the term morceau is used only by Betsimisaraka accordionists, not *valiha* players. This perhaps suggests that at some point in the past a foreign linguistic term was incorporated to explain and identify performance on a newer, perhaps at the time more foreign musical instrument. Antandroy do not make generic distinctions in modes or forms of their musics. They conceive all their musics foremost as *resaka amindrazana,* conversation with their ancestral spirits.

I spent a great deal of time with an Antandroy *valiha* player, Vinelo, who had resettled in Tamatave-ville from Ambovombe. Like Velontsoa, Vinelo worked as a guardian. He was employed at the *quincaillerie* of Dida, a privileged wealthy Merina who took a great interest in musical performance in Tamatave. Sometimes at night Vinelo and I, often along with several other Antandroy guardians working in the same area, would take short breaks from guarding to go drink wine at a nearby bar. Vinelo and I developed a strong connection that included taking long walks through Tamatave, laughing and joking together, performing leisurely together on our respective instruments, and even preparing a small public concert that Dida arranged for us. Vinelo and I spent many late nights outside his tôle and cardboard encampment set against the wall of Dida's *quincaillerie,* playing *valiha* and *kaiamba* together or simply watching and commenting upon the goings-on in the street.

Neither Velontsoa nor Vinelo seemed accustomed to verbally explaining their musics or musical experiences, at least to an outsider. Once Vinelo instructed me to bring *maro kasety,* many cassette tapes, to the small house he rented on the outskirts of Tamatave-ville. He simply said to turn on the recorder, and over the next several hours he simulated a progression of *valiha* performance for *tromba* ceremony. He played almost nonstop, interjecting verbally only infrequently. The following information is taken from this session Vinelo recorded for me:

The major mode diatonic scale and playing within it is called *manontolo,* which means "as a whole" or "all in one." *Manontolo* also refers to an effectiveness and appeal to all the ancestral spirits. A specific motival segment called *tabelo* is commonly played in *manontolo* at the commencement of a *tromba* ceremony. Vinelo said, "Raha fa hiantso tromba dia izay ny atao amin'ny aloha," meaning that when one wants to call *tromba, tabelo* would be the first thing played on *valiha.*

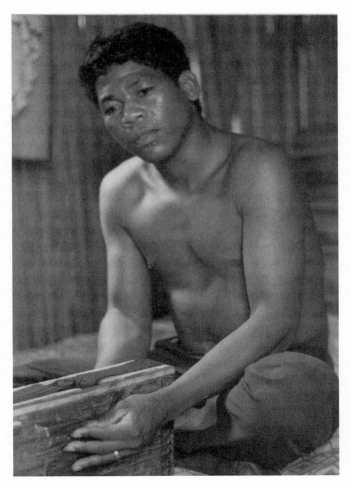

Photograph 6. Vinelo performing on *maro tady.*

Vinelo then showed me two elaborations upon the opening *tabelo.* These were slight transformations in melodic and rhythmic content that might be conceived as shifts in motif, for they resembled *tabelo* yet were clearly different. These altered motives were called *be goreve* and *mampi-tagny,* and Vinelo said about these, "Raha fa vignitra ilay tromba dia izay ny atao," meaning that these two segments are used to appease angry or displeased *tromba.* Vinelo then demonstrated several other such motival divergences from the opening *tabelo,* each of which he associated with particular *tromba.* For example, Andriamisara is the name of a powerful royal *tromba* who comes to both Antandroy and Betsimisaraka, as well as the title of the *valiha* segment that calls this spirit. Vinelo explained, "Raha fa tonga Andriamisara dia izay ny atao. Tsara fagnahy sy mahay mitsabo olona izy" (When Andriamisara comes, this is what to play for him. He is good-natured and can heal people.)

Komiverika, Kokolampy, Mandalanaka, and Ray Mandenta, all names of specific spirits or types of spirit entities, are as well titles for other motival segments in *manontolo*. Each newly introduced motif is replicated for some time, though with much internal variance in subsequent expressions of it before moving on to another motif. The newly introduced segments or motives often seem to evolve from the previous one—in other words these motives usually sound melodically and rhythmically connected to what precedes them. Vinelo's performance here conveyed a formal and complex sense of musical development, transformation, and progression.

Vinelo said that at some point in a ceremony a *tromba* might say to him, "Mahatavy resaka," which is an order to "make the musical conversation thicker." To do this, Vinelo had to diverge from previous musical material, not only in melodic and rhythmic character but in modality as well. This called for a shift of tonic to the second scale degree and so to a minor modality. Within *mahatavy resaka* there are also numerous motival divergences; some of these are *kamoro* (*morona* means a boundary or spatial edge, though I'm not sure exactly to what this title refers), Tsarerirery (the name of another *tromba*), *namana* (friend), Toliara (southwestern province of Madagascar in which many Antandroy live), and *maro havana* (many kin). With a shift to the fifth scale degree as tonic, Vinelo played "Salama tompoko," a greeting directed to *tromba,* and "Andeha hody izaho," (I'm going home now), a tune used either in the closing phase of a ceremony or as send-off to a particular spirit who is departing the present ceremony. All these divergent sections are based on preconceived motival structures, which themselves necessarily have to be filled in with improvisational alterations. Each Antandroy *valiha* player has to recollect the same repertoire of motival structures, yet each also has to individually articulate and improvise upon them.

Vinelo and Velontsoa both frequently invented new *valiha* material, new phrase or motif structures that would be replicated numerous times while the musician improvised within this replicated structure. Vinelo was playing two such newly created phrase structures, at that time called "reggay" and "mandôlina Kassavy." Both of these titles convey a global influence transmitted by the national radio station—Bob Marley's reggae and Kassav's by-way-of Paris Antillean *zouk*. These titles bespeak as well a twofold mediation by which foreign musical ideas, once mediated electronically through the radio, could be transformed and then performed for the *razana* by Vinelo and Velontsoa.

Antandroy as well as other east coast Malagasy expressed little concern over traditions being static or flexible, genuine or spurious (Handler and Linnekin 1984). Writing about Africa, Chris Waterman has implied the potential for all traditions to be flexible, since "all human identities, no matter how deeply felt, are from an historical point of view mixed, relational, and conjunctural" (1990b: 367).[5] Constant introductions of new sounds, musical forms, materials, and ideas are characteristic processes that in part define tradition in Madagascar.

Sung Texts

I am concerned here with the performative power of words (see, for example, Stoller 1989) and with the significance of the participatory role of singing in "the perceptual embodiment of the transformative [ritual] process" (Roseman 1991: 150). Ceremonial participants enhance and intensify their own feelingful experience of placing themselves in a consubstantial past with ancestral spirits, in part by communicating vocally with these spirits. Singing; spoken/chanted *tsodrano,* or benedictions; formulaic *kabary,* or introductory speeches; and talking directly with spirits while they inhabit a medium's body are primary modes of such discursive communication in *tromba* ceremony. The human voice thus creates potent *maresaka.*

In both Antandroy and Betsimisaraka ceremonies, singing is not always fixed in text nor by its positioning in a ceremony. In other words, a participant generally can sing what she or he wants at whatever moment it is desired or deemed necessary. One such ceremonial need to sing arises if a *tromba* spirit is not readily responding to the invitation to inhabit a medium's body. Singing in *tromba* ceremony is usually sporadic, spontaneous, and somewhat fragmented in nature—not like a song with recognizable form, but more like short bursts of vocalized sentiment spilling out onto the ceremonial proceedings. These sung texts contrast with the more formulaic *kabary* that opens these ceremonies and the often more cohesive *tsodrano* that are commonly made to ancestral spirits throughout.

Specifically in Betsimisaraka *tromba* ceremonies, sung lines are likely to mirror melodically and rhythmically what is being played instrumentally on accordion or *valiha.* While singing in *tromba* ceremony could be improvisational and individually expressive in character, there are also common stylized collective Betsimisaraka chants such as "Avia aty tompoko" (Come here, my master). Other sung lines address specific *tromba,* such as: "Milalao, milalao, milalao Andriamarofaly" (Play, play, play Andriamarofaly). Addressed to the royal spirit Andriamarofaly, this sung phrase in melody, alliteration, and even content is reminiscent to me of a nursery rhyme.

This verse seems to imply a sort of kinship crossing-over, in which living mediums assume a parental role to an ancestral spirit, inviting him to play like a child. Indeed, some *tromba* are actually child spirits who once embodied play with toys, speak in baby talk, and sometimes whimper and cry like spoiled children.[6]

Most texts sung during Betsimisaraka *tromba* ceremony thus create rather brief image forms, involving either a particular spirit or some evocation of festive interaction. Overall, these sung phrases are extranarrative in nature. Their significance is lodged not in a story told but in the meaningful impact of specific words enunciated in particular ways.[7]

In Betsimisaraka *basesa* specifically for ceremonies other than *tromba*, ceremonies that most often do not involve possession of mediums by spirits, sung phrases are usually longer and convey a more elaborate image or metaphor. There is usually a single verse that is sung several times, paralleling the melody employed in what I have called the head of these compositions. The following is the text of "Tanoran'i Dadilahy" as sung by Roger Jean Louis and his family:

> Izaho ny tanoran'i dadilahy
> o ya ye o ya ye
> Izaho tsy ho andry tsy mba variagna
> o ya ye o ya ye
> Raiso ankafaliana izy e fa hidola

> I am grandfather's youngest
> o ya ye o ya ye
> I won't sleep or be distracted (daydream)
> o ya ye o ya ye
> United in joyfulness he'll dance with us

In this verse, past and present are suggestively infused into one another with the kinship term *dadilahy*, which could refer simultaneously to an elder living Betsimisaraka as well as to elder ancestral spirits. The singing of kinship terms often simultaneously evokes familial *and* ancestral relationships, contributing feelingfully to bridging spirit and living worlds. Singing of such relationships could also imply the value of interiorizing otherness on the east coast, for *dadilahy* could refer to non-Betsimisaraka Malagasy ancestral spirits, Sakalava for instance, who were being internalized in varied ways into the Betsimisaraka family in the ceremonial present. Non-*tromba* texts such as this one evoke the imprinting of aural images of *disembodied* ancestral spirits onto a non-possession ceremonial consciousness. Perhaps a more extended narrative evocation of ancestral personalities in these texts in some sense takes the place of the actual appearance and embodiment of ancestral spirits in *tromba* ceremony.

When Antandroy sing during *tromba* ceremony, it is usually in the form of chanted *tsodrano* (benedictions) to the *razana*. These expressions do not commonly follow the instrumental melodic shape of the accordion or *valiha;* in fact, they are more lyrically spoken than melodically sung (see List 1963 on fluidity between speech and song). Like Betsimisaraka *tromba-istes,* Antandroy do not usually sing texts that are semantically, narratively, or melodically elaborate in their ceremonies. When texts are sung, spoken, or chanted, their significance and sentimental effectiveness arise largely from their role as an integrative component in the total soundscape of the multidimensional ceremonial *maresaka*.[8] For instance, Vinelo told me, "Tsy maintsy mihira fa manao maresaka amindrazana" (It's necessary to sing to create *maresaka,* to converse with the razana). Vinelo then went on to list other acoustic necessities for calling *tromba,* including *kaiamba* and *valiha* playing, hand clapping *(mitehaka),* and vocal *tsodrano.*

Antandroy *tromba* spirits themselves sometimes sing. One powerful Sakalava *tromba* that came regularly to Tompezolo commonly sang short melodic phrases, in which the quality of the current musical performance was commented upon. Some Antandroy compositions, like "Andeha hody izaho" (I'm going home), which has no text, could implicitly convey messages without sung words, in this case that a *tromba* is leaving the body of a medium to return to its tomb.

Micro-poetics and Improvisation

In mind of the pervasive importance of musical performance in daily or ceremonial life in Tamatave, I evoke the term *micro-poetics* to refer in part to small-scale or short-duration musical structurations and maneuvers that can also comprise or reflect an expansive lived-in poetics of everyday or ceremonial life. As a system of constant small-scale rhythmic alterations and subtle melodic turns and manipulations, a musical micro-poetics of performance mirrors and encodes other cultural principles for creative articulation among east coast Malagasy. For one, micro-poetic improvisation involves expressive freedom within a framework of relatively fixed replicated structure, a poetics that extends beyond musical improvisation into improvisations upon daily life throughout the past in Madagascar.

Among both Antandroy and Betsimisaraka, musical performance is based in part upon the musician's ability to reiterate powerfully driven replicative phrase structures while micro-poetically improvising on rhythmic and melodic material within these structures. This imbrication of replication and improvisation also plays a crucial part in the makeup of the aesthetic of *maresaka*. Indeed, the daily greeting, "Inona ny maresaka?" asks in part "What's *new?*" And in spite of the common reply, "Tsy misy" or "Nothing's new," the respondent usually then goes on to enunciate the recent goings-on of family and friends. Thus, this common daily interchange itself entails performative discursive improvisation.

Micro-poetic improvisation within replicable short-duration phrase structures echoes on a musical scale a more general propensity among Malagasy in Tamatave to collect fragments into meaningful wholes, to recycle, revalue, and maneuver sets of signs while operating within larger imposed structures. Micro-poetic improvisation calls for interpretation and creativity within a largely unnegotiable *maresaka*-inducing repetitiveness of form necessary to *tromba* performance.[9] While musical micro-poetic improvisation is based upon maneuvering within relatively fixed structures, as well as from structure to structure, it resounds as well in everyday tactics throughout the past for operating effectively and creatively within other relatively fixed structures, for instance, that of colonial dominance and, more recently, within structures of widespread material poverty, illness, and environmental devastation.

By introducing the concept of micro-poetics I do not advocate a performative system that could be overly self-referential, "too caught up in poetics to be able to discern broader social and political contexts" (Bauman and Briggs 1990: 67).[10] To the contrary, encompassing social and political fields in Madagascar lend meaning to micro-poetic improvisation, a mode of improvising that applies as well to an everyday extramusical aesthetic in which materials, ideas, and meanings are imaginatively and often spontaneously recirculated and improvised upon.

Proper improvisatory activity in part determines musical competence. A player who effectively and consistently alters the material within short-duration phrase structures is thought to be more *mahay,* or musically skilled; thus, his or her playing is more exciting than that of one who is not as musically adventurous. Some examples of Antandroy modes of improvisation are illustrated in Velontsoa's playing of *midegana* represented in figure 5. A recognizable two-measure phrase is replicated throughout, though with variations in each articulation of the phrase.

Some other examples of Velontsoa's improvisations within *mira feo* are diagrammed in figure 6. Vinelo told me that the *mira feo* mode *is* "karaha ilay feo gorodora" (like the voice of the accordion). This is in part because *mira feo* contains a doubled fifth scale degree—both left hand

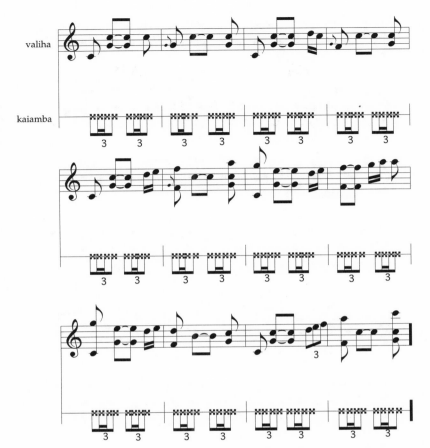

Fig. 5. Improvisation within replicable small-phrase structure of *midegana* performed on *valiha* by Velontsoa.

and right hand on the *valiha* have access to a string tuned to this degree—which allows one to produce a continuous drone or ostinato as could also be produced on reconditioned Antandroy accordions (all explained fully in chapter 5). As with other tunings or modes, there are well-defined divergent motives to perform within *mira feo*, such as one entitled *sejirina*, which is specifically meant to *mampisôma tromba*, to incite *tromba* to dance or to party.

Among Betsimisaraka there are two distinct styles of improvising. The improvisational activity acceptable within accordion *basesa* for *tromba* ceremony differs from that for non-*tromba* accordion *basesa*. In *tromba* ceremony, the left hand on the accordion consistently pumps a constant driving

Fig. 6. Improvisation within replicable short-duration phrase structure of *mira feo* performed on *valiha* by Velontsoa. Note freedom of Velontsoa to vary rhythmic and metrical orientation throughout this representation. *Kaiamba* pulses often do not align symmetrically with *valiha* phrases in this segment of *mira feo*. Note also augmented fourth scale degree characteristic of *mira feo* turning.

accentuation of each eighth note pulse of the 6/8-like component of the tripartite rhythm diagrammed previously. With the right hand, short melodic motives are replicated numerous times, always with subtle motif-internal micro-poetic improvisations, largely in rhythm and phrasing. Figure 7 illustrates a short-duration phrase structure from Jily's performance on accordion of a *tromba morceau* entitled "Volon'aomby," a reference to valued zébu cattle.[11] As in Antandroy performance, musical phrases such

Fig. 7. Phrase of "Volon'aomby," a Betsimisaraka *tromba morceau* performed on accordion by Jily. The uppermost staff represents the right-hand side of the accordion; the middle staff, the left-hand side (left-hand button and direction of bellows motion are indicated). The left hand plays each pulse of an apparent 6/8 meter, in phase with the *kaiamba* rhythm.

as these are replicated countless consecutive times, with subsequent introductions of phrase-internal alterations.

In contrast to *morceaux* specifically for *tromba*, such as "Volon'aomby," non-*tromba* accordion *basesa*, for *tsaboraha* or other largely nonpossession ceremonies, consists of a replicable "head" and then a linear improvisational section that diverges noticeably from this head, to which the performer eventually returns. I derive the term *head* here intentionally from jazz practice to suggest that Betsimisaraka accordionists have potentially been influenced by some specific outside musical ideas. While the terms *head* and *improvisation* were not marked linguistically by Malagasy on the east coast, Betsimisaraka musicians did distinguish between sections in their music with descriptive phrases such as "miverina amin'ny voalohany izay," meaning a return to the initial section. Also, the improvisation sections were commonly said to *mihetsiketsika foagna*, meaning that these sections structurally and processually are more free to "move around."

In Betsimisaraka *tromba* compositions for accordion, improvisation is contained within the replicable short-duration phrase structure, while in non-*tromba* compositions the improvisation creates completely new musical ground and material independent of and distinct from the replicable head. In addition, in non-*tromba basesa*, the left hand commonly alternates from emphasizing each eighth note pulse of an apparent 6/8 meter to accentuating an interrhythmic meter of three pulses, or it might accentuate only this triple meter throughout the whole composition. A *basesa* played this way—accentuating a triple meter—however is still distinguished from a *valse*.

Figure 8 represents the head of Roger Jean Louis's performance of "Tanoran'i Dadilahy." The left hand of the accordion adheres to an apparent 3/4 meter, which actually combines in this representation with the *kaiamba*'s 6/8 meter to form an inter-rhythmic density, another mode of or contribution to *maresaka*.

Figure 9 represents an improvisational segment from Roger's playing of "Tanoran' i Dadilahy." In this segment, Roger diverges greatly from the melodic and rhythmic construction of the head of this composition.

The particular mode of linear improvisational development on accordion, with return to a head, illustrated here is not used in *tromba* ceremony (except occasionally in the highly unusual style of Tsiariagna, an accordionist

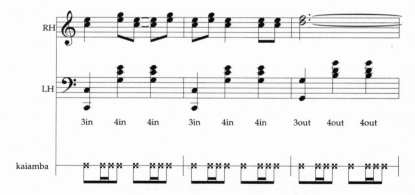

Fig. 8. Head of "Tanoran'i Dadilahy" performed on accordion by Roger Jean Louis. In non-*tromba* compositions such as this, the left hand could switch freely from accentuating a triple meter, as shown here, to accentuating each eighth note of an apparent 6/8 meter (in phase with each pulse of the *kaiamba*).

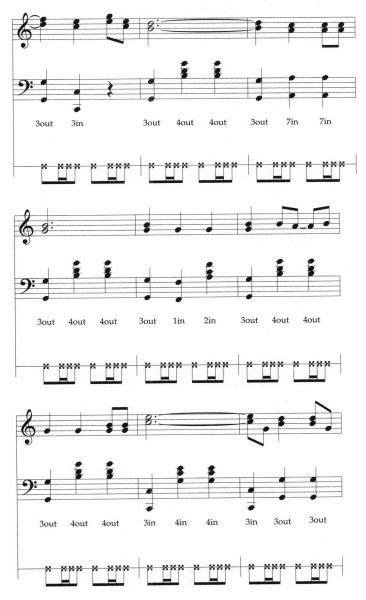

Fig. 8 (continued). Head of "Tanoran'i Dadilahy."

Fig. 8 (continued). Head of "Tanoran'i Dadilahy."

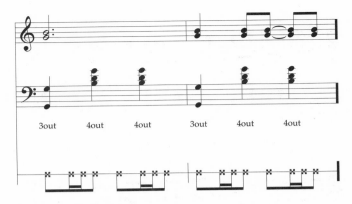

Fig. 8 (conclusion). Head of "Tanoran'i Dadilahy."

Fig. 9. Improvisation section of "Tanoran'i Dadilahy," performed on accordion by Roger Jean Louis.

Fig. 9 (continued). Improvisation section of "Tanoran'i Dadilahy."

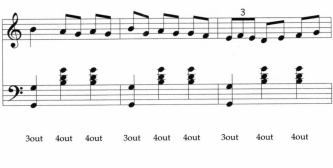

3out   4out   4out   3out   4out   4out   3out   4out   4out

Fig. 9 (conclusion). Improvisation section of "Tanoran'i Dadilahy." In the second measure shown here, Roger briefly varies the left-hand rhythm.

to be discussed later). Nor is it used in Betsimisaraka *basesa* performance specifically on *valiha;* thus, *valiha* music is not categorized into either *tromba* or non-*tromba* forms. The *valiha* is often thought of as a more "traditional" (in other words, historical) instrument than the accordion. Recall Tombo Daniel's evaluation that *valiha* represents "original," "pira" (pure) Malagasy music.

Among Betsimisaraka accordionists I commonly heard experimentation with nonceremonial, even non-Malagasy compositions and musical forms, such as polkas or the tune "Que Sera Sera." I heard only *vakondrazana,* the ancestors' music, performed on the *valiha*. The accordion, a newer instrument in Madagascar possesses a versatility distinct from that of the *valiha,* namely, its capacity to create a left-hand, essentially rhythmic part across a right-hand, largely melodic one. This has provided a particular means with which Betsimisaraka, as well as Antandroy, create new performative genres and styles to meet their current expressive needs (S. Stewart 1991).[12] In addition, the majority of accordionists in Tamatave, both Antandroy and Betsimisaraka, performed versions (quite playfully) of the Malagasy national anthem, "Ry tanindrazanay malala o," a marchlike European-influenced composition. I never heard this anthem played on *valiha*. *Valiha* or accordion performance, then, could cull different recollections of, associations with, and comments upon varied pasts.[13]

Among both Antandroy and Betsimisaraka, constant micro-poetic reor-ganizations of musical time and alterations in musical articulation create *maresaka,* an order arising from constantly reordering. Such small-scale musical refigurings are basic performative components in engendering other larger scale temporal alterations in *tromba* ceremony. Micro-poetic maneuvers in essence might be thought of as musical phonemes in a system of bringing past and present into one another. Even daily nonceremonial time is commonly experienced differently in Madagascar. Malagasy on the east coast rarely wear watches (ones that work at least) and seem unfamiliar with the experience of being late or having to rush. Some Malagasy would joke about *rendez-vous gasy,* a "Malagasy meeting," in which someone would be indeterminately late, a joke that plays upon a European sense of punctuality, upon a strange urgency to be on time. This was not a self-deprecating joke—Malagasy here were joking about their difference from Europeans, about their sense of being *in* time rather than *on* time.[14]

Maresaka among Merina in Tamatave-ville

Since I have suggested that the Merina dialect of the Malagasy language has sometimes evoked oppositional-like sentiment from some non-Merina people, it is pertinent to mention as well Merina musical practices in Tamatave-ville. While I was there, commercial musical performances in Tamatave-ville were arranged, promoted, and controlled by Dida, a Merina settler from Antananarivo. He also ran a small studio at which local Tama-tave bands could practice as well as tape their sessions, using his set of mu-sical instruments, available for an hourly rental fee. The majority of the young Tamatave musicians who patronized Dida's studio were also Me-rina—I can think of only one or two who were Betsimisaraka and none who were Antandroy. While there were personnel for perhaps three full popular music bands in Tamatave-ville, the musicians could rarely afford to pay for studio rental time. In addition, there occurred only infrequent pub-lic occasions or commercial events for which a band could perform. Dida did sponsor his own house band that performed for dinner parties thrown by wealthy Karana (Indian) merchants or by Dida himself. The repertoire of this band consisted of a mix of local *basesa, salegy* from the north of Madagascar, covers of hits from better-known Malagasy popular stars from Antananarivo, and covers of some Western pop artists such as Stevie Won-der and Ace of Base.[15]

Dida occasionally helped to stage musical events at the Tamatave Alliance Française, the local French social club. These musical events were infrequent and catered to a small audience composed of mostly temporary French residents in Tamatave-ville—instructors at the Lycée Français or business people—and wealthier Merina residents there. The vast majority of Betsimisaraka and Antandroy could not afford the admission to these events and so were virtually excluded from them. Furthermore, most Betsimisaraka and Antandroy would not have been interested in the content of many of the programs at the Alliance.

One particularly memorable show orchestrated at the Alliance was billed nostalgically as "An Evening with Edith Piaf." The singer for this show was a Merina woman named Nirina. Wrapped in a formal black evening gown, Nirina imitated Edith Piaf's repertoire and vocal style for about an hour, backed up by young Merina musicians who resided in Tamatave. The desired effect, Dida told me, was to re-create a club scene of the 1930s or 1940s in France, a scene imagined into being in Tamatave through the prompting of the French director of the Alliance.

This performance represented a complex interweaving of differing desires. For one, the director of the Alliance was attempting to evoke a collective French nostalgia for a colonial-era performer and for a distant, past homeland, though one imagined into being here primarily through Malagasy actors. Dida himself was imagining through this event his own dream of a French-style nightclub in Tamatave, a place of his own distinct from the French-controlled Alliance Française, a desire he explained to me explicitly days after the show. For Dida, this show evoked a nostalgia for a future in which he likely would never be able to live and for a separation from a French-controlled club he quietly disdained yet often effectively exploited to his own ends.

Wealthier Merina in Tamatave-ville were sometimes overcome with what appeared to be a sentimentality for French musics, especially from the colonial era.[16] A fondness for Piaf, like being a member of the Alliance Française, did not, however, convey a Merina desire to be more French. Indeed, other Merina members of the Alliance Française, in addition to Dida, sometimes voiced cautious disdain for their French club associates. Rather, what might have seemed to be an expression of colonial desire among Merina was in part their own display of class distinctiveness, meant to separate Merina by taste from other Malagasy in Tamatave.[17] Dida implicated his own exclusionary aesthetics with his lack of enthusiasm for, and even occasional condescension toward Betsimisaraka and Antandroy ceremonial musics on the east coast. This is not to deny that Merina members of the Alliance Française in Tamatave could truly enjoy colonial-era French musics.

However, these Merina live disconnected from their central homeland, as sometimes unwelcome "guests" on the east coast. The socially strategic implications of Merina musical preferences in Tamatave are complicated, involving also Merina sentiments for the past and, in particular, for the foreign Others who inhabited it. This is elaborated on elsewhere (Emoff, n.d.).

A Merina fondness for Edith Piaf and other colonial-era musics is part of a self-empowering strategy, one that commonly includes distancing oneself from other Malagasy (a distancing played out spatially within the exclusive grounds of the Alliance Française). Like Antandroy and Betsimisaraka on the east coast however, Merina there seek out and appropriate from varied pasts that which they can use to their own ends to empower themselves in the present. Dida's performances at the Alliance Française, which acoustically mimed the colonial era, became occasions to voice a more modern, particularly politicized and class-distinctive *maresaka,* which was yet reliant upon processes of recollecting, salvaging, reassessing, and combining. *Maresaka* itself, whether in linguistic, musical, everyday, or ritual applications, is an aesthetic that relies upon *composition,* not simply in the conventional musical sense of creating specific works but in the piecing together of variegated histories and different practices, of reconnecting (with) fragmented components of the past.[18]

CHAPTER FIVE

Material Media of Maresaka
The Value in Things

ॐ

The form of musical instruments in Madagascar varies greatly: *valiha* made from a section of bamboo approximately four feet in length (bearing a physical resemblance to some Malaysian and Indonesian instruments);[1] metal-bodied or pine box versions of the *valiha;* accordions; Malagasy reworkings of European violins, clarinets, and trumpets (which are most commonly played in Merina *hira gasy* performances in the central Haut Plateau region though are rarely used on the east coast), and a variety of other stringed and percussive instruments. Between apparently disparate endpoints, one "indigenous," another European, there are varied composite instrument forms that draw upon both ends. Malagasy, however, do not conceive of their instruments, those that are based in part upon European forms, simply as European things. Remnants of the colonial, such as accordions, are appropriated and revalued to be given new lives that are foremost Malagasy. Such once foreign things, though, are always still partially imbued with colonial power (see Thomas 1991).

Most Malagasy ceremonial music that I encountered relied upon some form of *kaiamba* percussive shaker. Sometimes the sound of the *kaiamba* itself is considered to be a particular mode of *maresaka* especially conducive to persuading *tromba* spirits to enter the body of a medium. In Betsimisaraka villages the *kaiamba* is sometimes called *tsikatrehana*. This particular instrument is usually made from a length of bamboo, approximately thirty centimeters long and seven centimeters in diameter, which is filled with hard, round seeds from the *abaradeda* plant (close relative of *Canna X generalis*). These seeds are forced through slots cut the length of the bamboo tube—the slots also act as sound holes through which the instrument's voice can escape. In Tamatave-ville, instead of bamboo, a Prochitox insecticide can of about the same dimensions, punched with holes, is used as resonant chamber for the *kaiamba*. Antandroy build their *kaiamba* from a small condensed-milk can, filled with either broken glass or roundish pebbles. This can, also punched with holes, is then fit into a slot cut in a hardwood stick approximately twenty centimeters long that serves as handle. The holes punched in Antandroy *kaiamba* serve not only to allow sound to escape but also to replicate specific formations of *sikidy* seeds, thereby stamping this instrument with readable signs of spirit presence and meaning.

The accordion—called *akordôgna* among Betsimisaraka, *gorodora* among Antandroy—and the *valiha* are the most desired instruments for *tromba* practice in the Tamatave region. A small guitar-like instrument, *kabôsy* among Betsimisaraka, *mandôlina* or *gitara* among Antandroy is also less frequently used there. The body of the *kabôsy* is often rectangular, but a scaled-down indented shape (like a small classical guitar) is also used. The Betsimisaraka *kabôsy* generally has six strings, two lower pitched single strings and two higher pitched courses of strings, each of these courses consisting of paired unisons. Its tuning, from lowest to highest pitched string, is usually i–i'-iii'(doubled)-v'(doubled). Like some *valiha* strings, the *kabôsy*'s are made of unraveled strands of bicycle brake cable.

The Antandroy *mandôlina,* although about the same size as the *kabôsy,* is an altogether different instrument. It generally has five or seven movable nylon or metal wire frets spreading fully across the width of the peghead end of the neck, while the rest of the neck is left unfretted. With this repositionable fret system Antandroy can readily alter the scale system of the instrument. The strings of the *mandôlina* are usually made of nylon monofilament, used otherwise in Tamatave-ville as fishing line or for mending fishing nets.

Some Antandroy musicians in Tamatave-ville had carved the bodies of their *mandôlina* to replicate a small, portable monaural "magnéto" or cassette player/radio combination, a machine owned by the relatively few Tamataviens able to afford one. These *mandôlina* were delicately detailed with carved "stop," "ff," "rewind," and "play" buttons, inset condenser mic, handle, output speaker, antenna, and radio tuner dial with varied bands and frequencies inscribed. These particular instruments were iconic mediums for the electronic reproduction and mediation of musics over the Merina-controlled national radio station in Antananarivo.

This mechanical embodiment represented in part a desire for ownership of a musical machine. Magnétos themselves are often prohibitively expensive, particularly for Antandroy. Often left behind in an age of musical mechanical reproduction, some Antandroy musicians iconically amplified the *maresaka* they created by modeling their instruments after an acoustically powerful yet difficult to obtain electronic device. They could thus enact the propagation of their music across the radio airwaves, along with imagining the prestige of having control over radio programming choices. Implicit in this mimetic appropriation was an acute musical criticism that some Antandroy in Tamatave-ville verbally expressed over the very absence of a public and economically profitable outlet for their own musics and over national as well as local neglect of their musical skills.

∽

Antandroy in Tamatave-ville were fond of another instrument, the *lokanga*, a three-stringed bowed instrument probably borrowed initially from neighboring Bara people in the south of the island. *Lokanga* performance in Tamatave is infrequent and largely for leisure, though this instrument still has spiritual associations. The evolution of *lokanga* in Madagascar most likely reflects the influence of an Arab bowed instrument such as the rebab, though the European violin, which had also made its way to Madagascar, cannot be discounted as partial model.[2] Since Antandroy in Tamatave-ville did not regularly perform on *lokanga*, I will not elaborate much upon it here, except to mention its accompanying breath-song/chant, another very powerful vocal mode of communication with ancestral spirits. This mode of verbal expression is called *ndrimotra*, from the verb *midrimotra*, to heal.

Antandroy employ a variety of different tunings on their stringed instruments. They often adjust the lowest pitched string on either the *mandôlina* or *valiha* to the sixth scale degree below what in Western terms would be the tonic degree, the next highest pitched string. This allows them to freely emphasize different modalities without retuning. Antandroy seemed more familiar and adept with varied scalar forms than did Betsimisaraka musicians, who might traverse different modalities while playing but rarely, if ever, did they adjust their stringed instruments to different tunings during performance. Upon reflection, these specific orientations to tuning might evoke some sense of obfuscation or inversion of local histories. Betsimisaraka had long known foreign contact in the Tamatave region, whereas Antandroy had remained more isolated from Europeans in the south (they commonly retain such isolation even currently in Tamatave-ville). Antandroy adeptness and creativity with employing varied scales, tunings, and modalities might seem musically more European-like, while Betsimisaraka disinterest in varying their scales and tunings might suggest a less-European musicality or musical curiosity. Perhaps these different preferences in musical practice imply that what appear to be European signs of musical proficiency or lack of it have attained unique value once deployed in Madagascar by different people there.

Valiha

The body of the Betsimisaraka *valiha* is most often made from *tôle*, a thin, malleable corrugated sheet metal used when available as the roof for some houses on the east coast. A length of *tôle* is wrapped into a cylinder approximately four-feet long and pounded into a rectangular shape; then smaller pieces of *tôle* are used to cover either end of the sound chamber. Since the available *tôle* usually has already been used as roofing material, it often has nail holes punctured in it, which serve not only as connecting points for the end pieces but as small sound holes in the resonant chamber. A larger sound hole might also be snipped out of the *tôle* body. Strings once again are made from unraveled strands of bicycle brake cables; these are wrapped as tightly as possible around nails at either end of the length of the instrument, and then thick wood bridges are wedged up under each string. This instrument usually has approximately twenty strings, ten each strung on either vertical face of the sound chamber.

Individual strings are tuned by moving each bridge to either lengthen or shorten the effective resonant length of the plucked part of the string. Cloth shoulder straps allow the instrument to be held and played at a small

Photograph 7. Jean Dedier, from the Tamatave countryside, with Betsimisaraka *tôle valiha*.

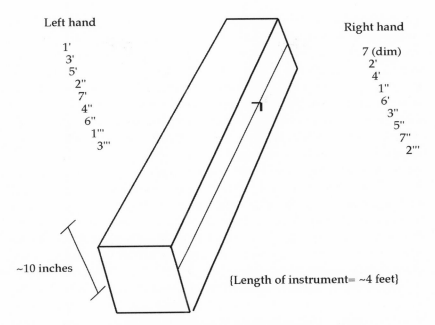

Left hand

| 1' |
| 3' |
| 5' |
| 2" |
| 7' |
| 4" |
| 6" |
| 1''' |
| 3''' |

Right hand

| 7 (dim) |
| 2' |
| 4' |
| 1" |
| 6' |
| 3" |
| 5" |
| 7" |
| 2''' |

~10 inches

{Length of instrument= ~4 feet}

Fig. 10. Tombo Daniel's *valiha* tuning, Cité Canada, Tamatave, November 28, 1993. The tuning of some Betsimisaraka *valiha* is inverted from the order shown here, so that it "begins" with the 1' scale degree on the right-hand side of the instrument. Individual *valiha* players usually build and tune their instruments to their own preferences and specifications.

vertical angle to the player's body. The particular tuning order of the *valiha* played by *tromba* musician Tombo Daniel is represented in figure 10.[3]

Betsimisaraka *valiha* players are undoubtedly familiar with the European major mode diatonic scale, to which accordions in use in Madagascar are tuned, though they consistently reorient and invert the ascending order of the tones of the scale, introducing varied "interruptions" in this diatonic order. When I questioned the origin of or reasons for these specific *valiha* tuning structures, I was commonly told, "Tsy haiko," (I don't know) or "Efa ela be karaha io izegny," (That's just the way it's been for a long time).[4] The diatonic tuning with "out-of- place" 1" and 2" scale degrees on Tombo Daniel's *valiha* might reflect an ideologic and performative autonomy from European ideals. These reorderings perhaps signal Betsimisaraka choices, to be influenced by such ideals discriminatingly and imaginatively though not to be overwhelmed by them. In contrast to Betsimisaraka *valiha,* the tuning of the Merina *valiha* (the resonant chamber of which is usually made of bamboo) adheres most often without disruption to the ascending order of the European major mode diatonic scale.

Interestingly, the bamboo for these Merina instruments is endemic to the Tamatave region, yet Betsimisaraka themselves choose *tôle,* a modern foreign construction material, over their own bamboo to construct their *valiha.*[5] Acoustically, the metallic *valiha* projects a voice with more intensity of mid- and high-range frequencies and more, different audible harmonics than the bamboo instrument. Recall Tombo Daniel's elucidation upon the benefits of tôle *valiha* over earlier Betsimisaraka ones constructed of bamboo. Also, *tôle* is often more durable than bamboo, and it resounds to Betsimisaraka and to their ancestral spirits as well with the prestige and honor of appropriating and assimilating a (once) foreign material into their performative practices. Merina favor bamboo for the construction of their *valiha,* a material that is more difficult to obtain from the central Haut Plateau region of the island where most Merina reside. Thus, one factor among Malagasy in valuing their musical instruments seems to be the degree of difficulty in finding and obtaining the materials with which to construct them.[6]

Antandroy *valiha* are built from *sapay* wood (from the French *sapin,* pine). These *valiha* are usually slightly smaller in dimension than Betsimisaraka *valiha.* Wood planks are hacked out and planed down by hand with a *meso,* a long-handled machete-like knife, and then with a gouge tool made from any piece of metal that can be rounded and ground to an adequately sharp edge. Large enough pine planks are difficult to come by, usually having to be brought from the Haut Plateau region. Again, the difficulty of obtaining pine planks for the *valiha*'s body becomes a term of value in the communicative power that the instrument will eventually possess. I assisted Velontsoa (minimally) in the construction of several *valiha,* an exacting process, though he always worked with unflagging patience and precision.

Optimally, the long planks to form the sound boards upon which the strings rest have to be planed to about 3/4 of a centimetre or less. This dimension is not measured spatially but aurally. Velontsoa would tap across the surface of the plank, listening for the resonance of the correct thickness. The various boards are then nailed together (*colle* or glue, is prohibitively expensive at the *quincailleries* in town). Pine, a soft wood, does not have great durability in the year-round high humidity and heat of Tamatave[7] but is chosen by Antandroy because its *feo,* or voice, can best *miresaka amindrazana,* converse with Antandroy ancestral spirits.

Antandroy *valiha* generally have twenty to twenty-four strings. These are extracted from much thicker wire than bicycle brake cable—either from automobile clutch cable or from a stranded cable approximately two centimeters in diameter found at Port Toamasina, the large commercial port in

Tamatave-ville. According to Antandroy, thinner cable can not *mahatavy resaka* (literally, produce thick conversation).

The pine resonant chamber has two square-ish sound holes cut on the top plank, one slightly larger than the other. The significance of these sound holes extends beyond their function as channels through which sound can escape from the instrument. As they are the two points of most concentrated sound wave emission from the *valiha*, these sound holes are also sacralizing points. *Toaka* (rum) or cigarettes, sometimes lit, are commonly dropped into the sound holes to please and honor *tromba* spirits. Even in everyday situations, Antandroy musicians might pour a benediction of *toaka*, *divay* (wine [from the French *du vin*]), or *labiera* (beer) into the *valiha* sound hole before they themselves would drink. In addition, other valued objects are commonly placed in these sound holes while music is being produced through them. For instance, I had given Velontsoa a large Buck knife, which he immediately put into the sound hole of his *valiha* and began to play and chant to the *razana*. He left the knife there over the next several weeks while using this *valiha* in both ceremonial and everyday occasions. As sound brings spirit-forms into the present, it also transfers physical items to the *razana* to be blessed and enjoyed by them.

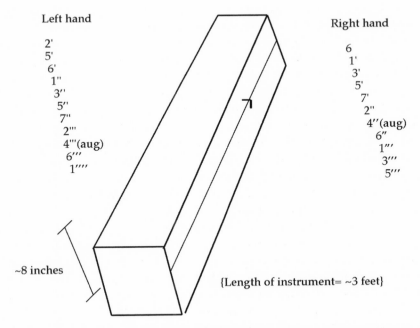

Fig. 11. Antandroy *mira feo valiha* tuning. This tuning is distinctive in its combination of augmented fourth scale degrees and doubled fifth degree on the left-hand side of the instrument.

As mentioned above, one standard Antandroy *valiha* tuning consists of the tempered major mode diatonic scale with sixth degree as lowest pitch. Scale degrees in this tuning alternate between right and left hands; though unlike those of the Betsimisaraka instrument, these scale degrees ascend sequentially (with the exception of the sixth), uninterrupted from their European order. Two other Antandroy tunings employ either augmented fourth degree or diminished seventh degree. Antandroy *valiha* players, when in the "standard" tuning often shift "tonic" to the fifth scale degree, contrastively modulating to a scale with diminished seventh degree. A fourth tuning mentioned in the previous chapter, *mira feo,* is also employed. This tuning or mode combines augmented fourth scale degrees with a doubled fifth scale degree that replaces the expected fourth degree in the left hand. In this tuning the performer can create a sustained drone or ostinato-type effect by rapidly alternating between two unison fifth scale degrees as played by left then right hands. At the same time, the performer can continue to play melodic phrases on other strings. *Mira feo* refers to the "doubled voice" of the fifth scale degree. (See fig. 11.)

Akordôgna and Gorodora

In 1829, Cyril Demian patented in Vienna a single-row diatonic button accordion, with five right-hand buttons (Macerollo 1980). Two-row diatonic button accordions were available shortly thereafter (by the mid-1830s). It has been suggested that these two-row diatonic models began to be disseminated in the European colonial territories, thus in Madagascar, after 1910, fourteen years after the beginning of French colonial control in Madagascar (Gianattasio 1979: 51). By 1912 the Hohner Company, a well-known German maker of accordions, was marketing its own early two-row diatonic button accordions (Maurer 1983: 108). Hohner accordions are the prevalent make in Madagascar. Malagasy with whom I spoke could not recall exactly when the accordion first appeared there, though one regularly voiced recollection was "Tonga niaraka tamin'ilay vazaha izegny" (It arrived here with White outsiders).

I encountered two models of Hohner two-row diatonic button accordions on the east coast: one the "Vienna Style," which has a wooden frame encasement; the other, the plastic-encased "Corso," described in the Hohner catalog as "a modernized version of the Vienna Style model." Plastic-bodied Corsos arrived in Madagascar after the first wooden-framed Vienna-style accordions, plastic being available for production use only by the 1940s. Antandroy favored the Vienna-style accordion (gorodora); Betsimisaraka generally preferred the slightly larger, newer Corso (akordôgna).

Hohner diatonic button accordions prepared for sale in France have traditionally differed in one structural aspect from those prepared for sale in the United States: the American versions had four accidental tones positioned at the lowest-pitched end of the right-hand buttons, two tones in each row (one tone on the push in of each lowest button, another on its draw out). These accidentals did not appear on the French versions. Instead, duplicate tonic or dominant pitches from the respective diatonic scale of each row were placed at these button positions.

Two of the Corso model accordions that I encountered in Tamatave had an alteration in the diatonic scale order in their inner row of buttons—the sixth scale degree here was deleted and replaced by a duplicate fifth scale degree of this row. The sixth scale degree was in place as expected in the outer row of buttons on these accordions. Rick Epping, accordion product manager of Hohner, Inc., in Richmond, Virginia, has told me that representatives of Hohner's operation in France confirm that, to their knowledge, no Corso models with missing sixth tone in the inner row were ever produced for their market (personal communication, 1999). Betsimisaraka accordionists informed me that such alterations in tuning were attributable to the unavailability of exact replacement reeds for repairing their broken accordions; consequently, an available fifth scale degree reed was used to replace a nonextant replacement sixth scale degree reed. Such alterations in tuning thus became "natural" elements in the performing style of the accordionists who owned these particular accordions. I have wondered about but been unable to ascertain a correlation between such an "aberration" in accordion tuning and the reordered scales used in Betsimisaraka *valiha* tunings discussed above.

Each of the two right-hand rows of melodic buttons, on both the Vienna-style and Corso accordions, has a range of two octaves. Both rows of buttons are tuned to a major mode diatonic scale, the outer row (further from the bellows) of eleven buttons a fourth below that of the inner row (closer to the bellows) of ten buttons. The left-hand has access to eight bass and chord buttons, factory-set as shown in figure 12.

Betsimisaraka whom I knew generally played their Corso accordions as they came tuned and structured from the factory, with little or no deliberate retuning. Most of these Betsimisaraka accordions had some reeds that had become de-tuned or even broken from wear, so that some unintentional alterations in tuning again became, by necessity, natural. Rabody Thierry who was living in the village of Betampona when I first met him, pointed out drastically de-tuned reeds on his accordion. However, he ingeniously played around the poorly or nonfunctioning reeds on his instrument. For example, he would incorporate the de-tuned reeds in intervals

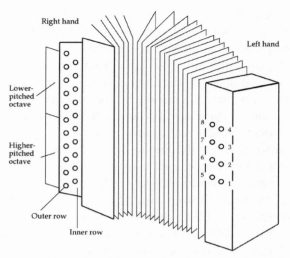

Right hand

Left hand

Lower-pitched octave

Higher-pitched octave

Outer row

Inner row

Fig. 12. Structure of the Corso and Vienna-style Hohner two-row diatonic button accordions as factory-set. The right-hand outer row is tuned a 4th below the inner one (for example, outer row C major, inner row F major). The Corso has three reeds for each right-hand tone, one tuned just slightly above and one tuned slightly below the scale pitch. This produces an out-of-phase tremolo effect and is referred to as "wet" tuning. The Vienna-style model has two reeds for each right-hand tone, one tuned slightly above the scale pitch, also producing an out-of-phase wet tremolo. The push-in and the draw-out of the right-hand buttons generally yield different pitches. The diatonic scale of the lower-pitched octave of either row of buttons, for example, is ordered as follows: 1 in, 2 out, 3 in, 4 out, 5 in, 6 out, 7 out, 1' in. (Antandroy, unlike Betsimisaraka, completely retuned both sides of their accordions. The specific configuration of Antandroy accordions in Tamatave-ville is illustrated in fig. 13.)

The factory tuning of the left-hand buttons is as follows (this model is based upon an accordion with outer row tuned in C and inner row in F): Bass tones are tuned neutral, for instance, 1 combined with 1' (the Vienna has 2 bass reeds per tone, the Corso, 3); chord button sets of reeds are tuned in combinations of 1, 3, and 5, sometimes in inversion (the Vienna has 3 chord reeds per tone; the Corso, 4).

Button	Push-in	Draw-out
1	bass, tonic of inner row (f+f')	bass, dominant of inner row (c+c')
2	chord, tonic of inner row	chord, dominant of inner row
3	bass, tonic of outer row (same as 1 out)	bass, dominant of outer row
4	chord, tonic of outer row (same as 2 out)	chord, dominant of outer row
5	bass, sub-dominant of inner row	same as 5 in
6	chord, sub-dominant of inner row	same as 6 in
7	bass, 6th of outer row (a+a')	bass, 2nd of outer row (d+d')
8	chord, major 6th of outer row	chord, minor 2nd of outer row

that aurally backgrounded or canceled out to some degree their out-of-tuneness. Thierry was the only Betsimisaraka I met who had a Vienna-style accordion; other Betsimisaraka played the Corso model.

Antandroy accordionists in Tamatave-ville completely retuned their Vienna-style accordions. They commonly asked me to bring them two Vienna-style accordions upon my return to Madagascar so that the reeds from one could be removed and worked into the other accordion to transform its tuning. These Antandroy also specified that they did not want the plastic-bodied Corso model, for it could not *mahatavy resaka,* produce thick conversation. This was an aesthetic distinction that referred to the timbre and relative tuning of the Corso. The Corso's triple-reed wet tuning in the right-hand buttons produces sonorities specifically ineffective for calling upon and conversing with Antandroy ancestral spirits. The Corso's ineffectiveness among Antandroy is also compounded by the fact that it is commonly tuned in a register lower than that of the Vienna-style accordion. Velontsoa explained that one important difference between Betsimisaraka and Antandroy musics in general is in the sound of the different accordions themselves: "Tsy mitovy ny feo ilay gorodora Betsimisaraka sy ilay gorodora Antandroy" (the *voice* of the Betsimisaraka accordion is not the same as that of the Antandroy accordion). Like vocal distinctiveness, determined in part by timbre, point of articulation, pitch register, and resonant chamber shape (all qualities that contribute to making one human voice recognizable and distinct from another), the voicings of different accordions also communicate in distinct ways.

Magnampy Soa and Very Soa both played accordion brilliantly, though only Very Soa had developed the specialized knowledge and skill to repair and retune these instruments. Very Soa told me that all the accordions he had ever had in his possession were *efa ela be,* or already quite old and worn. He had never had a new one. He kept a small box of old accordion parts and reeds for repairs. Sometimes, due to the scarcity of accordions throughout the island and especially in the south, his own accordion would disappear for weeks or even months at a time while it was borrowed by relatives or friends for a ceremony in Ambovombe.

When Very Soa had in his possession two Vienna-style accordions, or enough parts from two, he would effect the following alterations. From the pairs of reeds in the right-hand rows of buttons in the to-be-played accordion (recall that the Vienna-style model has only two reeds per right-hand button; the Corso has three), Very Soa removed the "wet" reeds, those tuned in the factory slightly above each "pitch" reed. These wet reeds contribute to an acoustic interference between out-of-phase wavelengths and thus a tremolo effect. He would then match each pitch reed in the lower pitch register of the to-be-played accordion with a reed one octave above it taken from the higher register of the parts accordion. Thus, in the lower register of each row of buttons each tone would be coupled with a tone an octave above it, a "dry" tuning. This new sound greatly contrasts with that of the factory-set pairing of reeds, varied in pitch only slightly so as to produce a tremolo.

For the higher register, Very Soa would retune each wet reed (the one tuned slightly above pitch) of the to-be-played accordion to the unison of its pitch reed. He would accomplish this retuning by delicately adding a slight amount of wood resin to the tongue of the reed, minutely increasing its mass and so lowering its resonant frequency to match that of the pitch reed. Therefore, the higher register would be tuned in unisons, also a dry tuning, which aurally greatly contrasts with the tremolo effect tuned into the accordion at the factory.

Very Soa's adjustments were precise and difficult to perform, particularly since he had no specialized tools with which to work. Even with tools available in the United States and in Europe, reed building and tuning are highly specialized skills. Most accordion builders do not make their own reeds but order them from a reed builder. Here, in Austin, Texas, where accordion players are abundant, there are only a few people who are qualified

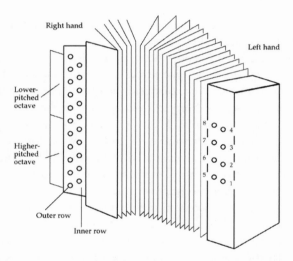

Fig. 13. Very Soa's alterations upon the Vienna-style accordion. On either lower octave register of right-hand buttons, Very Soa coupled each reed with a reed tuned an octave higher. Each higher octave register reed he coupled with its own unison. These reed configurations, which do not produce the wet-tuned out-of-phase tremolo of the Corso model, comprise, in Western terms, a "dry" tuning. Very Soa altered the left-hand reeds as follows (* indicates deviation from the factory-set tuning illustrated in fig. 12).

Button	Push-in	Draw-out
1	bass, tonic of inner row (f+f')	bass, dominant of inner row (c+c')
2	chord, tonic of inner row	chord, *tonic* of inner row (f,a,c)*
3	bass, tonic of outer row (same as 1 out)	bass, dominant of outer row
4	chord, tonic of outer row (same as 2 out)	chord, *tonic* of outer row (c,e,g)*
5	bass, subdominant of inner row	same as 5 in
6	chord, *neutral 6th* of inner row (d,a,d')*	same as 6 in*
7	bass, *2nd* of outer row (a+a')*	bass, 2nd of outer row
8	chord, *minor* 6th of outer row (a,c,e)*	chord, minor 2nd of outer row

to tune and repair accordion reeds. Very Soa's accordion transformations are illustrated in figure 13, transformations that significantly refigure the voicing capacities of the Vienna-style accordion.

Very Soa also altered the harmonic structure and order of the accordion's eight left-hand chord and bass buttons. Both Corso and Vienna-style accordions have been factory-designed specifically to facilitate playing compositions based on I-IV-V harmonic structures. By replacing the factory-set dominant chords on left-hand draw out buttons 2 and 4 (fig. 13), Very Soa forestalled the capacity of the left hand to produce European-designed harmonic accompaniments for melodies played by the right hand. This new tuning was conducive rather to playing drones or ostinato-like patterns. For instance, by alternating from pushing in on button 1 to drawing out on button 2, Very Soa could maintain the same harmony while changing direction with the bellows. One must recall that on these diatonic accordions (as factory-set), free melodic movement necessarily requires one to regularly alternate bellows direction, since not all notes of the diatonic scale are accessible on either just the push-in or draw-out motions. The left-hand buttons have been factory-set with this need to systematically change bellows direction in mind, concurrent with the need to alter harmony accordingly. By Very Soa's adjustments, the left hand could no longer harmonically follow, on European terms, the material played by the right hand.

Very Soa also made other changes in the factory tuning of the left-hand buttons. On both the push-in and draw-out of button 6, he replaced the factory-set subdominant major triad chord with a neutral sixth harmony of this row. On an accordion with outer row tuned in C and inner in F, this transformation would alter a harmony composed of the tones B-flat, D, F to one composed of D, A, D'. This transposition and modalizing of a major sonority then allows button 6 to be harmonically compatible for instance with the minor second sonorities of the push-in and draw-out of button 7. Button 6 then is also harmonically compatible with the push-in of button 8, which Very Soa had transformed from the factory set major sixth of the C row to a minor sixth harmony. The factory-set major sixth triad contains a pitch, its third scale degree, not within the diatonic scale of either right-hand row of buttons. For instance, on an accordion with outer row tuned in C and inner in F (A–C-sharp–E) would be the harmony to which I am referring. By lowering this accidental pitch C-sharp a half-tone, Very Soa actually returned to and reclaimed the pure diatonic scale for his accordion. Since Antandroy most often have an acute sense of pitch—they exactingly tune and retune their instruments, accordions as well as stringed instruments—it is likely that Very Soa heard the accidental pitch in the major sixth chord as errant to the desired order of otherwise complete diatonicism of the Vienna-style accordion. Thus, he felt the need to correct it. About retuning this accidental tone he would say only, "Izay tsy mety" (That note is not possible [it doesn't belong or fit]).

It was not possible to accurately play Betsimisaraka musics, which tended to rely more upon a I–IV–V harmonic structure, on an Antandroy accordion, nor could I reproduce Antandroy accordion music on my own Betsimisaraka-style accordion that I had brought from the United States.[8] While the Vienna-style accordion had been factory-tuned to produce European sonorities and harmonic structures, Very Soa harmonically and timbrally disengaged these French ways of sounding, mechanically transforming the diatonic accordion into an aural medium of Antandroy spiritual and communicative efficacy.

Antandroy friends in Tamatave-ville commonly asserted that non-Antandroy musics were not *mafy* or hard—in this case, they were not hard-driving in tempo and energy. Hence, other Malagasy musics from around the island could not *miresaka amindrazana,* or converse specifically with Antandroy ancestral spirits. When Magnampy Soa and I occasionally would sample my recordings of non-Antandroy Malagasy accordion musics, he would listen intently, seeming to enjoy these other ways of playing, though he would invariably make the evaluation "Tsara io mosika io fa izy tsy mahay" (That music's all right, but the player isn't competent). By this Magnampy Soa did not mean that the player was not a good musician. In a more refined way he was suggesting that these other musicians were not able to produce the proper musical intensity, the particular modes of *maresaka* needed to communicate with Antandroy ancestral spirits.

Antandroy accordionists extended the sonic limits of their instruments in other ways as well. They would occasionally snap or slap the bellows on both draw out and push-in motions to create a syncopative percussion, for which these bellows had not been designed. Antandroy would often rapidly and repeatedly jerk the bellows to produce a quavering voicing. With their reworked accordions, Antandroy would occasionally play a melodic motif with the left hand as a sort of counterpoint to the right-hand motif, a difficult technique to perform on this type of accordion.[9] In addition, Antandroy played their accordions at an unbelievably rapid tempo for which the diatonic Vienna-style accordion was not structurally designed. Indeed, I had never heard any diatonic accordion anywhere pushed to such extremes of rhythmic and improvisatory intricacy at such rapid tempos.

The appearance of European instruments and materials in Malagasy practices has not represented a coercive or detrimental wave of colonial effect upon local traditions. Antandroy alterations in accordion structure, in

Photograph 8. Very Soa making accordion adjustments.

factory-set delimitations built into these instruments are themselves altering maneuvers through which traditional European constraints upon ways of music making are reevaluated and transformed. Indeed, in France or the United States the two-row diatonic accordion is commonly thought to be a self-limiting and simple folk instrument, an opinion commonly expressed by Europeans I met in Madagascar. In Very Soa's or Magnampy Soa's hands, the two-row diatonic button accordion was transformed into an instrument of Antandroy virtuosity, capable of producing music beyond the scope of its European designers. Both Antandroy and Betsimisaraka musicians cleverly and dexterously *exceed* French-conceived limitations on colonial instruments and materials, things that had often been left in Madagascar essentially as colonial refuse.

CHAPTER SIX

Recollecting

ﾟ

Practical memory is regulated by the manifold activity of *alteration,* not merely because it is constituted only by being marked by external occurrences and by accumu-
lating these successive blazons and tattoos inscribed by the other, but also because
these invisible inscriptions are "recalled" to the light of day only through new circumstances . . . Perhaps memory is no more than this "recall" or call on the part of
the other, leaving its mark like a kind of overlay on a body that has always already
been altered without knowing it. This originary and secret writing "emerges" little
by little, in the very spots where memory is touched: memory is played by circumstances, just as a piano is played by a musician and music emerges from it when its
keys are touched by the hands. Memory is a sense of the other. (de Certeau 1984: 87)

Past personalities and occasions become stimulated and embodied in
tromba ceremony in part when an array of forces play upon the ceremonial
body. For example, memory surfaces when varied sounds; the taste of rum;
the scent of cigarettes, incense, and foreign perfume; and other physical
sensations convene upon and in this body. Select recall of the colonial era
also can be encoded into performance practices in Tamatave, to play into
the feelingful experience of ceremonial recollection. "Practical memory" in
tromba ceremony can be "inscribed," by both ancestral and colonial Other.
Like a tattoo, this memory is effectively blazoned upon the body—*tromba*
ceremony indeed has its painful moments. Antandroy in Tamatave sometimes even tattoo themselves, to recall specific connections to ancestry and
place (chap. 11).[1]

Memory leaves its mark upon *tromba-istes* "like a kind of overlay on a
body that has always already been altered without knowing it." Powerful
spirits call upon the living to re-mark corporeally upon them, to heal the ill
body or psyche. However, a *tromba* also can *cause* one to become ill:
tromba commonly make potential mediums ill as a sign of interest in possessing that person. Illness itself is an often occurring imprint on and into
the body in Tamatave (chap. 10). In *tromba* ceremony another mode of
corporeal overlay arises as often deleterious physical demands are made

upon the body, ranging from the extreme of auto-inflicted injury, to the physical difficulty of sitting in one cramped position hour after hour, to the difficulty with which a spirit enters a medium's body (hyperventilation, the medium's head snapping around wildly, etc.). Overlays of varied inter-group and colonial interactions also have historically altered or imposed forces upon the Malagasy body. Less overtly, the transformative power inherent in some colonial things has placed other subtle overlays on the Malagasy body—for example, at a micro-poetic level, the acquired physical agility and dexterity necessarily developed by Malagasy to master the structural makeup of newly introduced diatonic accordions, or the calluses necessarily developed to play on metal-stringed *valiha*.[2]

Yet, concurrent with its painful or difficult elements, *tromba* practice also evokes the joyousness of reuniting with revered ancestral spirits. Some Malagasy on the east coast say that in *tromba* ceremonies they and their ancestors *misôma* or *midôla*, dance or play joyously together in the present. Memory is effectively played, or played with, by *tromba* musicians, who aurally empower varied pasts, at once both painful and joyous, into being reconstructed and enacted in the present. This can also mean playing with older European musical events and forms, such as colonial dances (*bals*) and the *valses* commonly played at them. Recall of the past, especially in Betsimisaraka *tromba* ceremonies, often involves playing with or upon the sometimes odd, humorous, or flamboyant behavior of different foreign personalities.

Michael Jackson has written that among Warlpiri in Australia, "memory is never merely a cognitive process, the past recollected in tranquility. Remembering is social. It entails concerted, concentrated, embodied interaction with kinsmen, affines, and countrymen to recreate modes of intersubjectivity that encompass both the living and the dead" (1998: 129). A distinction between recollection and memory in Tamatave is in order. Ceremonial recollection here is reliant specifically upon a social trafficking in *images* and upon the collective actualization of such historical images (see Casey 1987). Recollection in *tromba* practice encompasses more than remembering things as they might flash upon a screen of awareness. Ceremonial recollection necessarily calls upon *enacting* varied pasts and often fragmenting, reassessing, and altering them in their enactment. Recollecting also involves collectively extracting from the past to empower, embellish, and make sense of the present.

Recollection in *tromba* ceremony is more a matter of socially *becoming* certain pasts than of merely remembering them. I do not mean to suggest that Malagasy do not express or experience other modes of remembering. I am setting the ground for a particular ceremonial and performative recollecting that relies upon embodying, then sometimes politicizing and critiquing images of varied pasts. This is all coordinated by social and thus spiritual interaction and by the sentience of individual as well as collective experience in the present.

Malagasy histories in *tromba* practice become multidirectional articulations, in which the past can exercise a vivacity of its own, imprinting itself upon the present or into other time periods. As suggested, history in *tromba* ceremony is not something simply to know but something to do, something with which to become involved. In a sense, the present and the past work reciprocally to transform or transfigure the other. Edward Casey more broadly alliterates a potential for fluidity and alterability in experiences of remembering:

But memory is not just something that sustains a *status quo ante* within human experience. It also makes a critical difference to this experience. The situation is such that remembering transforms one kind of experience into another: *in being remembered, an experience becomes a different kind of experience.* It becomes a "memory," with all that this entails, not merely of the consistent, the enduring, the reliable, but also of the fragile, the errant, the confabulated. Each memory is unique; none is simple repetition or revival. The way that the past is relived in memory assures that it will be transfigured in subtle and significant ways. (1987: xii)

Casey later explains what he calls the "thick autonomy" of remembering—thick with the integration of varied memory-ful body-oriented sensations and autonomous by the variability and multiple focus of memory. This, he contraposes with a more passive or photographic model of memory, which would rely primarily on fixed or incontrovertible images. Such a thick autonomy of recollecting imbues east coast Malagasy spiritual practices.

In this chapter, I want to elaborate upon some acoustic and other elements in playing out recollection, in specific east coast ways of evoking "a sense of the other," to which de Certeau likens memory. Such a ceremonial sense of an Other fits comfortably with a more widely felt historical consciousness and aesthetic of intermixing and *métissage* in Tamatave. Difference itself can be taken on, in *tromba* ceremony and in daily life, as a qualitatively consumable attribute. The combining aesthetic of *maresaka* can also translate into human behavior and socialization during *tromba* events. I will illustrate here some specific ways in which east coast Malagasy not only relive but refigure their pasts by recollecting (from) them. I keep close at hand Casey's elaboration upon truth, and thus some implications about what can be "real":

Truth emerges in and through the act of remembering itself. This is what we mean when we say that a given memory is "true to an experience," or that we are "truly remembering" something. In such cases the truth resides not in statements that may accompany the remembering, or in items of evidence, but *in the remembering itself*—in its relation to the past with which it is reconnecting, whatever the precise evidence or expression in words may be (1987: 282).[3]

Looking Back and Becoming

Many times in the Analalava region [northwestern Madagascar] . . . I felt I was a ghost—besides myself, an image of all the vazaha who had lived and worked there before me. Many encounters with people, especially first encounters, were surrounded by this ghostly aura, in which the significance of our words and actions had historical, ancestral vibrations. (Feeley-Harnik 1991b)

Madagascar has sometimes been characterized in commercial and educational media by its "out-of-timeness." For example, I've seen more than one naturalist television special that begins with a voiceover romanticizing "this wondrous land out of time." Vividly expressing her own sense of a multidirectional temporality while in Madagascar, anthropologist Gillian Feeley-Harnik sees herself reembodied, placed back into a history of contact in Madagascar that she herself has not actually experienced. Imagining her own ghost merging with other ghosts, she expresses here a sense of being infused into the past and of the past being embedded into her experience of the present. Indeed, her own perceptions of the present seem to depend somewhat on this past-sense. And it is specifically *first* encounters that are affected by a ghostly aura of historical *vibration* in Feeley-Harnik's remembrance. This may resonate with the importance of discursive encounter among Malagasy and perhaps even with the significant role played by acoustic vibrations in the recollection and realization of things.

In *tromba* ceremony Malagasy often recall the spirits of powerful Sakalava royalty from Malagasy kingdoms that ruled northern and western regions of the island from the seventeenth through the nineteenth centuries (see, for example, Brown 1979, Feeley-Harnik 1978, 1988, 1991a, and 1991b, Grandidier 1910 and 1959). Sakalava had at times mounted viable resistance to early Merina expansionism into the northwest of the island. As ancient Sakalava royalty had resisted outside forces, one might be tempted to incorporate resistance itself as an interpretive framework by which to evaluate *tromba* practice. I will question resistance as praxis at length in the following chapter. In the present then, spirits of Sakalava royalty return to inhabit mediums in *tromba* ceremony to heal the sick, foretell the future, advise the living, and intercede in everyday disputes and problems. Not all *tromba* spirits are Sakalava; some had also been Merina royalty, colonial officials, and other powerful people from Madagascar, as well as from other places. As royal *tromba* spirits rarely are actually Betsimisaraka or Antandroy like the mediums who call them, the evocation of these spirits allow Malagasy in Tamatave in part to enact their sentiments, past and present, toward other groups and individuals.

There are also numerous nonroyal spirits who possess varied powers and who exercise varying influence over *tromba* proceedings. These might include recently deceased immediate relatives and even spirits of White outsiders. Honorine, a Betsimisaraka medium to whom as many as twenty-five different *tromba* came, frequently became possessed by a *silamo* (Muslim) spirit named Sadam Hoseny and by an American-like spirit named Georges Klintsky who resided in the ocean off the coast of Greenland. These spirits themselves conversed regularly with me while Honorine was possessed by them—I will return to them in chap. 8. Recollecting in *tromba* practice brings up not only Malagasy pasts, but it can involve imagining French, Islamic, American, or other foreign pasts as well.

Since *tromba* spirits have human personalities, the action of a *tromba* ceremony is grounded in the potential moodiness and unpredictability of sometimes exaggerated human behavior. A Betsimisaraka medium possessed by a child spirit once became very agitated by my presence at a *tromba* ceremony and began to throw a disruptive tantrum, screaming in a high-pitched voice and stomping throughout the *tromba* house. I was instructed by the presiding *tromba* to take the child spirit upon my knee and to tell him a story to calm him down. The medium was a rather heavy woman, and the sight of her sitting on my lap caused outbursts of laughter and joking from many of the other participants. Once a very powerful Sakalava spirit (the medium also was a woman) insistently directed that I choose one of his young female attendants to take as a wife. Thus, I myself was sometimes a medium in the spontaneous dénouement of ceremonial procedure (and my own behavior might become incorporated into varied negotiations in the course of the ceremony). In a more extreme instance, once I was sitting on the floor during a *tromba* healing ceremony with Velontsoa, beside an Antandroy woman who I did not know well at the time. She became possessed by a *bilo*, a very powerful though potentially temperamental spirit among Antandroy. *Bilo* are not royal Sakalava spirits; they are a sort of dangerous disembodied force that comes largely to cause illness. This *bilo* had become angry with the medium because she had failed to fulfill some of its demands upon her for material things, which she simply had not been able to afford. The woman (the *bilo*) picked up a sharp knife and began to stab herself repeatedly in the shoulder, retribution from the angry spirit force, until the knife could be wrestled from her grasp by the rest of us. *Bilo* are also distinct from *tromba* in that they often come uninvited, to inflict an injury or illness upon someone by possessing them. *Tromba* spirits themselves sometimes cause illness, but these illnesses are usually inflicted by them in disembodied form from afar, not through direct possession of a person by the *tromba*. Thus, the proceedings of a *tromba* ceremony would unfurl unpredictably, humorously, even shockingly and would rely to a certain degree, like musical performance, on expressive improvisation.

Recollecting in *tromba* ceremony commonly extends beyond grasping "a sense of the other," to *becoming* the other, in at least two senses. For one, *tromba* mediums give themselves up to distant spirits and situations as they literally become embodiments of them. *Tromba* ceremony also can draw upon the ability to reflect back favorably upon (becoming-ly of) older musical principles, genres, instruments, and social events. Reciprocally, these other, often once colonial things, as integral components of *tromba* practice, can mirror favorably back upon these very *tromba* proceedings.

Following Benjamin's view that the "gift of seeing resemblances is nothing other than a rudiment of the powerful compulsion in former times to become and behave like something else" (1978: 333), Michael Taussig has written:

> Pulling you this way and that, mimesis plays this trick of dancing between the very same and the very different. An impossible but necessary, indeed an everyday affair, mimesis registers both sameness and difference, of being like, and of being Other . . . all identity formation is engaged in this habitually bracing activity in which the issue is not so much staying the same, but maintaining sameness through alterity. (1993: 129)

Taussig continues that "the full effect occurs when the necessary impossibility is attained, when mimesis becomes alterity. Then and only then can spirit and matter, history and nature flow into each other's otherness" (ibid.: 192). In *tromba* ceremony, becoming an Other can enhance and maintain sameness. Here, exchanging one's spirit for that of a distant personality is meaningful in part because of the very recollections of how difference has combined throughout the past in Tamatave. While east coast mediums become embodiments of royal Malagasy ancestors or other foreign figures, *tromba* musicians simultaneously reflect back becomingly upon musical instruments, forms, and occasions of the colonial era, even to "become" in some instances the French musician performing at colonial social events.

Desire and Selective Recollecting

Tromba ceremony is often fueled by desire, a longing not only to remember the ancestral past (*taloha*) but to become immersed in it, indeed to become it. This desire is circumstantially fulfilled in part by the medium's reverential giving up of her or his body to *tromba* spirits, to reconstruct a joyous connection with ancestors and more recently deceased family members. This joyousness, though, is filtered historically through periods of colonialism, intergroup strife, and numerous other obstacles to everyday existence in Madagascar. In *tromba* ceremony, Malagasy can delve into the past and experience it selectively, in composites of varied features, events, and personalities. *Tromba* transcends historical/temporal sequentiality. Yet Michael Lambek (1998) suggests ways in which temporal sequentiality is played out in *tromba* ceremony. For instance, older, more powerful spirits can use seating order to instate their seniority, as they sit in front of and sometimes elevated above other, more recent *tromba*. Such sequentiality also can be emergent in patterns of deferential behavior toward these older spirits. The combination of overt indications of temporal sequentiality with actions that transcend such sequentiality might even lend experientially to the blurring of boundaries between past, present, and future among *tromba-istes*. I began to wonder if such a selective and often nonsequential historical gaze, along with recollections of capacities for taking colonial and foreign things into *tromba* ceremony, to absorb and rework their power, might explain in part the conciliatory demeanor that most *tromba-istes* seem to have found for their colonial past.[4]

Re-dressing Models

[S]inging origins is not done so much to gain control over the object of the Origin-History song, but first and foremost to create that object through its soulful *evocation* . . . such that "calling them up" is to conjure with their image, hence their soul, and hence give birth to the real. I am suggesting, in other words, that the chanter is singing a copy of the spirit-form, and by virtue of what I call the magic of mimesis, is bringing the spirit into the physical world. (Taussig 1993: 104–5)

Some Betsimisaraka, *tromba-istes* as well as non-*tromba-istes*, adorned sections of wall space in their houses with a display of collaged together magazine pictures or calendar photo cutouts (when and if they could find them). One type of illustration particularly favored for this purpose, specifically in tromba houses, featured Asian or European models, usually bejeweled and dressed in extravagant, brightly colored gowns, often standing in front of a sports car or posed in front of some modern architectural backdrop. These cutout wall displays usually were very close to or directly over the *tromba* alter. Antandroy in Tamatave-ville did not adorn their houses at all with magazine cutouts.

These partial magazine pages themselves stand as one type of sign among Betsimisaraka, in that they are quite rare and difficult to acquire. Simply having them comes with a certain amount of prestige. Magazine cutouts also could take on a masking quality, as they are amassed and concentrated on old, worn, soiled walls of *tromba* houses. These well-worn walls themselves frame and intensify the inequity between the glossy excesses contained in the photos and ever-present daily realities on the east coast of material absence and excessive wear.

Images of Asian and European models in *tromba* houses in effect are signs of signs—here the image(ing) is real while the printed reality is imaginary (Taylor 1993: 179). These images are models, more accurately models of models, for which there is no (apparent) original. Most Betsimisaraka could only distantly imagine such embodied opulence, though they never actually experience or view it themselves in the Tamatave region. Fragments of magazine advertisements do not connect the ceremonial present to some specific reality as advertised in them. These displayed images are in part prestigious representations, as items very difficult to obtain, of an intangible and unspecific real imagined to be out there somewhere.[5] Combinations of magazine photos then generate a fluidity of signs with which *tromba-istes* can interpret and give new meaning to both the past and present. These wall collage displays and the re-dressing practices that are related to them, could embody the re-dressing of varied modes of power.

Gillian Feeley-Harnik asserts that, among Sakalava in the north, "clothing styles express a broad range of opinions concerning relationships among Malagasy and between Malagasy and Europeans" (1989: 81). While they are colorful decorations that amuse, entice, impress, and appease *tromba,* images of foreign glamour and excess spilling from *tromba* altar photo collages can also serve Betsimisaraka as models for ritual behavior. Magazine photos of brightly and stylishly clad foreign women could recollect and reinforce older tenets of *tromba* ceremony. Here the foreign, the excessive, and the unattainable provide mimetic fuel for articulating and even validating certain preestablished customs of re-dressing in the desired garb of particular *tromba,* for modeling the "foreign" clothing styles and comportments of Malagasy royalty. Thus, these photos might even be imagined into *tromba* ceremony as foreign affirmations of and reflections back upon Malagasy practices. Through such photo combinations, Betsimisaraka also could recollect or imagine varied histories of foreign contact, as waves of Europeans and Asians in particular have come throughout the past to visit or settle in the Tamatave region. Quite often these Europeans and Asians have known greater economic privilege than most Betsimisaraka (though not to the extent represented in the *tromba* altar collages).

Betsimisaraka *tromba* ceremonies are thus characterized by large crowds of interacting *tromba,* elaborate re-dressing rituals, and an integration of emotional expression that ranges from introspective reflection to much drunken boisterousness and partying. The combination of these characteristics mirrors a connection with or mimesis of often boisterous *baolina (bals)* from the past, thrown by French colonials in the Tamatave region. The linguistic marking of the French term *bal,* still used by some Malagasy, and its Malagasy derivative *baolina* also seem to attest to some level of recollection—direct, retold, or imagined—among Tamataviens of older European social events.

The *diner-dansant* appears to be a present-day vestige of the colonial *bal* held in Tamatave-ville or in small towns like Fénérive-Est. This is a dance party, reserved most often for French or Merina businessmen, government officials, other foreigners, such as the few American Peace Corps volunteers or environmental conservationists in the area,[6] and the few Betsimisaraka who could afford the admission price. Antandroy in Tamatave-ville were not interested in these affairs (and there was no Antandroy community in Fénérive-Est). Popular Malagasy bands, if available, would perform for these events, or cassettes were played on a magnéto. The general aesthetic of a *diner-dansant* is quite European-influenced in form and procedure— place settings, European-style food and formality, and dressing up in one's finest European-style clothing, a dressing up that is always noticed by other Malagasy, dressed down and peering in from outside these events.

Sammy Maurice, about seventy years of age, was the oldest man in Betampona, a Betsimisaraka village in the mountainous region northwest of Fénérive-Est.[7] On a breezy Betampona peak overlooking the Indian Ocean to the east and the surviving bit of rainforest to the west (every other hilltop still smoldering, decimated by recent slash-and-burn agriculture), Sammy Maurice stooped, barefoot. He was drawing maps in the dirt and showing me the location of different important places in the region as he recalled the *bals* that French colonials had organized:

Tonga teto matetika ny vazaha frantsay. "District Administrateur" nagnanô tragnô taketô antampon'ny Betampona avaratra ary nagnanô tragnô teto. Isaky ny asabotsy mandeha mampandihy baolina taketô—nisy tragnô lehibe taketô taloha ny fiangonana protestanta teo. Isaky ny asabotsy "atao mampandihy baolina"— tamin'izay ny tanora.

French colonials came here often. The district administrator had a house here at the highest point in the northern section of Betampona, and he had another house there[Sammy pointed to another hillside]. Every Saturday night there were dances here—there was a big dance hall here before the Protestant church went up over there. Each Saturday it was, "see that there is much dancing together"—back then in my youth.

Sammy Maurice continued by saying that both French colonials and local Malagasy attended these French-sanctioned *bals* that were commonly held in Betampona as well as in other locales throughout the Tamatave countryside.

Sammy Maurice recalled an abundance of *trandraka*, the Malagasy *tenrec*, or quill pig, in Betampona in those days. But when one ate *trandraka*, she or he would exude an odor that was thought to be unpleasant to Europeans, so young Malagasy would not eat it prior to a *bal* to avoid offending their colonial hosts. Sammy said that both men and women exercised elaborate cosmetic preparations for the *bals*. For instance, men would apply *pômady* to slick down or Europeanize their hair; women would fix theirs in *voampelaka*, an elaborate, formal, and time-consuming braiding process. Most Betsimisaraka in Betampona usually had in their possession one set of European-like clothes, reserved for such occasions or for Malagasy ceremonies such as weddings. Sammy was insistent that these external alterations were not necessarily internalized, for along with such dressing up, Betsimisaraka remembered and performed older traditional dances, such as *bararatra* at these integrative colonial functions.

From recollections of colonial *bals* commonly voiced by elder Betsimisaraka and supported by the presence of a current form drawing on such *bals*, the *diner-dansant*, I began to gather that images of colonial celebrations have become entangled with or integrated into Betsimisaraka ceremony, as a certain implicit remembering on-the-occasion-of. Certain colonial events appear to have settled upon Betsimisaraka ceremonial consciousness and become fuel for commemorative-like modeling:

On Christmas day, for example, one may experience an atmosphere of "Christmas past" without being able to specify *which* Christmas, or group of Christmases, one is thus indistinctly recalling. It is as if the significance of the occasion precludes more explicit acts of remembering or at least renders them difficult, replacing them by a diffuse familiarity in which the past is present not in person but by insinuation only. We should also notice, finally, the considerable commemorative power of remembering on-the-occasion-of. Such remembering is not necessarily an express act of commemoration (e.g., as it might be on Memorial Day); but it often plays this role because of the very nature of the situation: to remember in this way, at this place and time, is *ipso facto* to commemorate past experiences that occurred in this same place at other times. (Casey 1987:62)

Recollections (or imaginings) of older dance events and magazine cutout collages over *tromba* altars clearly indicate that Betsimisaraka *tromba-istes* actively evoke and incorporate outside worlds. I am suggesting here that colonial era social events also contribute form, process, and meaning to current *tromba* practices among Betsimisaraka. While colonial *bals* themselves are not personally remembered by younger *tromba-istes*, these, as well as other European-like events, become re-placed as "a diffuse familiarity in which the (colonial) past is present not in person but by insinuation only."

Antandroy in Tamatave-ville on the other hand, are for the most part unfamiliar with the concept of European-style *bals*, nor do they display signs of foreign excess in their houses. This is not to say that Antandroy in Tamatave-ville are *not* affected by an aesthetic of incorporation but that they allow themselves to be selectively affected in different ways (chap. 11). Antandroy *tromba* ceremonies, as more solemn events in which only one medium becomes possessed, are not implicitly replicative in form or proceeding of larger boisterous colonial fêtes, characterized in part by many foreigners interacting joyously with one another.

Tompezolo—Recollecting (from) the Past

Tompezolo told me that Christian icons in her *tromba* altar—the statues or pictures of Jesus and the Virgin Mary, for instance—are specifically for one of her *tromba* who had been *kristiana*. Even revered *tromba* spirits could embody what are considered by most Antandroy *tromba-istes* in Tamatave-ville to be *vazaha*-like traits or preferences. By displaying and replicating how Christianity had been appropriated and taken in by this particular Malagasy royal ancestral spirit, Tompezolo was able to interiorize an essence of Christian power, earlier European proponents of which had commonly condemned *tromba* practice in Madagascar. Tompezolo also on occasion expressed her own recollection of Merina king Radama II's affinity for European religion in the latter part of the nineteenth century.

Thus, Tompezolo did not display Christian icons in the sacred space of her *tromba* altar as commemorative affirmations of Christianity. Rather, these icons were signs to her of how Malagasy people from the past had adopted and applied, indeed altered, Christianity to their own ends. Tompezolo was able to negate some of the deleterious effects of Christianity in Madagascar by revaluing it in a different light, in which it represented to her a freedom of choice exercised by other powerful Malagasy personalities. Christian icons are powerful, therefore, not only as things taken into *tromba* ceremony to variably embellish it with their immediate presence. These things also symbolically incorporate varied pasts into the present, transforming an often deleterious force throughout the past into a useful sign of current spirit power. Christian icons in her *tromba* altar represent Tompezolo's accommodation of and respect for the actions of Malagasy royalty and other historical figures.

Tompezolo's altar also contained several silver coins. Silver and silvery objects exude a doubly valued composite essence among Antandroy in Tamatave-ville. The power of foreign capital is combined in silver objects with the ancestral significance and power with which silver is always already endowed by its connection to the Zafimbolafotsy lineage of ancestral spirits ("grandchildren of silver"). Particularly desirable and valued are older, out-of-circulation French coins from the era of colonial occupation in Madagascar. Tompezolo asked me on occasion to bring her other silver coins from *ampitany* (out there) to add to the incorporative and combining power of her altar. Sometimes foreign silver coins, when attainable, were nailed into the doorway of Antandroy *tromba* houses.

Antandroy *ombiasa* construct amulets called *aoly* (*aody* in Betsimisaraka speech) for healing purposes, protection, or good fortune. Such a device consists of a cow's horn filled with a curative mixture of herbs and ground tree barks (a mixture called *aoly aby*). Into this sticky mixture, old scissors, safety pins, or straight pins are commonly inserted. These are all things that represent by hue the combining powers inherent in silver. The simultaneous use of scissors and safety or straight pins in a single *aoly* creates an image of conjoined opposites—scissors rend, safety pins hold together (the tears of overuse, for example). These silvery things also have similar value and power in co-functioning to repair old or create new clothing. Healing power in these particular *aoly* also draws upon combining substances from different ecologies—silvery commercial objects, representing a foreign industrial production line, and Malagasy herbal mixtures, representing the Malagasy wilderness.

Velontsoa had creatively combined varied sources of power into a particular *aoly* he had made. From the sticky herbal center of this device protruded a broken-off segment of a portable radio antenna, a medium of the technologized transmission of modulated waveforms and their transference into audible sound. As a component of this *aoly,* the (silvery) radio antenna fragment stood as medium of empowerment in its capacity to combine varied forces—the transmission and amplification of sound through radio broadcast, Zafimbolafotsy ancestral power, in addition to the power of colonial capital. In this composite object, Velontsoa had constructed a combining healing whole stronger than any of its different colonial, ancestral, electronic, acoustical, and natural or herbal parts.

Velontsoa's *aoly,* with its protrusion of radio antenna, also took on the power of a sound-transmitting device that it copied, a machine often unaffordable among most Antandroy in Tamatave-ville. As with Antandroy *mandôlina* detailed with the markings of a portable radio/cassette player, Velontsoa had empowered this *aoly* with the propagation of electronically produced and mediated sound waves over the national radio station. Recall that the Radio Nationale, emanating from the capital, Antananarivo, is controlled by Merina and that Antandroy ceremonial musics are virtually never broadcast over it. This electronic extension from within a spiritual object again represented empowerment, over the possession of a prohibitively expensive musical device and the prestige implicit in Velontsoa's imagined control of his own music symbolically sounding over the national radio station. Velontsoa also had created an amalgamated power reliant upon the reciprocal transmitting capacity of this *aoly*—sound traveled to the *razana* through the antenna while ancestral and foreign healing powers were simultaneously transmitted through this same device into present.

Tompezolo as well reassigned value to varied other things in her *tromba* altar. The red, green, and white Malagasy flag/handkerchief she kept there was not an indication to her of a nationalist sentiment. To the contrary, it was a colorful offering to *tromba* spirits by which a sign of the national and modern became subordinate, specifically to ancestral powers from the pre-national past. Tompezolo had once said about this handkerchief, "Iah, mety karaha fagneva gasy io, fa tia mamaoka ny tarehy ilay tromba" (Yes, perhaps it's like the Malagasy flag, but *tromba* like to wipe their face with it).

Tompezolo, as well as other *tromba-istes,* both Antandroy and Betsimisaraka, would sometimes hold small hand mirrors outward over the *tromba* altar, sometimes to reflect to the *tromba* spirit its embodied form but also to mirror outward onto the external world. Mirrors pointed outward thus serve as clarifying and focusing devices, through which *tromba* could better visually regard this embodied world, which they only temporarily visit from afar. Sunglasses are often worn by mediums to protect the vision of certain spirits who find the external world too brightly illuminated, even visually painful, without its being shaded or polarized. Such visual preferences attest to the acute sensitivity of the medium/spirit to physical sensation, to the tactile external world, and by extension to its vibrations, hues, volumes, and timbres.

Ceremonial recollection for Tompezolo, as well as other Antandroy in Tamatave-ville, is in part a matter of collecting remnants that, once assembled, can bring varied pasts together in the present. Both Antandroy and Betsimisaraka are expert *bricoleurs,* making use of what is on hand, though they each do so selectively in distinct ways.

The Nature of Mimesis

I am hesitant to conclude that mimetic appropriation, specifically in Betsimisaraka *tromba* ceremony, is intended primarily as parody (for instance, of European *bals*). Taussig, for one, sees a connection between mimesis and parody: "[P]arody is where mimicry exposes construction, suggestive of a new sort of anthropology, post-post-Frazerian, that defines its object of study not as Other but as the reflection of the West in the mimetic magic of its Others." (1993: 69).

Might parody, however, implicate a specific critical or otherwise evaluative intentionality, one that might even be assumed in analysis rather than
necessarily in the minds of those people acting mimetically? My own hesi-
tance is informed by Nicholas Thomas's admonition:

the appearance of parody in the copying of institutions, practices, and objects from
one's own tradition may distort the intentions of those doing the copying. . . . [In]
these cases copying is appropriation, a project engaged in to specify alterity and to
incorporate the powers of the other. The political seriousness of the intercultural
transaction is diminished if acquisition and reproduction are understood primarily
as burlesque imitation. (1991: 187)

Thomas specifically questions whether interpreting the actions of Haouka
spirit mediums in Jean Rouch's *Les maîtres fous* (1954) as parody "would
entail a radical misreading of the cult's orientation" (ibid.). I agree with
Thomas that local meanings are likely complex and distinct, and that "entanglement" might often more suitably explain some dynamics of contact
between colonial regimes and colonized people:

The notion of entanglement aims to capture the dialectic of international inequal-
ities and local appropriations; it energizes a perspective situated beyond the argument between proponents of the view that the world system is essentially determi-
nate of local social systems and those asserting the relative autonomy of individual
groups and cultures. (1991: 201)

In *tromba* ceremony, spirit mediums become foreign others, not simply
intending to burlesque and ridicule them or to create carnivalesque inver-
sions of historically familiar structures of power. Rather, this becoming is
meant to shape an integrative power of the Other, to have the present become entangled in complex pasts that are themselves an imbrication of varied forces that can have Sakalava, French, Merina, and American visages.
All such becoming, then, is framed within the social power created through
immersion and joyous interaction, engendered aesthetically as an effusion
of ceremonial *maresaka*. It is inevitably the curative power created in the
present that is most vital to *tromba-istes* in Tamatave.

Recollecting the Real

Narrativity can be invested in material artifacts and relations that have a story-
telling capacity of their own. . . . If narrativity can be embedded in iconic arrangements of material artifacts and/or actions, one can speak of the making and narrating of history as two sides of the same process. This implies an imaginary
dimension to the production of specific performances as historicized and historicizing practices. (Feldman 1991:14)

I take "imaginary" here not as unreal but as becoming real in the imagining. *Tromba* ceremony itself becomes a mediating form through which

meaning passes (K. Stewart 1996). The real, both past and present, is not simply enunciated or reiterated in these ceremonies, it is imaginatively produced by them. Realities are alterable and altering here, for instance, as colonial social events become or reflect becoming-ly upon the invocation of sacred Malagasy ancestors. In another reality from the past, the colonial powers represented by these social events actually had fervently opposed and even prohibited such ancestral practices. *Tromba-istes* are mediators of the real, reordering histories of dominance, exploitation, and condescension into more productive narratives that interconnect the foreign and the ancestral. Thus, even though *tromba* spirits are not accustomed to having *vazaha* such as myself appear at *tromba* ceremonies in Tamatave, my presence at these ceremonies did not usually seem particularly disruptive or irreconcilable. Even when it was momentarily so, this was quickly and easily ameliorated. Foreign presence and how it can be incorporated into the ceremonial moment are already vital processual components of *tromba* practice.

Edward Casey has noted that "things put the past in place; they are the primary source of its concrete implacement in memory" (1987: 206). Multiple meanings inherent in things, such as accordions or foreign-produced perfume, for instance, work as complex signifiers in integrative recollections of the past. Thus, accordions can narrativize upon both a colonial *bal* and Malagasy ancestral spirits; perfume can stimulate recollections or imaginings of colonial celebrations as well as of previous *tromba* events in which specific memorable things occurred. The sound-producing capacities embedded in things such as accordions, bicycle brake cables, roofing sheet metal, insecticide cans, each with its own stories to tell, resonate in the present with ceremonial joyousness and healing efficacy, though the power of each is also rooted in its colonial origins, as well as in Malagasy abilities to alter these things. Lifting sound from nonsounding materials, transforming the voicing and structure of musical instruments, revaluing signs of Christianity, taking magazine photos in as objects for self-reflection, Malagasy creatively recollect (from) varied pasts. Altering creates ancestral power, while altered things serve as mediums through which the past can gaze becomingly back upon the present.

Ceremonial joyousness is not only a product of an intersubjectivity of feeling between *tromba-istes* and ancestral spirits.[8] Specifically among Betsimisaraka, it can reflect recollections of joyous colonial celebrations historically glimpsed, overheard, and even participated in by Betsimisaraka. In contrast, Antandroy *tromba*, which has developed in isolation from *vazaha* practices, is much more somber in nature, yet it can also reflect varied modes of intersubjectivity between Antandroy and others.

The previous varied scenarios from both Antandroy and Betsimisaraka *tromba* practices illustrate iconic rearrangements of the variable meanings inherent in and recollections extractable from things and actions, of the narrative opacity and flexibility in things that Malagasy create. Subsequent chapters delve more into the particular ways in which meaning is emergent in *tromba* ceremony as Malagasy recollect and reawaken (once) foreign powers. In particular, the following chapter elaborates upon ways in which Malagasy extract musically from the past to empower the present.

CHAPTER SEVEN

Power, Resistance? Valses

Kiki has been expressing a profound fear lately, that she will become possessed by *tromba* against her will. Her apprehension has been aroused in part by an aunt, an unrelenting drunk, who has been trying to torment her with fabulated stories about people who have frequented *tromba* ceremonies and then involuntarily become spontaneously possessed. Kiki has begun to eat pork the night before accompanying me to a ceremony, since pork is *fady* (taboo) for many *tromba* and thus would make the body unclean and repulsive to them. The evening after the last *tromba* at Honorine's house, Kiki said she was feeling inexplicably agitated and that she was having a very strong urge to drink rum, even though she has never before liked to drink alcohol. She fears that her compulsion was actually that of a *tromba* who has become interested in possessing her.

(From my notes, January 5, 1994)

Ironically, many current understandings of discursive domination (following Foucault) or hegemony (following Gramsci) are at least in part informed by notions of order that seem antipathetic to the posture of critique, for our notions of power appear both totalizing and a priori. "Power" is virtually synonymous with order, even though as used currently, the term implies a critical stance on order. Thus in denaturalizing order, we must also denaturalize power, attending to its own fissures and dispersals. In turn, we should not see resistance as a pure counterpart to power, for there are dangers in reifying our concepts of struggle. But if order can be seen as an effect of power rather than its condition, then resistance, too, can be freed from the (teleological) requirement that it establish a new order in order to be recognized as significant. (Dirks 1994:501)

Assessments of power in colonial and postcolonial locales once commonly followed externally demarcated rifts between weak and strong, subjugated and dominant, Other and European. *Local* concepts of power and order and of how these work (and can be reworked) might draw upon other parameters, which certainly can differ cross-culturally. Of vital significance, power can be conceived and (re)ordered performatively. In Africa, for instance, Fabian (1990), following the local proverb "le pouvoir se mange entier," shows how power has been imaginatively conceived and enacted in dramatic performance in Zaire (now Democratic Republic of Congo). Erlmann (1996) delves into ways in which *isicathamiya* performers in South Africa have performatively incorporated the hegemonic apartheid order there. Drewal (1992) and Apter (1992) have written on unique ways in which Yoruba in Nigeria conceive of (and indeed perform) power. Arens and Karp (1989) have assembled a volume illustrating ways in which transformations in experience, identity, and action have shaped unique concepts of power among different Africans.

Cannell (1999), referring specifically to the Philippines, suggests that conceptualizations of power there can evolve from "a *relationship* in which both powerful and less powerful are liable to affect each other" (p. 25). Similarly, Dirks, in a chapter entitled "Ritual as Resistance: Subversion as Social Fact," contends that power is a relation, "indeed, an endless series of relations" (1994). Similarly, *tromba* practice in Tamatave often thrives upon relationships in which various powers act reciprocally on one another. The present moment is surrendered to domination from powerful distant foreigners. Concurrently, the present exerts forces upon these foreigners, as *tromba* spirits are constrained in the medium's body or as these spirits become actors in the cross-temporal configurations of *tromba* proceedings. The Malagasy ceremonial body itself is simultaneously a medium for both subjugation to and control of varied pasts.

While undeniably injurious, colonialism itself did not necessarily disengage the recollections, beliefs, and practices of distant peoples. In colonialism's destructive wake, dominated peoples might yet have maintained unique historicized, extracolonial ways of conceptualizing and working with power. Perhaps colonial "subjects" were even able at times to sidestep, transcend, or consume outside power. Guided by an older local aesthetic, east coast Malagasy have often imbricated remnants of colonial and later European powers into their *tromba* practices, enhancing the incorporative strength of this practice itself rather than simply adhering to or replicating colonial structures of power. By suggesting that east coast Malagasy have conceptualized empowerment in ways that might predate or elude such colonial structures, I do not mean, of course, to paint an image of a "traditional" society unaltered or untouched by varying forces of modernity. Charles Piot (1999), for one, illustrates how a "traditional" society in Togo has existed "within modernity."

Postcolonial struggles cannot uncritically be thought to replicate conditions of colonial domination, and I certainly do not mean to extend a colonized consciousness onto Malagasy people in the present. Yet, east coast Malagasy are still commonly faced with foreign intrusion and expropriation, with specters of colonialist presence. IMF and World Bank representatives, for instance, have attempted to invest in (and thus control) Madagascar's economy.[1] There are varied environmental conservation projects currently being deployed in Madagascar by foreigners. Even the sometimes questionable practices of Indian merchants and traders in Tamatave are brought into postcolonial narratives of power and control there. *Tromba-istes* of varied ages and experiences can rework and express in *tromba* practice their familiarity with colonial or colonial-like powers from the past, traces of which often extend into the present. *Tromba* practice *is* politicized—for instance, as the gestures and excesses of foreign personalities are sometimes hyper-enacted, critiqued, incorporated. A French personality might arrive in a *tromba* ceremony to demand material excesses of the ceremonial participants, such as expensive whiskey, foreign cigarettes, or items of clothing. While *tromba* is fueled by east coast ideas about familiar enough modes of power and how these have taken shape in the present, this practice is not primarily or predominantly an expression of resistance *against* outside power, either past or present.

The argument might be made that it is "symbolic" power being discussed here. *Tromba* spirits, however, have the power to affect alterations upon physical as well as conceptual worlds of experience. *Tromba* practice is not conceived merely as symbolic gesture among Malagasy in Tamatave—it generates a combinative power that can ameliorate situations, as in healing the sick or in righting social problems.

Attuned to the potential for differing perceptions of power, Nicholas Thomas warns, "Critiques of Orientalism and associated colonial discourses need to avoid reproducing one of the central assumptions of those ideologies: that prospectively or already colonized places are *tabula rasa* for the projection of European power and European representations" (1991: 36). During my first weeks in Madagascar, I heard echoes of Thomas's caution in the words of an older Merina man at a *famadihana*[2] ceremony in the village of Lazaina, near Antananarivo: "Christianity for one didn't need to be forced upon us—this spirit, Jesus, sounded familiar to us, he fit well with our pre-existing beliefs and practices involving our own ancestors. We *took* Christianity ourselves because it suited us and our own spiritual beliefs" (from my notes, translated from French, September 25, 1993). This Merina man's expression of religious volition might not have represented a historically contiguous sentiment in Madagascar—recall the staunch anti-Christian prohibitions of Queen Ranavalona I in the mid-eighteenth century (chap. 2). However, he was clearly staking claim to a particular Malagasy history and belief system, both of which, for him, superseded and to some degree operated independently of missionization and colonization in Madagascar.

I have come across some African-manufactured world maps on which the African continent occupies an unusually enlarged, central, and focal position, while the rest of the world is distanced into spatially shrunken or even somewhat distorted cartographic peripheries. These maps perhaps graphically intone a desire, displayed in a reordering of the world's geographic proportions (originally designated by European mapmakers), to reorient and redistribute other modes of power throughout it. In a recent book on popular music, Tony Mitchell problematizes center/margin distinctions, as do such reorienting maps:

Arguments about the appropriation of indigenous popular music often construct a simplistic opposition between 'margins' of authentic local cultural expression and a 'centre' controlled by market and commoditization forces in the global music industry. These arguments are frequently defined in terms of the imposition of Anglo-American music on the rest of the world, and the exploitation of traditional, culturally distinctive and often politically oppositional forms of 'roots' music by globally dominant and Western market forces, recording industries and musicians. They are usually linked to what has been referred to as the cultural imperialism thesis, which claims that the power of market capitalism—dominated by USA, Japan and Western Europe—not only 'dumps' its own cultural products on an unsuspecting world but appropriates, technologizes, contaminates and commodifies the cultural products of Third World and economically weaker nations and channels them into a global economy which denies recognition or reward to the products' originators. As John Tomlinson has indicated in his book on the subject, the cultural imperialism thesis originated in the 1970s as a left-wing academic shorthand term to describe what was seen essentially as a one-way process of economic and cultural dominance spreading from a single centre of power across the globe. (1996: 49)

By following a line of power as it disseminates from a "Western" center across the globe—a line based in Mitchell's criticism largely upon Western market notions of productivity and commodification—local and other means of deconstructing and reassembling the variegated sign vehicles upon which such power depends and travels might be overlooked, denuded, or denatured. What of unique local complexities of articulation, what de Certeau (1984) has referred to as varying *combinatoires d'opérations*? *How* might third or fourth world cultures individually "be seen as involved in an intercontinental traffic in meaning" (Hannerz 1987: 547)? Do commodities and information emanating from "the center" necessarily remain imbued with the center's precepts of power, value, or significance once they reach these "peripheries"? Do the very concepts of center and periphery accurately describe local realities of power and how it works, as Arjun Appadurai (1996), for instance, and others have come to question? Might such concepts even represent restatements of an older colonial dividing-up of the world?

On the east coast of Madagascar, distant or foreign powers often provide fuel for creative articulation and reevaluation. Malagasy ceremonial power commonly arises from the very *processes* of deconstructing and reassembling other modes of power. Of course, this is not to contend that Malagasy in Tamatave welcomed colonial domination for the workable foreign-ness it introduced. Yet even colonial power might have in some sense come as a relief to Betsimisaraka, since French colonials broke the nineteenth-century Merina stronghold in the Tamatave region. Some Betsimisaraka speak with some rapprochement toward Europeans. French presence often has been less repugnant to Betsimisaraka than servility to Merina, their own neighbors. While Malagasy have certainly expressed overt forms of resistance to colonial control—for instance, the 1947 anticolonial insurgence—the workings of power in *tromba* practice are too complex to reduce this practice primarily to a symbolic counterforce.

In material terms, east coast Malagasy reinstate new power into things that have long been disempowered by deterioration, disempowered at least from an initial colonial or foreign usefulness. This is visually and sonically evident, for instance, in decades-old accordions, with soiled, worn, and torn bellows, broken buttons and reeds, and rusting, frayed, or missing parts. The accordion has long since shed its aura as a specifically colonial instrument (recall that it was introduced into Madagascar after the early 1910s). Yet it still can echo with recollections of the colonial era. The nature of power in things rests in the abilities of Malagasy to awaken though reorder older, often mechanically weakened voices in them and thereby amplify and enhance powerful ceremonial *maresaka*. To imaginatively revalue once colonialist and postcolonial things, then, facilitates the fortification of the present, with the curative and advisory power brought by ancestral spirits.

⸙

Unique ideas about power among Betsimisaraka are influenced by the recollection that there had been no powerful local Betsimisaraka *royaumes* or *mpanjaka* (kings) in Tamatave as there had been in Sakalava and Merina territories. Rather, Betsimisaraka historical consciousness is often grounded in part upon recollections of a loose confederation of the "many (different) who don't separate." Royal ancestral power is something always already distant and exterior to Betsimisaraka, something to be brought near and internalized. In *tromba* ceremony, Betsimisaraka could imprint a local royal order onto a present that could not claim royal histories of its own. My Merina friend Dida even had a theory that among Betsimisaraka the absence of memories of a royal past contributes greatly to what he expressed as a general demeanor of inferiority and apathy among Betsimisaraka. This opinion resounds with early colonialist evaluations of Betsimisaraka, as well as current, pervasive Merina condescension toward coastal peoples.

In recollecting from the past, Betsimisaraka in particular could empower themselves in a specific fashion. During the colonial era, Betsimisaraka might have been somewhat nervous, lesser guests at colonial social events. In *tromba* ceremony, Malagasy royal court and colonial *bal* could overlap, thus in part allowing Betsimisaraka to more equitably partake in a colonial social world. In mind of Lévy-Bruhl's emphasis on the effect of participation upon collective experience, in *tromba* ceremony Betsimisaraka could intensify such an effect by participating consubstantially and simultaneously in both ancestral and colonial pasts (or a colonial past as represented in current form such as the *diner-dansant*). To recollect the past in *tromba* ceremony means not only "to recognize—indeed create—the power of whomever the object of remembering is" (Cole 1996: 4). Such recollection allows *tromba-istes* to immerse themselves in and to interiorize these powers. Indeed, the Malagasy ceremonial body becomes a primary medium for the diffusion of varied modes of power in *tromba* practice.

I intend to examine in this chapter ways in which some Malagasy on the east coast (re)naturalize their worlds of experience, in part by reordering signs that were once external or that still carry traces of the foreign to fit into their own schemes of power. More broadly, I want to consider that varied people living under dominant regimes or with recollections of them likely employ uneven and differentiated ways of figuring and ordering power. In augmenting, intensifying, or otherwise sustaining their own local order, distant peoples might have *ways* of naturalizing power not necessarily reliant upon or simply derivative from European-like models. I want to question whether political, social, and economic domination necessarily forces *cultural* resistance from dominated peoples. I also want to consider varied ways in which local histories might play into determining how power is ordered and interpreted locally. Additionally, this chapter will take up Malagasy methods of integrating everyday and ritual realms, neither of which operates exclusive of the other. The everyday finds expression in the ritual, the ritual in the everyday—each contributes to the empowerment of the other.

It is also important to note that colonialist regimes themselves have been uneven and differentiated, fueled by differing ideologies. British control in

India, for instance, has a complex history distinct from French domination in Algeria. Thus, what is broadly referred to as *a* condition, colonialism, more accurately tranlsates into various individual colonialisms, which encompass unique local circumstances, ambitions, and styles of appropriating and ruling, among other things (see Thomas 1994). In particular, Paul Rabinow has suggested that French colonization in Madagascar was geared specifically toward pacification of the colonized and development of commerce in their territories (1989). As colonialist regimes took varied courses, the means devised by different peoples for coping with them could as well be uneven. Malagasy reactions to colonization, for instance, were likely informed by the general Malagasy aesthetic of communicative indirectness and by a discursive preference for avoiding direct conflict. This is not to conclude that Malagasy necessarily resorted to clandestine modes of resistance to French colonialism or to negate that they might have engaged in more direct ways of talking back to the presence of colonialism.

⁊

Kiki seems to have completely overcome her fear of tromba. She has become even closer with Velomaro and Delphine, and with Tompezolo (she used to fear Antandroy in general as there's a widely circulated myth in Tamatave about their supposed savage character). Now she is constantly looking forward to the next tromba ceremony, and even expresses an anxious longing if more than a few days pass without attending one. She vigorously and joyously participates, playing kaiamba, clapping, singing, and conversing with tromba. She now says that even the thought of pork makes her ill. She will now accompany me to a bar to indulge in a Three Horses beer, something she never used to do. Her aunt's vehement displeasure with tromba (her aunt is Christian, which seems to play into her hatred/fear of tromba) has apparently become displaced in Kiki by something very powerful, something apparently lodged in part in the social experience of participatory immersion, both during and outside of tromba ceremony.

(From my notes, March 15, 1994)

⁊

Musical Transformation

I remember wondering before ever leaving for Madagascar how the equal-temperament-based diatonic tuning of button accordions introduced into Madagascar might initially have been received. The earliest Southeast Asian and South African settlers there likely were familiar with scales ordered differently from this European one. The accordion must have affected some transformations in previously existing Malagasy musical systems, repertoires, and styles of performing. For example, its foreign structural design and timbral qualities must have evoked a need to develop new techniques, corporeal agility, and aural skills to play it. And before colonial introduction of industrial cable, the "strings" of the *valiha* had been made from long, thin strips cut lengthwise directly into the body of the instrument's bamboo, left attached at either endpoint, and wedged up under two wooden bridges. This older instrument, still occasionally performed upon in Madagascar, produces wholly different timbres than the newer metal-stringed *valiha*. I wondered if assigning sonic value to otherwise a-musical bicycle brake cabling and assimilating this foreign-introduced material into a local practice might have represented to Malagasy a creative, intentional turning around of the overtly deleterious face of colonialism. I thought about how sonic transformations in musical systems might have reflected or been involved with social, ideological, political, or spiritual transformations, and how the mutability of musical practices might have been related to other modes of cultural change.

Diffusionist theories in the early 1900s, those of Stumpf and von Hornbostel, for instance, commonly generalized that "non-Western" musical practices were for the most part static, at least until they might be affected by the spread of European influence. By this mode of thought, local transformations in these static musical systems apparently would have been "unnatural." Some early theories of musical change conveyed an apparent fear that outside forces would impoverish, dilute, or subsume "pure" local traditional practices. A common sentiment among some observers was that these traditions needed to be protected and preserved. Later, Wiora (1965) viewed the twentieth century as primarily an "age" of musical homogenization. Lomax (1968) was concerned about encroaching "cultural gray-out," and with supposedly disappearing musical diversity. Thus, in some later theories of musical change, local non-Western musics were envisioned as suffering from the spread of "westernization." Such beliefs in effect tend to strip local peoples of their agency in making their own musical decisions, in being influenced only as much as they might choose to be. Indeed, the cultural gray-out premise itself might evoke images of a colonial-like dispersion of foreign power as it overtakes weaker peoples across the globe. "Evolutionary" theories of change in African cultures also usually did little to address local peoples' volition or agency, often reflecting an ideology that in some sense justified colonialism. Africans were supposedly forced into a beneficial evolutionary stage, though one in which they would always be inferior to or lagging behind Europeans (Kubik 1986).[3]

Concerned with the pressure placed upon "world musics" by Western musical influence, Bruno Nettl writes, with some likeness to diffusionist modes of thought, "During the last hundred years, the most significant phenomenon in the global history of music has been the intensive *imposition* [my emphasis] of Western music and musical thought *upon* the rest of the world" (1985: 3). Certainly some Western musics might be conceived to have been forced or enticed upon Others, for instance, hymn singing in mission schools. Even in these situations, though, there were often specific local politics informing choices made by people to participate in these schools. Such participation was not necessarily simply an act of submission. And new modes of local performance commonly arose out of European contact, practices not simply "westernized" but sometimes even more localized through the very act of incorporation (see Erlmann 1996, 1991; Waterman 1990a, 1990b). Although Nettl seems concerned with the means by which other cultures have reacted to Western "pressures," his stance itself sounds perhaps neglectful of local concepts of power. By such logic or language, might one also reciprocally conceive of the "imposition" of African-like rhythms, syncopations, or musical layering upon James Brown's music?

As with practices of bricolage (chap. 1), modernization comes not simply from European contact. Africans, for instance, influence each other in a modern world. "Modernized" musical practices can also be built upon "traditional" musical structures. Such newer practices thus can still evoke recollections of and connections to varied pasts. Chris Waterman, for one, describes a musical "reindigenization through modernization" (1990a: 84) that occurs in Yoruba jùjú music in Nigeria. Rather than weakening existing traditions, transformative musical processes might engender ingenious interpretive moves made by people in transforming worlds. Newer expressive modes in actuality are least likely to be simple de-purifications of older traditions. This is not to deny that serious cultural destruction, such as language death, has resulted from modernizing forces. People can, of course, operate imaginatively under conflict or transformation, not only by providing symbolic balances to *displace* superior forces (see de Certeau 1984, Stallybrass and White 1986) but by expressing themselves as well in ways that might precede or even exceed conditions of domination.

Several Malagasy popular musicians—in other words, musicians who are able to perform before large crowds for some though often not much profit—told me that their commercial musics are in essence also based upon *fombandrazana,* or Malagasy ancestral customs, and so are simply modern forms of older traditions. Jaojoby, a popular musician from Diégo Suarez, described the *salegy* dance music from that region as *miresaka amindrazana* (conversing with the ancestors). Antandroy *tromba* musicians in Tamatave-ville also use this term, *miresaka amindrazana,* to refer to the spiritually discursive power of their own musics. Jaojoby called his popular music *vakondrazana électrique,* or electrified Malagasy traditional music. Since the *razana* like all *vakondrazana,* Jaojoby reasoned, they also like modern *salegy.* Jaojoby added that *salegy* is so effectively manifest with the rhythms and sonorities of *tromba* music that he had seen people in the audience at his shows, induced by his music, become possessed by *tromba.*[4] So even popular, overtly "westernized" musical performances in Madagascar can create perceptual fields that bring precolonial spirit worlds into the present. For many people in Madagascar, Malagasy music of any kind always has the potential to evoke images of these spirit worlds.

Transformations in musical practices thus are "natural," in other words, "historical," or part of historically contiguous processes among Malagasy. Indeed, transformation in varied ways is a vital process in *tromba* ceremony. Of course, *tromba* musics performed on accordions and industrial-cable-stringed *valiha* cannot be overlooked as modernized modes of expression, though they are vital components in practices themselves with premodern histories.

Female Bodies, Male Maîtres

For Merleau-Ponty, human existence is *carnal.* This carnality creates a cleavage in the subject that faults self-consciousness. Rather than a self-contained entity, the body is a "gaping wound [*blessure béante*]" that always remains "incomplete [*inachevée*]." While the reflective subject attempts to close in on itself by incorporating every other and assimilating all difference, the living body resists closure and necessarily remains open to what is other than, and different from itself. This "openness" *(ouverture)* is the dehiscence or fission [*déhiscence ou fission*] of [the body's] mass." As a result of its holey-ness or gappiness, the living body cannot be defined in terms of the binary opposites that structure conceptual reflection. The body is neither "subject nor object," neither *"in itself"* nor *"for itself,"* neither *res extensa* nor *res cogito.* Rather, the body is the *mean* between extremes—the "milieu" *(milieu)* in which opposites like interiority and exteriority, as well as subjectivity and objectivity, intersect. Never reducible to the differences it simultaneously joins and separates, the body is forever *entre-deux.* (Taylor 1987: 69)

Among Betsimisaraka the majority of *tromba* mediums are women (though there *are* powerful male mediums, such as Velomaro), while most *tromba* spirits are male. At Betsimisaraka *tromba,* though, there are usually some men participating, as musicians, attendants, or simply as devotees. Among Antandroy there is a greater percentage of male mediums as well as female spirits.

Andréa, a Betsimisaraka woman and spirit medium in Tamatave-ville,

Photograph 9. Jily performing on accordion at one of Andréa's *tromba* ceremonies.

commonly became possessed by some of the most powerful Sakalava and Merina royal *tromba*. Andréa's *tromba* ceremonies are especially noteworthy because few men ever attended them. Andréa also preferred to hire Jily, a woman accordionist, to play for her ceremonies. This choice was clearly as much about Jily's musical acuity and the preferences of Andréa's particular *tromba* as it was about Jily's being a woman. Yet it was primarily the spirits of kings, of powerful men from the past, that came to possess Andréa and the other women mediums at her ceremonies. While outwardly privileging the presence of women, Andréa's ceremonies were at the same time implicit with the spiritual presence and subsequent internalization of maleness. In general, men were more present as participants, though not necessarily as mediums, at other Betsimisaraka *tromba* ceremonies. Tatasy or other male musicians commonly performed at the *tromba* ceremonies of Velomaro and other Betsimisaraka.

Andréa's *tromba* house itself appeared to be divided into gendered sections. Diagonally opposite walls of the house were adorned with stereotypical European images of either maleness or femaleness. Just above her *tromba* altar Andréa had placed a collage of magazine cutouts of nude or seminude European women, professional models provocatively posed and gazing seductively back at the viewer (see photo 10). There were as well a few magazine cutouts of shirtless and very thin male European models in

Photograph 10. Andréa possessed at *tromba* altar.

the outer margins of the montage over Andréa's altar—pairs of men, in this case in mutual amorous-like embraces. Andréa found these male models to be reminiscent of womanliness. She once told me (when not possessed), "Karaha viavy ilay le'lahy, malem-lemy 'zareo" (Those men are like women, they're rather soft). These images of female-like males in mutual embrace connotatively modeled an inversion of a common practice in Andréa's and others' *tromba* ceremonies, in which a Malagasy king, in a woman's body, embraces or is otherwise quite physically affectionate with other male spirits, also in women's bodies.

These nudes above Andréa's *tromba* altar were counterpositioned across the room, on the wall diagonally farthest from the altar, by a series of colonial-era schematic diagrams of automobile engines and chassis. These diagrams gave an exploded view into varied layers of the internal workings of older European machines. They stood as veritable deconstructions of a pervasive representative of foreign power and rare local privilege, the mass-produced automobile, which in Madagascar most often means imported French-made Peugeots or Renaults. In these particular diagrams the structural integrity or solidity of a model of French power gave way to varied gazes into an agglomeration of mechanical parts. Thus, somewhat like the collages of nude or seminude European models, these automotive schematics displayed a hidden (European) inside as visible outside.

Few people in Andréa's *tromba* community or, for that matter, in Tamatave own, drive, or even ride often in automobiles (except for infrequent collective journeys by taxi-*brousse* to visit family or friends in the villages). Furthermore, the maintenance, operation, and possession of automobiles in Tamatave is mostly the domain of men, rarely, if ever, that of women. The exploded views of automobiles in the schematics seemed to represent conventional male power, here publicly disassembled into component parts. About these schematics, Andréa would say only, "Raha le'lahy izay" (Those are men's things). It is interesting to note that to keep older automobiles operational, men commonly must improvise with pieces of other, often nonautomotive things to replace car parts that are frequently wearing out. Replacement car parts themselves are often difficult to find and always prohibitively expensive. The exploded automobile views hinted at a (male) capacity to reassemble that which is broken down, a power reliant upon creatively improvising with replacement parts (of other things) that are significantly different from the originals.

Recall that photos of *well-dressed* European models, samples of which were displayed on other walls of Andréa's *tromba* house, could be multi-meaningful signs (of signs) in Betsimisaraka *tromba* re-dressing practices, as models for ritual behavior and as favorable reflections back upon it. The re-dressing performed by mediums in *tromba* ceremony, though, commonly occurs behind a visual barrier of several *lamba,* held up by *tromba* attendants. While Andréa and her circle of *tromba-istes* did practice re-dressing in the costumes of different *tromba* spirits, their *tromba* never emulated the scantily clad or nude European models in Andréa's altar photo collage. *Tromba* undressed privately, never as exhibition.

⁓

Dressing up practices among Betsimisaraka evoke for me a scene from Jean Rouch's film, *Les maîtres fous*, in which his voice-over is offered as a Haouka initiate's confession: "I never wash, I'm dirty, I'm not elegant." Rouch shows here varied examples of colonial pomp and Haouka imitation of it. During a British colonial ceremony, Haouka dancers are shown "amid the crowd looking for their model. And if the order is different here from there [at a Haouka possession ceremony], the protocol remain the same." Rouch questions whether these Haouka mediums have found a "panacea against mental disorders" . . . "a way to absorb our inimical society." Could this capacity or propensity for absorption of otherness be a component in practices and beliefs that predate or otherwise overstep the colonial political and social order, invasive as it had been?

(From my notes, March 23, 1994)

Images of foreign women, whether well dressed or nude, were not simply material for undifferentiated ceremonial mimesis by Andréa and other *tromba-istes* in her community. Rather, these images were individually interpreted, and distinct meanings were extracted from either type of photo. As mentioned, the nude models seemed to stand in part as an externalization of that usually hidden, a view of inside as outside, specifically a distanced European inside. And they were clearly chosen by Andréa over the photos of well-dressed models to be displayed in the most honored and highly visible focal area just above the *tromba* altar.

The foreign model cutouts and perhaps the automobile schematics as well also bespoke a seductive control over a desirous male gaze. Andréa once told me, "Tia viavy *vazaha* ilay tromba" (Tromba do like *vazaha* women). Andréa's photo arrangements were not simply prestigious signs of material wealth, as difficult-to-obtain magazine leaves. They were also snares with which to capture male attention. But while male *tromba* spirits took control of Andréa, enticed in part by her photo nudes, her body itself imposed certain boundaries and limitations upon these *tromba*. For one, it physically constrained them within the spatial delimitations of the cramped space of the *tromba* house, as well as within the gendered definition of the female body. Becoming the male *tromba* spirit meant not only that Andréa was possessed by maleness but that she took control to some degree over a male Other.

In addition, the actual control over the dénouement of Andréa's *tromba* proceedings were largely under Jily's musical direction, as she created the ceremony-essential *maresaka* to direct the heightening or relaxing of ceremonial tension and as she played the proper compositions to appeal to and invoke particular *tromba* spirits. Andréa's ceremonies could visually as well as aurally reign in maleness, stimulating male engagement yet physically constraining and controlling the male spirit in the female body.

Other Betsimisaraka mediums confirmed that *tromba* spirits sometimes came into the present specifically to *mitady viavy,* to search for women. Detty, a Betsimisaraka medium once became possessed by a spirit that had been a *viavy makorely,* a Malagasy prostitute, while her sister Jenny simultaneously became possessed by a Sakalava king who had come into the present specifically to search for women. There ensued much "manly" discourse between the royal male spirit (in Jenny's body) and the other men present, including myself—like men drunkenly eyeing and discussing a woman at a bar and planning strategies for approaching her. There was also much "womanly" discourse between Clarissy, the prostitute, and myself over, for instance, the oddities of men, for she had chosen me to be her confidant and advisor in this matter.

For her part, Clarissy reacted shyly to the approaches of the king, frequently withdrawing from discursive interaction with him to self-consciously check her appearance in a small hand mirror or to consult with me. In the course of this event, Clarissy warned me about Malagasy men: they are untrustworthy and generally no good *(ratsy fagnahy)*, and they have no money *(tsy manambola le'lahy gasy)*. She lamented the unlikelihood that she would ever find a *vazaha* to marry — *vazaha* men are supposedly more nurturing to and considerate of women. En-gendered and other boundaries were clearly being played with in this interchange, for example, as a woman medium's body made sexual advances upon another woman's body. Also, I was included by Jenny's *tromba* and the other men in their man-talk and simultaneously by Detty in her woman-talk, sometimes being drawn in mid-conversation from one to the other. Detty in particular was talking to me as though to another woman, for advice, support, affirmation. No other man at this proceeding was engaged by the others in what seemed a dually en-gendered discursive role. Thus, it appeared that my own presence was specifically being called upon in part to blur gendered boundaries. Perhaps I was even being discursively incorporated into this ceremony to enact a lessened distinction between *vazaha* and Malagasy, to create a feel for a combinative interactional power that immersed all people present, whether spirit, *vazaha*, man, and/or woman, in intersubjective experience. As for the control exerted by the woman medium's body over the possessing male spirit, there would be rather obvious physiologic constraints upon a male spirit (in a woman's body!) being able to attain sexual gratification. There was also perhaps an implication of prohibited sexual encounter between sisters, though no physical fulfillment was enacted in this event.

At other times, Detty also became possessed by Sakalava (male) royal spirits. Sometimes while Jenny was possessed by the royal spirit mentioned above, who liked to search for women, Detty simultaneously became possessed by this king's younger brother, and so brothers (sisters) together would embark upon a mutual woman-seeking mission. Detty's body, perhaps somewhat like my own presence, served as an integrating ground not only between male and female, royal and everyday, but also sometimes between *fomba gasy* (Malagasy ways) and *fomba vazaha* (European ways). Jenny and Detty were in part re-enacting common encounters between *vazaha* or sometimes wealthier Merina and Malagasy prostitutes. Such encounters occurred each evening on the main street of Tamatave-ville only a few kilometres from Detty's house. Detty had to frequent this corner because she worked as a seamstress for a *karana* shop owner there.[5]

~

Returning to Andréa, while her *tromba* proceedings might have appeared woman-centric, the effect was more of a simultaneous becoming, of woman becoming man and man becoming woman. Rita Astuti (1993) discusses a complex ritual process among Vezo in western Madagascar in which differences between men and women are transformed into sameness. Rather than specifically intending to invert or subvert male power by becoming royal male spirits from the past, Andréa and her associates were creating a complex multigendered ceremonial body, in part so that a specific mode of power could emerge from it. This power drew upon combining varied layers of experience, past and present, male and female, royal and common, ritual and everyday, Malagasy and European. Andréa's photo arrangements illustrated metaphorically a fragmentation and simultaneous unification of distinct *essences* of women and men, as nudes or car schematics. Andréa's photo collages stood in part as graphic tableaux of tenets of ceremonial *maresaka,* an aesthetic by which varied pasts are fragmented and recombined with new meaning in the present.

It is pertinent to mention theories of role inversion here. Marina Roseman, for instance, has written of Temiar possession in Malaysia:

During the spirit seance, a female patient temporarily transcends her everyday domestic subordination to her husband. She employs the sonic and kinetic language of the male role as part of her cure by dancing the warrior's ritual dance (bersilat) to the warrior tune (lagu ulubalang). This symbolic inversion, the affectation of a prototypically masculine form of behavior, allows the female patient a temporary symbolic ascendancy (1991: 17).

For one thing, women *could* attain more than symbolic ascendancy over men in daily life in Madagascar. The *filoha* (chef) of the village of Betampona was a woman named Rasoamandry. She was also the village schoolteacher along with other important duties she took on. At the national level, Mireille Rakotomalala, a Merina woman, had become a governmental *deputé,* and then the Ministre de la Culture in Antananarivo. Mireille has also written on Malagasy music, including an entry in the recent *Garland Encyclopedia of World Music* volume on Africa (see Rakotomalala 1986a, 1986b, and 1998). Many Betsimisaraka women are also commonly in charge of working their own rice fields, of doing most of the work related to family and household, and of earning capital often by transporting items to market for sale.

A considerable number of Betsimisaraka women, especially in the towns, live without men and thus sometimes have to take on augmented daily responsibilities. Francine, also from the village of Betampona, was raising a teenage daughter by herself. Her husband had left years earlier for an independent existence in Tamatave-ville. Francine fermented and sold *betsabetsa* (a mildly alcoholic drink made from sugarcane), she made fine sisal mats and baskets for sale, and she carried bananas and other items into Fénérive-Est to sell at the market there. Jily was another woman raising a daughter on her own in Tamatave-ville and had assumed responsibilities better divided between two people. She not only earned capital by playing accordion at *tromba* ceremonies, often traveling long distances to perform for ceremonies in the villages, but she also worked her own rice fields.

❧

In Betampona now for awhile. Francine has a delightful humor. In a conversation about religious beliefs today, over glasses of her homemade betsabetsa, she playfully criticized, "Mivavaka' 'jareo fô, izaho iraiky fô tsy mivavaka anefa tsy mamonolona. Izaho tsy mivavaka, tsisy fotoagna. Miasa foagna izegny"; "Others pray [in the church], I for one don't pray, but I haven't killed anyone. I don't pray, there's no time. It's work all the time for me."

In other words, church is primarily for sinners seeking absolution; hard work is its own absolution . . . ?

(From my notes, April 12, 1994)

❧

That Betsimisaraka women mediums take in male spirits to create a transcendent ceremonial power parallels daily circumstances in which some women have to be both man and woman, to carry on singlehandedly the responsibilities of each. The significance of these combinings in *tromba* ceremony does not reside simply in the power released or dramatized in shedding one gendered role for another. Rather, Betsimisaraka women create a unified power that is at once male and female, at once ceremonial and everyday, a power that spills onto conditions of daily life in which exigencies of material poverty must be overcome by women, quite often without the assistance of a man. Role inversion in itself would be inadequate to explain these gender components of Betsimisaraka *tromba* practice.

In Mark C. Taylor's terms (which introduce this section), "the body is the *mean* between extremes—the 'milieu' *(milieu)* in which opposites like interiority and exteriority, as well as subjectivity and objectivity, intersect.

Never reducible to the differences it simultaneously joins and separates, the body is forever *entre-deux*" (1987: 69). In varied ways, Andréa, Jenny, and Detty, as well as other *tromba-istes,* are able to become *entre-deux,* to open themselves to varying modes of difference, and thus to empower the present. East coast Malagasy more broadly maneuver *entre-deux* as they might recollect their pasts and indeed imagine themselves in varying combinations of Southeast Asian, African, European, Indian, Chinese, and even spiritual qualities.

Power in Antandroy Tromba

Antandroy in Tamatave-ville are often thought and even feared by some other Malagasy to possess communicative powers with ancestral spirits that far exceed those of any other *tromba-istes.* While Antandroy, like Betsimisaraka, do rely upon recollecting (from) the past by reassessing and interiorizing it, to thereby create power in the present, their performative practices are distinct from those of Betsimisaraka.

Antandroy in Tamatave-ville did not express direct recollections of colonial *bals,* nor were they interested in finding significance in magazine cutouts. They did, however, incorporate fragments of external things, especially from surrounding Betsimisaraka practices. For example, Antandroy *tromba* musicians were quite fond of some Betsimisaraka musical compositions. They reworked these into their own musical performances (though the converse did not occur). A particular Betsimisaraka *basesa* melody (outlined in fig. 14) was a favorite of Antandroy *valiha* players and sometimes of Antandroy accordionists as well. Velontsoa once explained while playing his version of this melody, "Hira Betsimisaraka voalohany izany" (That was a Betsimisaraka tune first). Velontsoa chuckled coyly when he said this; perhaps he was enjoying a subtle irony in his ability to incorporate something from a group of people that generally would have little to do with Antandroy in Tamatave-ville. One of Tompezolo's *tromba* was particularly fond of this once Betsimisaraka tune and would even improvise sung texts to it.

As mentioned, Antandroy *tromba* would commonly place the heads of their mediums upon or very close to the accordion or *valiha,* or they might rest the whole body on the *valiha,* internalizing into the ceremonial body the physical compression of sound wave.[6] The Betsimisaráka tune illustrated in figure 14 was particularly effective in inciting Antandroy *tromba* to enact this mode of embodiment. One component of the internalizable power embedded in this Betsimisaraka, then Antandroy, musical segment is its metrical organization, based in part upon shifting between *valse*-like and 6/8-like metered moments.

Fig. 14. Segment of Betsimisaraka tune favored also by Antandroy musicians in Tamatave-ville.

Antandroy sometimes empower themselves spiritually by taking in fragments of musical ideas from their Betsimisaraka neighbors in Tamatave-ville. Antandroy versions of Betsimisaraka compositions are vastly different, however, for instance, in improvisatory technique, tempo, and timbre (played on Antandroy *valiha* constructed of different materials).

Antandroy *tromba* ceremonies could also intone a coalescence of ritual and everyday experience, though in distinct ways. Antandroy men are as likely to be *tromba* mediums as Antandroy women in Tamatave-ville. Antandroy men also commonly become possessed by either male or female spirits, of both royal and nonroyal descent, as do women. Thus among Antandroy, both men's and women's bodies could equitably become mediums for convening a dually gendered spirit power.

In daily life it is much less common for Antandroy women in Tamatave-ville to be without a husband. These women work resourcefully and diligently on a daily basis, though more consistently in conjunction with a man who also works in some capacity, often as a guardian. Thus, relatively equal opportunities between Antandroy men and women to participate in *tromba* parallel an accord experienced between men and women in Antandroy daily life.[7] Also, Antandroy women often take specific musical roles in Antandroy ceremonies in Tamatave-ville, as vocalists or *kaiamba* players, for instance, though not as performers on *valiha* or accordion. Even here, Antandroy women tend to work musically in accordance with men. For instance, in *fa-havoazana* or Antandroy burial ceremonies, women sing specifically to incite men to dance.[8] At Andréa's ceremonies, Jily's accordion performance was not coordinated with the activities of men. Indeed, on a spiritual level, she was performing more in control of than in coordination with male *tromba* spirits (yet to create combinative, not "inversional," power).

Spiritual connections are never far removed from Antandroy daily life. Antandroy commonly maintain a continuous discursive, musical, gestural contact with their *razana* even outside *tromba* practice. Velontsoa, for one, explained that, no matter when he plays music, it is *resaka amindrazana*, communication with ancestral spirits (and a good deal of his daily time was spent playing *valiha*). Among Antandroy the ritual clearly spills into the everyday, as everyday situations imbue ritual action.

Antandroy in Tamatave-ville are often known to have the best fruit at the market, to construct the sturdiest mats and other woven items, to make the best guardians for local businesses. Antandroy are somewhat revered powerful healers and artists while they are also disdained and distrusted strangers. Oddly, it is northern Betsimisaraka who are most often purported to be *mpamôsavy*, or evil spell-casters in the Tamatave region, *not* Antandroy. Even though their spirit powers are not specifically believed to be maleficent, Antandroy are still feared for their excess of such power. In the following section, I turn to a vital musical facet that has been vastly empowering to both Antandroy and Betsimisaraka, one that has allowed each to be more *entre-deux*, though in unique ways.

Valses

༄

Throughout the Tamatave region I've been told a story in which early French colonials in the area, upon observing local Betsimisaraka dance and music performances for the first time proclaimed, "Quelle bassesse!" Of course these colonial observers meant this as a criticism—it expressed their repulsion with the "lowness" or "baseness" of Betsimisaraka modes of artistic expression. Betsimisaraka frequently overheard colonials decreeing such disgust with their local performance practices, and in a clever turn around of European derisive intent they reflectively named their genre of music and dance "*basesa*" (Betsimisaraka pronunciation). Betsimisaraka here imagined "bassesse" ironically into a compliment instead of an intentional insult. This act of incorporation attests in part to the power inherent in the colonial word, though more to the ability Betsimisaraka have cultivated for extracting their own meanings and intentions from it and from other colonial sources. Furthermore, naming one's sacred ceremonial genre of musical performance after a colonial derogation seems to convey other important things about empowerment, interiorizing the Other, and reassessing and redressing its vitality, which in this instance had initially been uttered with such a negative inflection.

(From my notes, October 21, 1993)

৶

All of the Betsimisaraka accordionists with whom I became familiar in the Tamatave region, both in town and in the villages, performed a repertoire of *valses*. These *valses* they clearly distinguished from *basesa* or other musical genres (these musicians used the French term *valse* though they did not speak French; there is no equivalent term for *valse* in Malagasy). Betsimisaraka accordionists played *valses* largely as a leisure genre, never for *tromba* ceremony and rarely in the course of any other sort of spirit-related ceremony. *Kaiamba* accompaniment, so vital to most other Malagasy musics, was most often left out when *valses* were played on accordion. Antandroy in Tamatave-ville, on the other hand, never in my experience performed *valses,* but Magnampy Soa and Very Soa seemed to enjoy it thoroughly when I would play a *valse* on accordion for them.

৶

I went to meet Roger Jean Louis, a Betsimisaraka accordionist, for the first time yesterday afternoon. He lives in a small *trano vato* (stone house) in the courtyard outside President Zafy Albert's Tamatave residence. He is paid a meager wage to guard this compound. He has a large number of children and apparently several "wives," only one of whom lives there with him. Two of his teenage daughters, Misy Vavy and Hortensy seemed particularly delighted to have me around to joke with (my Malagasy is getting a little better). Roger told me that on Thursday evenings his whole family, in full costume, regularly practices ceremonial *basesa* music and dance together and that I'd be welcome to attend this week's upcoming "répétition." Roger has the biggest and best known accordion *basesa* troupe on the east coast. His troupe even employs several different-sized drums.

Roger insisted that I stay and eat dinner with him. He took the one piece of meat out of his own bowl and placed it in mine. Later he also insisted that I stay the night—he said he did not want me wandering alone around central Tamatave-ville this late. Roger spent the evening teaching me the beginnings of *Viavy Rose,* a well-known Betsimisaraka *basesa,* on his own accordion. He played slowly and repeatedly so that I could try to memorize each phrase. With his accordion eventually in my hands, Roger sat back, grinning as I tried to replicate what he'd shown me. "Efa mahay 'anao," he complimented kindly though prematurely, "you know what you're doing."

(From my notes, October 26, 1993)

᰾

Roger Jean Louis was once discussing differences and similarities between *basesa* and *valse* with me. He explained that in comparison to the *valse*, *basesa* had a *lanjany*, or weight, to it. Here he was referring in part to the way that each is danced—unlike the *valse*, *basesa* is a heavy-footed dance. Roger was adamant that "tsy avy taninao ilay hira!" (that type of music [*basesa*] does not come from your country!). It was vital to Roger to make a clear distinction between *valse* as a genre more *vazaha*-like and *basesa* as distinctly Malagasy. He explained, however, that he thought there had been a *fifandraisana*, a historical connection between *basesa* and *valse*, and he specified that "ilay basesa mihetsika sy miezakezaka noho ilay valse—tsy mitovy ny rythme" (the *basesa* moves more and requires more effort than the *valse*—the rhythm isn't the same). Here he was referring again to the accompanying dances as well as to techniques for performing either genre on the accordion. Betsimisaraka *basesa* performed on accordion requires constant manipulations of the tripartite rhythmic elements illustrated previously—on emphasizing one component of this rhythm, then another. Betsimisaraka *valses*, on the other hand, require a consistent 3/4-like metrical emphasis. *Basesa* moves around rhythmically more than the *valse* does, and more rhythmic variation requires more physical and creative effort on the part of the accordionist and, subsequently, on the part of the dancers.

Most Betsimisaraka I knew were accomplished *basesa* dancers, though none of them remembered how to dance the *valse* proficiently (Roger remembered only that *valse* was not like *basesa*). This absence in itself is notable, for most other genres of Malagasy musics have particular dances associated with them. Indeed, these genres are often defined or conceptualized in part by their accompanying dance, evident in Roger's musical evaluations, in which he implicates qualities of both sound and movement. The *valse*, however, is connected to a dance mode only in the recollections of some older Betsimisaraka. Thus, Betsimisaraka have selectively recollected and put into practice only certain elements of the *valse*, those sonically valuable to them. The *valse*'s accompanying dance steps, perhaps not aesthetically translatable or embody-able to Betsimisaraka, had for the most part been forgotten.

Jily told me that she thought the *valse* had come to Tamatave from the

Diégo region in the north of the island, though she herself first heard it played on accordion by older Betsimisaraka men in the villages of the southern Tamatave region when she was a child (this would have been approximately the 1960s). Many Malagasy regard Diégo as the region of the island in which French colonials and other *vazaha* have been most welcomed throughout the past. Like Roger, Jily spoke of a connection between *basesa* and *valse*. She told me, "Ka salegy nagnara ilay valse" *(Salegy* [the predominant music and dance genre from the Diégo region] came after [or followed] the *valse).* Jily meant not only that the *valse* historically preceded *salegy* in Diégo but that *salegy* "followed" *valse* in some formal and performative aspects. In other words, *salegy* had to some degree evolved from the *valse,* though she would not elaborate further upon details of this evolution.

Jily and other Malagasy also told me that *basesa,* as well as other Malagasy musics from around the island, were themselves forms of or had descended from *salegy.* Jily, Roger, and others recollected a historical continuity passing from French *valse* to *salegy* and to *basesa.* French *valses* had certainly been overheard and even performed by Betsimisaraka at colonial *bals* held regularly throughout the Tamatave region (chap. 9).

Recall that in accordion *basesa* for *tromba* ceremony, the left hand continuously emphasizes each pulse of a 6/8-like meter. The triple rhythmic component itself is more subtly stated as it operates in combination with others. In non-*tromba basesa,* though, the left hand can commonly switch freely from accentuating this 6/8-like meter to explicitly pumping the *valse*-like triple. The accordionist here would seem to play upon an intertextual linkage to the *valse* and indeed to her or his own *valse* repertoire. It is possible that non-*tromba basesa* represents a particular sort of transformational genre, one in between *tromba basesa* and French-inspired *valses.*

Christian Malagasy commonly attend *tsaboraha* ceremonies, at which non-*tromba basesa* is performed and in which ancestor reverence is still very much a vital process, whereas possession by *tromba* is not. Perhaps such ceremonies call for a combining *basesa* that favors the occasional explicit enunciation of *valse* rhythm, as part of a hybridizing musical practice, to complement a somewhat "syncretic" religious belief (Protestant and Catholic Malagasy who attend *tsaboraha* are extolling a belief system that openly combines ancestral and Christian tenets). All the Betsimisaraka *tromba* accordionists I knew also had a repertoire of non-*tromba basesa,* whereas accordionists who would not perform for *tromba,* only for non-possession ceremonies, usually did not have a repertoire of *tromba basesa* (though they might recall one or two such compositions).

Valses are played by Betsimisaraka only on accordion—they are *not* performed on *valiha* or other Betsimisaraka instruments (though the triple-pulse rhythmic component is also vital to performance practices on these other instruments). Again, accordion practice bridges some specific aural gaps between Betsimisaraka and the colonial era, which *valiha* practice itself does not appear to span.

As French-imported accordions have become vital to *tromba* practice, the colonial *valse* has influenced the conception of modern Betsimisaraka *basesa*. Yet this genre, initially European, has potency in *tromba* ceremony only when it is fragmented, taken in, and re-expressed in varying combinations as something distinctively Betsimisaraka. Indeed, at moments of heightened spirit activity in a *tromba* ceremony, it is specifically the triple-meter component of the complex rhythm that would commonly be accentuated. Among Betsimisaraka this often means clapping a *valse*-like triple pulse directly into the ears or onto the body of the medium, especially to coax a hesitating *tromba* into the medium's body.[9] Intensification of a triple meter among Betsimisaraka calls upon a power innate in yet extracted from a familiar colonial musical form.

⁖

Among Antandroy a *valse*-like rhythmic component is a different sort of sign (of a sign). It is *not* specifically a medium of colonial power but a sign of Antandroy acuity for interiorizing from *other Malagasy*. In Antandroy *tromba* practice, emphasis upon a triple pulse is also articulated by hand-clapping or with the *kaiamba*, for instance. This pulse is often intensified during moments in which *tromba* spirits are particularly active, dancing, drinking, smoking, and conversing, and also when an obstinate spirit is being coaxed into the present. These usually are moments in a ceremony in which a feverish musical pace and intensity have been attained, concomitant with the heightened emotional intersubjectivity of interacting with beloved spirit personalities. A *valse*-like rhythm at these heightened moments works, like a picture of Jesosy or statue of the Virgin Mary in Tompezolo's *tromba* altar, as an evocation of capacities of other Malagasy to recycle things.

Antandroy, of course, know that the accordion did not originate with other Malagasy. However, taking in once European things is effective among Antandroy in part because such things have already been incorporated by other Malagasy. Antandroy thus enact *hommage* to incorporative skills from the past and from other parts of Madagascar. By deploying a fervent triple pulse at emotionally charged moments of contact with ancestral spirits, Antandroy in Tamatave-ville draw upon an acoustic sign of spirit power known to be effective among their Betsimisaraka neighbors. In addition, when Antandroy emphasize a triple pulse, it is much more rapidly and ardently articulated than by Betsimisaraka. Antandroy applications of the triple rhythmic pulse are so rapid as to disallow an aural association with the *valse*. In Betsimisaraka musics, the triple is accentuated slowly enough to orchestrate a recollection of or association with *valse* time.

It is pertinent here to recall Vinelo's newly created musical material inspired by Jamaican reggae and French Antilles *zouk*, musics he knew from radio broadcasts. These broadcasts themselves were often structured in sequences of disparate songs, often with little thematic, geographic, stylistic, or other cohesiveness. This was due in part to the limited availability of recorded resources in Madagascar but perhaps as well to the very combinative performative style of the Malagasy radio programmer. Strikingly, Vinelo told me that reggae and *zouk*, the genres upon which he based his own "reggay" and "mandôlina Kassavy," were Malagasy musics from other parts of the island (he said "Tsy tany ampitany ilay hira fa hira gasy izany" [These tunes aren't from 'out there'—from outside Madagascar. Rather, they're Malagasy songs]). Vinelo's belief that these were (different) Malagasy musics takes an ironic twist, in that he knew they were not being sung in Malagasy. These were "Malagasy musics" reliant particularly upon the linguistically incorporative skills of other Malagasy, who usually sing in their own local dialect of Malagasy. Vinelo had empowered his own new compositions, which he played for ancestral spirits, by modeling these compositions on what he believed to be other Malagasy musics, ones already once empowered because they themselves resounded with potent signs of Malagasy competence with linguistic incorporation and recycling.

Antandroy in Tamatave-ville construct spirit power in the present often by filtering into their performance practices perceived to be already (other) Malagasy. Indeed, the accordion itself is more accessible to Antandroy in Tamatave-ville, a relatively busy port town, than in Ambovombe in the south, where things are often more difficult to obtain. Recall that Very Soa often lent his own accordion to relatives in the south because they had none of their own. Among Antandroy, in practice the accordion is often as much associated with Tamatave-ville or with Betsimisaraka as it is with France or with *vazaha*. Betsimisaraka modes of incorporation are more often based upon combining with that realized in some capacity to be or have been European.

Making Copies

In 1969, French ethnologue Gerard Althabe published a book on *tromba* titled *Oppression et libération dans l'imaginaire*.[10] Althabe's premise was that the advent of independence from French colonials in 1960 brought about a crisis in village structures of power in Fetroamby, a small Betsimisaraka village in the southern Tamatave region. This postcolonial crisis supposedly involved the villagers' dismay at being confronted with newly appointed Malagasy *fonctionnaires*, state or local officials who in varied ways locally replicated the colonial order (collecting taxes and enforcing other laws). Althabe was concerned with what appeared to be a sudden postcolonial surge in *tromba* practice in this particular village, in which he thought *tromba* had not previously been widely practiced. He saw *tromba* specifically as a postcolonial internalization by Fetroamby villagers of colonial dependence ("une intériorisation, dans l'univers villageois, de la situation de la dépendence liant un maître à des serviteurs" [108–9]). Fetroamby villagers, apparently already so conditioned to domination, had replaced their servility to colonial masters with a new postcolonial order of subservience to their own "imagined" Malagasy spirit masters ("cette intériorisation d'un maître imaginable malgache" [ibid.]). While he suggested that choosing one's own master was an act of self-empowerment, Althabe in essence made *tromba-istes* into postcolonial casualties, subjects yearning for the familiarity of domination over the discomfort of independence.[11]

Feeley-Harnik has observed in the northwest that *tromba* "service expresses the power of Sakalava royal ancestors to enslave people, but also the power of their followers *to capture royalty and define it on their own terms*" [emphasis added] (1991b: 455). I would add that east coast *tromba-istes* have not so specifically desired to "capture" royalty or other modes of foreign-ness. Rather, they have sought to enact combinations of Self and Other, to integratively create a power of incorporation. Althabe overlooked the value of the enactment, the performance itself as an interpretive procedure through which Fetroamby villagers might have defined a new postcolonial order on their own terms.

Althabe likely had been influenced by Jacques Lacan's psychoanalytic theory (1966), particularly Lacan's thoughts on differing psychical domains, described briefly as the *imaginaire*, involving the production of images, the *symbolique*, the realm of signifiers upon which discursive interchange is based, and the *réel*, that which a subject perceives as real. In Lacan's writings the *imaginaire* is not exclusive of the real. Althabe, on the other hand, suggested that the *imaginaire* among Fetroamby villagers was a realm of the nonreal, one that existed essentially as fantasy, with no history of its own independent of colonial presence. Althabe indeed neglected several significant Betsimisaraka histories. For instance, during Madagascar's *première république*, under the presidency of Philibert Tsiranana, which began at the brink of the postcolonial era in 1960 and continued until 1972, Madagascar was still often largely under the political and economic aegis of French advisors and entrepreneurs. Knowledge of this lingering French control was abundant in Betsimisaraka villages on the east coast, according to current recollections and reports in Tamatave. Thus, there might not truly have been a sense of liberation at all among east coast people, who, I was told, commonly perceived themselves to still be under French control during the period to which Althabe refers.

An increase in *tromba* practice in Fetroamby just after decolonization might also have reflected the lifting of bans on ritual practice previously imposed by the French colonial regime. Recall, that prior to 1960, *tromba* practice had been proclaimed *interdit* by French colonials, and violators were subject to severe penalties (Estrade 1985). I was told that *tromba* had often been practiced clandestinely before 1960 throughout Tamatave so as to sidestep colonial prohibitions. Althabe's assumptions about the scarcity of preindependence *tromba* practice in Fetroamby might reflect the secrecy of this practice during that period.[12] Velomaro confirmed that he in particular had practiced *tromba* prior to 1960 in Tamatave; he also said that he had noticed no change in the frequency with which *tromba* ceremonies were performed in Tamatave after 1960. Feeley-Harnik has suggested that among Sakalava the practice of *tromba* spirit possession ceremony actually spread rather than diminished during the colonial era (1989: 103n).

Althabe also neglected to consider Merina intrusion as its own mode of colonization on the east coast. A historical sense of domination in Tamatave predates the arrival of French colonials, a sense that Althabe's theory neglects. He did, however, note the significance of mimetic behavior in postcolonial Madagascar. Specifically, he found Malagasy *fonctionnaires* to be affected by

un pouvoir qui se manifeste dans le mime des étrangers: les signes de ce pouvoir étant recherchés dans des objets d'origine étrangère dont ses acteurs s'entourent; c'est là un phénomène qui est loin d'être nouveau dans l'histoire malgache. (1969: 35n)[13]

a power that manifests itself in the mimicry of foreigners: the signs of this power being sought in objects of foreign origin that these agents covet; it is a phenomenon far from novel to Malagasy experience.

Perhaps mimetic power in Tamatave has arisen from the very *process* of making copies and from altering the original in the copying. I recall Taussig's comments here:

[S]inging origins is not done so much to gain control over the object of the Origin-History song, but first and foremost to create that object through its soulful *evocation* . . . such that "calling them up" is to conjure with their image, hence their soul, and hence give birth to the real. I am suggesting, in other words, that the chanter is singing a copy of the spirit- form, and by virtue of what I call the magic of mimesis, is bringing the spirit into the physical world. (1993: 104–5)

Antandroy accordionists combine different tuning systems, harmonic structures, timbres, and performative dynamics in their accordions, ones beyond the scope of the structural capacities of these instruments as they come from the (European) factory. Other *tromba-istes* also "conjure" with—in other words, alter and combine images of the spirit(s) of colonialism. Betsimisaraka do so, for instance, in recollecting and improvising upon colonial *bals* and the *valses* performed at these events. The following chapter contains examples of other explicit ways in which east coast Malagasy create a foreign *subject* through its soulful evocation.

Opposition and Resistance

Distinguishing the elements of resistance and accommodation in the formation of collective or personal identities at the site of any ethnographic project has become the almost slogan-like analytic formula for addressing the paradoxical modernist vision of "everything everywhere, yet everywhere different." (Marcus 1998: 61)

While performance may not occupy the privileged place among the subversive practices of the powerless that some authors have attributed to it, it may, as recent ethnographies of performance indicate, assume a key role in the dialectic between structure, as the givenness of the world, and agency. Even where this performative mode of interrogation does not query the legitimacy of social inequity per se, it does at times generate alternative power relations. . . . Collective resistance, although it may provide direction and impetus to the action of the powerless, does not necessarily create integrated, consensual communities. (Erlmann 1996: xxii)

Power means not *having* to act or, more accurately, the capacity to be more negligent and casual about any single performance. (Scott 1990: 29)

While traces of the foreign take shape in *tromba* practice in Tamatave, there is little indication that *tromba-istes* have conceived of this practice primarily as reaction or resistance to the powers represented in such foreign traces. Rather than domination's symbolic counterforce, *tromba* practice provides an evaluative system with which signs connected to the foreign can be reworked and rearticulated in unique, "alternative power relations" (in Erlmann's terms). Among both Antandroy and Betsimisaraka, power itself is prominently emergent in sound, its transformative and historical dimensions, its spiritual efficacy, its role in engendering recollection, its creativity. Although I cannot attest to the character of *tromba* practices during the colonial era itself, I can comment upon the appearance of varied modes of power as they are currently represented throughout Tamatave. I am not denying that resistance has historically been voiced and enacted on the east coast of Madagascar. I am suggesting that creating symbolic resistance to colonialism and other powers has not been a predominant, purposeful, or consensual factor of *tromba* practice among Antandroy and Betsimisaraka in Tamatave.

Paul Stöller (1995) writes fervently of cultural resistance in performative practices in West Africa. Specifically, he determines mimesis in ritual behavior and spirit-connected plastic arts among Songhay in Niger to be an "embodied opposition" to colonization and later to the postcolony state. Stoller elsewhere (1989) also conveys the sentience and sensuousness of West African spirit possession practices—elements pertinent to recollecting in *tromba* practice—and he does evoke varied histories of colonialism in West Africa. Yet resistance theories in which other people are portrayed merely or primarily as reacting against more powerful forces might denude the actual complexities of people, their practices, and beliefs.

Addressing a recent tendency to deploy resistance in theoretical frameworks for making sense of peoples' practices, Abu-Lughod (1990) writes of a "romance of resistance," a perhaps seductive compulsion to champion the reactive power of the weak. George Marcus, cited above, likewise asserts that resistance has become an "almost slogan-like analytic formula." Sherry Ortner (1995) criticizes some studies based on resistance theories for their tendency to be ethnographically "thin," essentially unsupported in real worlds of experience. Furthermore, should resistance be determined to be a factor in creative expression, is it necessarily the only or predominant one?

Resistance in practice might occur alongside other meanings, histories, politics, or modes of interpretation. Concerned with lacunae in histories, Nicholas Thomas writes:

It is often supposed, in both conservative and radical thinking, that imperial intrusions have had such shattering and pervasive effect upon the dominated groups that the form of local, precolonial society is of limited significance for subsequent development; even when struggle and resistance are recognized, the responses of the colonized are taken to be merely reactive. While the real balance of forces at particular phases of colonial history requires specification, and there clearly are times when indigenous peoples cannot do much to shape the events which overtake them, I am committed to the view that local events and representations are never totally encompassed or determined by the violence of colonialism, and that the distinctive forms of indigenous sociality and politics contribute in a crucial way to the dynamics of accommodation and resistance constitutive of colonial history. (1991: 35)

Ross Chambers, influenced by de Certeau, also writes critically of resistance:

[T]he discourses of power are not simply open to disturbance, as communication is subject to "noise," but the disturbance introduces change. It does so, moreover, without challenging the system, since it consists of making use of dominant structures for "other" purposes and in "other" interests, those of the people—all of us—whom power alienates or oppresses. (1991: xiii)

Chambers then distinguishes between resistance and opposition:

Oppositional behavior consists of individual or group survival tactics that do not challenge the power in place, but make use of circumstances set up by that power for purposes the power may ignore or deny. It contrasts, then, with revolution, which is a mode of *resistance* to forms of power it regards as illegitimate, that is, as a force that needs to be opposed by a counterforce. (1991: 1)

Opposition in this sense is manifest in "advantages taken" by people in occupied places to rework materials and ideas appropriated from a dominant force. It is an other or differing position taken on the use, value, and meanings extractable from things, and takes place in "that space of 'play' or 'leeway' in the system" (ibid.:xi).[14]

De Certeau (1984) distinguishes further between strategies—the behaviors of those in control of given situations—and tactics, the imaginative choices made by those operating within such control. Opposition becomes a tactic for creative articulation in occupied places, one that operates beyond or independent of defiance or subversion.

Both Chambers and de Certeau evoke varied means with which the "powerless" are able to locally empower themselves, symbolically or otherwise. Chambers contends convincingly that creative expression, particularly as discourse, "has characteristics that enable it, in an important sense, to elude both repression and recuperation, or more accurately to 'maneuver' within the 'room' that opens up *between* the two" (1991: 3). Achille Mbembe has also recognized the complexity and even ambivalence of postcolonial situations:

[T]he postcolonial relationship is not primarily a relationship of resistance or collaboration, but it is rather best characterized as a promiscuous relationship . . . acts of the dominated do not necessarily lead to resistance, accommodation, "disengagement," the refusal to be captured, or to an antagonism between public facts and gestures and those *sous maquis* [of the underground]. (1992: 5)

Writing specifically on Africa, Terence Ranger suggested that, while the song texts of Beni dance performance in Kenya and Tanganyika (now Tanzania) "can express African resentment of or opposition to colonial rule," Beni performance itself

was not *essentially* an oppositionist phenomenon. It was too profoundly assimilated into African societies for it to be exclusively or even mainly concerned with the externalities of opposition. Hence the Beni texts and Beni history more generally also reveal significant tensions within African societies, and significant aspirations (often toward modernity). (1975: 165)[15]

Beni dance was quite mimetic of colonialism in formal, processual, even musical attributes. Yet, Ranger recognized that Beni performance was a historicizing expression of deeply felt African sentiments, one that exceeded the mere enactment of resistance to colonial forces on the east coast of Africa.

Jean Comaroff has described an "articulation" that has grown out of the "clash" between colonial and African systems among Tshidi in South Africa, based upon

the joining of distinct systems, themselves dynamic orders of practice and meaning, into a unitary formation, the novel product of particular historical circumstances. In the process of conjuncture, formerly distinct formations become subsumed in an indissoluble unity. In the interaction of global and peripheral systems, the conjuncture is one between unequal orders, and between systems in contradiction. (1985: 153)

While such conjunctures were certainly facilitated, even forced by colonial contact, I question more broadly whether political and social imbalances necessarily translate primarily or solely into "contradictions" that become played out in Africans' practices (Comaroff specifically addresses religious practice here). Africans and others certainly are not subject only to being subsumed in conjunctures that represent disparities between orders of power, orders in which they are always conceptually the less powerful.

Power might have more than one nature. If resistance can be determined to be a motivating element in the creative production of culture, must it displace and subsume other processes in this production? Comaroff's interpretation and other similar ones might in some sense adhere to and even replicate a colonial order, in spatially dividing up the world into "peripheral systems" that are always implicitly overshadowed by a "central" original power. Distant others are liable to be conceptually recolonized when their expressive forms are seen exclusively as resistant to, and therefore dependent upon, for instance, European domination and always in some sense subsumed by such conditions of domination.

In Veit Erlmann's *Nightsong* (1996), *isicathamiya* singing star Joseph Shabalala speaks of "a power which rises above us all" (p. xx). While there is no question of the hegemonic impact of missionization (to which *isicathamiya* in part owes its harmonic structure) and apartheid upon performers in South Africa, perhaps Zulus, as well as other Africans, conceive of power, spirituality, or alienation on their own unique terms. And perhaps these terms could exceed Western understandings of power as alliterated, for instance, in concepts such as hegemony or resistance. And if *isicathamiya* is primarily a resistant practice, might it at times step outside this particular capacity, to evoke as well issues and sentiments that extend beyond the impact of the dominant order in South Africa, to engage "a power which rises above us all"?

On spirit mediumship in Papua New Guinea, Bruce Knauft writes, "Viewed more phenomenologically and taken on their own terms, the aesthetics and experience of spirituality come to center stage, not as resistance or counter-hegemonic agency but as the expression of cultural meaning and sociality" (1998:197). It is indeed the very *aesthetics* of spirituality from which meaning emerges among Malagasy in Tamatave, an aesthetics of recollecting (from) that encompasses and expresses more than reaction to colonization or to postcolonial inequity.

Tromba practice in Tamatave is, in Chambers's terms, oppositional in nature. A primary tenet of this practice has been to create room to maneuver—its own space *entre-deux*—between the past and present, between the ancestral and the everyday, between the foreign and the familiar. *Tromba* in essence transcends boundaries delimited simply by a colonizer/colonized dichotomy. In the very altering of Other modes of power, *tromba-istes* on the east coast create invaluable ceremonial *maresaka,* healing power, and the inevitable joyousness that arises when living and spirit worlds commune. James Scott suggests that "power means not having to act. " Perhaps from performance a certain truth can emerge, inherent in the performing itself rather than in a specific, texted content or plot. In *tromba* ceremony, power indeed arises from the very processes that go into enacting and musically stimulating and integrating varied pasts.

CHAPTER EIGHT

Clinton, Bush, and Hussein in Tamatave

⌇

> [T]he conjunction of temporalities, including the present, allows each period to serve as a locus of commentary on the others. . . . In the resulting arena for heteroglossia, multiple voices and alternate points of view are expressed and made available for consideration, without being subordinated or silenced by others. This is a condensation of historical time within the space of the present, but emphatically it does not thereby flatten or confuse historical voices.
>
> What this means is that historical consciousness is not reducible to a single attitude, but arises through the interplay of multiple voices. It is neither single nor static, but open. It is no mere response to the present, nor is it something that can be reduced to a term like *resistance*. Thus the anthropologist cannot state what it is, but can only describe the forms through which it is produced. (Lambek 1998: 108–9 on Sakalava *tromba*)

Honorine, a Betsimisaraka woman in her mid-thirties and a *tromba* medium who resided on the outskirts of Tamatave-ville, had as many as twenty-five different *tromba* that came to her. Her *tromba* spirits had a wide range of varied personalities, including that of an ill-mannered child of a Sakalava king, a sometimes arrogant French colonial administrator from Mahajanga in the northwest of the island, and a Frenchwoman who liked to wear *six* separate barrettes in her hair, who demanded an ashtray that had to have ridges in the corners on which to rest her cigarettes, and who drank only whiskey (available but very expensive in Madagascar). Whiskey is usually demanded only by certain European spirits. Local rum is much more affordable and is the preferred drink of most Malagasy *tromba* that like to imbibe alcohol.

Two of Honorine's spirits were quite unusual. One was a *silamo*, or Muslim, spirit named Sadam Hoseny; another a *vazaha*, was a non-Malagasy spirit named Georges Klintsky. I took Georges Klintsky to be a composite/condensation of George Bush and Bill Clinton; the latter at that time had recently won the U.S. presidency from Bush. In light of more recent scandals involving the White House, Veit Erlmann has suggested to me that perhaps Georges Klintsky actually stood for a combination of Bill Clinton and Monica Lewinsky—*tromba* spirits are, after all, capable of seeing into the future.

Sadam Hoseny was modeled in part after Iraqi leader Saddam Hussein, who in the recent past had been engaged against Bush and the United States in the Gulf War. The appearance of these two powerful leaders from very distant places at first baffled me; for one reason, most if not all of the *tromba* I had encountered previously in Madagascar had been spirits of people already deceased. Moreover, detailed news from outside Madagascar was not usually well circulated throughout this *tromba* community. Malagasy newspapers from Antananarivo, such as the *Madagascar Tribune* and *Le Midi,* were sometimes available at the *bazary be* in Tamatave-ville, though Honorine and her circle of *tromba-istes* did not, in my experience, buy or read them.

I later discovered that Honorine possessed a small black-and-white television set, on which fragmented images of the Gulf War had been broadcast into her home via French satellite (though French was not spoken by Honorine or her family). Also transmitted had been televised segments from the Clinton–Bush election. Honorine was the only *tromba*-iste I knew in the Tamatave region who had a TV, and indeed she was the only medium to whom Georges Klintsky and Sadam Hoseny ever came. Older Malagasy royal *tromba* spirits came to many mediums in this community, as well as to other mediums throughout the island. Thus, Klinstky and Hoseny were somewhat of a surprise in that they did not *mifindra* during Honorine's ceremonies, they did not "move" from medium to medium as many other *tromba* often were able to do.

When possessing Honorine, Sadam Hoseny, also sometimes called simply "Silamo" by other *tromba* participants, wore a white turban formed with a linen sheet, and he usually spoke in an aggressive chatter that I could not comprehend. He would sit cross-legged—not at all a common way for Betsimisaraka to sit—and would have several attendants surrounding him. With me he was sometimes garrulous. He occasionally became impertinent when I could not understand him, though he was never aggressive or threatening. Marie Yvonne, a Betsimisaraka *tromba* medium, *ombiasa,* and very good friend, would usually mediate when Sadam Hoseny spoke to me, in speech that actually was Malagasy but with much vocal distortion, a throaty, sometimes guttural articulation of Malagasy words perhaps imitative of some Arabic consonant pronunciations.

Hoseny was a self-absorbed character, eyes always bulging with intensity. He was often preoccupied with ordering his attendants about or with provoking or engaging in some mode of verbal commotion or confrontation with other participants. This was often over the quality of the proceedings or the whereabouts of his ceremonial things. Hoseny usually kept by his side, for instance, an imported box of incense, which was rare, expensive, even exotic in Madagascar. It appeared to me that Hoseny was, in part, articulating gestures and behaviors characteristic of a French TV depiction of a despotic ruler.

The most powerful *tromba* at Honorine's ceremonies usually seemed unaffected by Hoseny's strange way of speaking and unusual mannerisms. They rarely paid him any noticeable attention, nor did they address him (Velomaro was often the medium for the presiding *tromba* at Honorine's ceremonies). Hoseny's appearance and exaggerated, often ridiculous or disruptive behavior would occasionally send other *tromba* and ceremonial participants into paroxysms of delight. At the same time these *tromba* participants tolerated him, addressed him with respect, and responded cooperatively to his requests and demands. Jean Dedier, the Betsimisaraka *valiha* player who usually performed for Honorine's ceremonies, told me that Hoseny preferred *hira vazaha,* or outsider's songs. Dedier, however, said he knew none of these on *valiha.* Hoseny seemed content to arrive and depart to Betsimisaraka ceremonial basesa.

Even though he inquired about my origins on several occasions, Sadam Hoseny, oddly I thought at first, did not seem to mind that I was an American who was essentially intruding into his ceremonial place. I apparently did not represent to Hoseny the very enemy with which Saddam Hussein was then embroiled on a global ground. In fact, Sadam Hoseny was not a despotic ruler to these *tromba-istes,* nor did Honorine's *tromba* ceremonies become a stage for replaying a war being waged on Kuwaiti and Iraqi terrain; nor was I an enemy of any sort. Rather, Hoseny and I were, in different capacities, representatives of foreign power, foreign personalities in the Malagasy ceremonial present as providers of, among other things, entertainment for royal spirits and other participants. We were mediums through which foreign power, as discourse as well as action, could be absorbed and refigured by both *tromba* spirits and the living. Hoseny and I engendered more *maresaka,* as lively talk and gesture.

Varied modes of talk in addition to other activity among the living, like musical performance, arouse the interest of ancestral spirits and entice them to enter into the ceremonial present and to remain there longer so as to partake in such discursive interactions. The verbal commotion as well as the bursts of laughter or astonishment that Hoseny provoked among *tromba-istes* themselves were *maresaka.* Several *tromba-istes* told me that even though presiding *tromba* might seem to ignore spirits like Hoseny, they were nonetheless pleased by his arrival and subsequent activities.

Discourse with or from foreigners such as Hoseny and I further heightened and intensified the power and efficacy of the current *tromba* proceedings by adding more volume, interaction, points of view, stories, information, modes of linguistic pronunciation and accentuation, and impetus for verbal reaction or response. Such discourse engendered a prestige and empowerment, of simply having distant foreigners appear before revered royal ancestral spirits in their resurrected, multitemporal courts. These particular instances of *maresaka* were all the more empowering because they opened a discourse of a global nature, yet one that reigned in and denuded the global of its potential or actual destructive force as projected on TV (recall the video game–like TV images of scud missiles in surreal formations of sparkler traces lighting up the Baghdad night).

Thus in Honorine's *tromba* ceremonies, Sadam Hoseny was not a global threat but often a rather comical stranger who embodied many characteristics of what it meant *not* to be Malagasy. Interactions with such foreign personalities could encode Malagasy sentiments about some of their own encounters with *vazaha,* who more recently might be French teachers or business people in Tamatave-ville who were there only temporarily.[1] Hoseny's insistence on having his incense nearby, which Honorine when not possessed had to purchase and keep on hand for him, once drew a sardonic comment from a powerful ancestral spirit, "Tsy vary izay!" meaning, "It's not rice (so what good is it to us)!" Rather than representing some critique of a particular foreign personality, ideology, or global struggle, interactions with Hoseny allowed sometimes for a more broad-ranged cultural critique, of *vazaha* in general and of foreign visitors and their sometimes strange ways and priorities. Indeed, the term *vazaha* could refer nonspecifically to a range of peoples from outside Madagascar and not specifically to any one type of foreigner.

Appearances by *vazaha* like Hoseny also allow *tromba* participants to enact their patience and tolerance, even for odd *vazaha* behaviors. Yet the insurgence of 1947, for instance, demonstrated that east coast Malagasy would differentiate between odd though sometimes incorporable *vazaha* behavior and, in this instance, the insupportable *vazaha* appropriation of ancestral land. Some of the eldest *tromba-istes* in Honorine's community, like Velomaro, had even partaken in this insurgence. In *tromba* ceremony, *vazaha* are not cast as colonial-like threats; they are usually tolerated, even appreciated, for the discursive *maresaka* they can generate, even if this is emergent as peculiar behavior, dress, or desire. Tolerance in the midst of vast difference and adversity was a quality lacking in decisions then recently made on a global scale by Bill Clinton, George Bush, and Saddam Hussein themselves. By taking in Saddam Hoseny and Georges Klintsky, Honorine not only absorbed the power of foreign leaders, she also reaestheticized this power.

While images of foreign figures in *tromba* ceremony could evoke among Malagasy essentialized critique of *vazaha,* such images could also denote more specific issues. For instance, there have long been adherents of Islam living in Madagascar, concentrated mostly in northern and southern parts of the island. Honorine and her friends were not unfamiliar with Islamic modes of dress, prayer (there was a mosque in Tamatave-ville from which amplified calls to prayer were broadcast daily), and *fady,* or taboo. There had been earlier waves of Islamic infusion into Madagascar by visitors and settlers who commonly had been traders, foreign in appearance and custom, who specifically brought foreign, unusual things to the island. Hoseny's fondness for exotic incense, his turban, and his mode of speech could be linked not only to images absorbed from foreign TV broadcasts but to the recollection and imagining of specific histories of difference and contact throughout the past in Madagascar.

Muslim Indian shopowners, Karana, have on different occasions throughout the past in Madagascar been the targets of mostly youthful reaction to dire economic and social conditions there. In 1994, while I was on the east coast, an angry crowd of Malagasy youth burned to the ground a whole block of Indian shops at the market in Tamatave-ville. This outrage stemmed in part from then Prime Minister Ravony's continued devaluation of the Malagasy franc—its value had plunged by a factor of nearly one-third in just the twenty months that I was in Madagascar—and from the resulting difficulty or impossibility of purchasing daily necessities such as rice. Many of these exasperated youth expressed their deflation over the prospect of having few or no educational or occupational opportunities in Madagascar, as well as their feelings of ineffectualness arising from not being able to provide for their families. In addition, Ravony's economic policies were often seen as a treacherous strategy aimed at arousing *vazaha* financial interests while ignoring the immediate needs of Malagasy in the countryside.[2] Among members of Honorine's *tromba* community, appearances by the *silamo* Hoseny likely were not conceptually divorced from recollections of such violent episodes, in which the dealings of Indian merchants were associated with national economic inequities. Themselves usually economically privileged, Indian shopowners were sometimes cast as *bouc-émissaires* in Madagascar, as daunting signs among other Malagasy of worsening economic conditions. Outside *tromba* ceremony many *tromba-istes* explicitly commented on such attacks on Karana shops, usually regretting the violence but also disturbed by Ravony's monetary policies. As mentioned, interactions with Hoseny were denuded of any potential for violent or truly transgressive behavior.

Honorine and her friends proclaimed a different sort of justice and social equalization in their *tromba* ceremonies. They were not concerned with scapegoating Karana shopowners for material impoverishment among Malagasy or with remarking upon an incomprehensible war in the Gulf States.[3] Hoseny in essence created new foreign ground on which to imaginatively construct more talk and interaction, themselves vital components in the potency of any *tromba* ceremony. Indeed, Saddam Hussein himself was eliciting much discourse, commotion, and engagement with others foreign to him in the outside world; his TV image was a viable model for ceremonial *maresaka*.

Hoseny was a somewhat ambiguous character. He was linkable to some transgressive sentiment and to recollections of difference throughout the past in Madagascar. Yet he was a forceful though constrained proponent for the proliferation of some basic tenets of and processes in *tromba* ceremony. He represented in part a dangerous force brought under control, taken in, revalued, and then dramatically recycled into a Malagasy scheme of empowerment.

∽

Georges Klintsky was eloquent and knowledgeable. In my presence he spoke only French, though, as I've mentioned, Honorine when not possessed spoke no French. Bush's or Clinton's speech segments on Malagasy TV were translated as French voiceover, though listening infrequently to TV would not account for Klintsky's/Honorine's fluency in French. Klintsky was also loquacious, but in contrast to Sadam Hoseny, his manner was austere and patient—becoming of the French TV depiction of a U.S. president? He sat straight-postured in a Western-style wooden dining room chair, while most of the other participants sat on the ground. Sitting elevated in a chair is usually reserved for the *tromba* spirits presiding over the ceremony. This is always a very powerful royal spirit, accompanied by his or her attendants, although they usually sit somewhat slouched over in their chairs in a contemplative pose, not upright and straight-backed like Klintsky. These few presiding *tromba* spirits, self-absorbed in reflection or concerned with other elements of propriety in the current proceedings, usually seemed to be ignoring Klintsky as they did Hoseny.

My introductory conversation with Georges went as follows:

GK: J'habite dans la mer près de la côte de Groenland. Toi, tu habites au Méxique!

RE: J'habite au Texas, pas loin de Méxique. Est-ce que vous aimez bien habiter dans l'eau?

GK: Je n'aime pas y habiter. La mer est trop froide, mais c'est où j'habite. Je préfére-rais habiter à Madagascar, mais les Malagasy sont impolis. Regard là- bas *(Il indique les autres qui s'assoient par terre tandis qu'il a une chaise)*. Les gens en Amérique sont "okay." Cette femme *(il indique Kiki)*, elle est ta femme?

RE: Non, elle travaille avec moi.

GK: Elle va t'accompagner en Amérique quand tu partiras? *(Beaucoup de rires des autres participants, les uns possédés, d'autres pas possédés)*.

RE: Je ne sais pas en ce moment.

GK: Il te faut l'emmener avec toi pour qu'elle puisse voir un autre pays. Pourquoi tu ne te marie pas avec elle?

RE: Nous sommes amis, comme frère et sœur.

GK: Merci bien. Mes amis m'attendent—je m'en vais. Je pourrais t'assister avec ton travail—je viens ici de temps en temps.

GK: I live in the ocean near the coast of Greenland. You live in Mexico!

RE: I live in Texas, not far from Mexico. Do you enjoy living in the ocean?

GK: I don't like to live there. The ocean is too cold, but that's just where I live. I'd prefer to live in Madagascar, but Malagasy are rude. Look down there *(he points to the others who are sitting on the ground, while he sits in a chair)*. Amer-icans are okay. That woman *(he points to Kiki)*, is she your wife?

RE: No, she works with me.

GK: Will she return with you to America when you go home? *(Much laughter from the other participants, some possessed, some not possessed)*.

RE: I don't know yet.

GK: You must take her with you so she can see another land. Why don't you marry her?

RE: We're friends, like brother and sister.

GK: Thanks a lot, then. My friends are waiting for me—I'm leaving. I can help you with your work—I come here from time to time.

It is important to note Klintsky's direct and rather aggressive or persis-tent questioning of me. This discursive style contrasts greatly with a prev-alent Malagasy discursive aesthetic of communicative indirectness and nonaggressiveness. Engaging in this direct, pointed discursive style, Georges Klintsky, like Hoseny, also embodied in part what it meant *not* to be Malagasy.

Klintsky's delving into my affairs, his disregard for the general Malagasy aesthetic of discursive indirectness, and his condescension toward other cer-emonial participants are also reflective of a belief I occasionally encountered in Madagascar, that Americans are aggressive and even *masiaka,* or mean-spirited. These impressions of Americans are often assisted by knowledge of Rambo-like movie characters starring at local video houses—often specifically American characters that are aggressive, usually engaged in some monumental battle, and virtually indestructible. Vinelo had a spirit who was half Sakalava and half American named *Be Koronta* (big fight). Be Koronta was a powerful healer, though he liked to provoke fights and was generally *ratsy fagnahy* (of a malevolent character). These latter aggressive qualities, Vinelo explained, were more attributable to Be Koronta's American side.[4]

Some *tromba* participants told me that Georges Klintsky was *masiaka* because he repeatedly refused their requests to share his knowledge of outside worlds with them. Elizabeth, a very kind and reserved Betsimisaraka woman, whose role it was to serve as attendant to *tromba* spirits at these ceremonies, lamented to me that she wanted to learn French but that Klintsky persistently denied her requests to tutor her (Klintsky apparently also spoke Malagasy, though I never heard him do so—he always insisted on speaking French to and around me). So Georges Klintsky was also an ambiguous character, paternalistic and kind to me (a fellow American?), sometimes rude, condescending, or *mahidy* (stingy) to Malagasy.

It was the result of no accident, confusion, or oversight on the part of Honorine or members of her *tromba* community that Georges Klintsky was a composite of (at least) two foreign personalities, George Bush and Bill Clinton. The constructing of coherent wholes out of combinations of compounded segments is a performative component of the aesthetic of *maresaka.* That Klintsky resided in the ocean off Greenland was quite baffling to me. Indeed, when not possessed, Honorine could not give any detail of where or what Greenland is. The Indian Ocean off the east coast of Madagascar is a sacred place to Honorine and her *tromba* associates; but unlike the cold Greenland waters described resignedly by Klintsky, Indian Ocean waters near Madagascar are warm, and it is usually Sakalava ancestral spirits that reign over this body of water. Klintsky's lament contained a sense of self-imposed exile, to another quite non-Malagasy place—cold, distant, and unknown—forced in part by what he deemed to be the insufferable rudeness of Malagasy who sit on the floor. Greenland, like Madagascar, is a large isolated island, and its appearance in Honorine's subconscious had likely resulted from some recognition of similarity or difference between the two islands that she had internalized.

I often thought of Klintsky as another sort of composite, a combination of TV images of current foreign political figures and recollections of older French colonials, who also came from some invisible distant and cold place to impose harsh judgments, regulations, and prohibitions on Malagasy and their expressive practices. Perhaps Klintsky's lament over not being able to live in Madagascar due to Malagasy "rudeness" in part mirrored back critically upon these French colonials, who had condemned Malagasy sacred ancestral practices and, in making prohibitions on *tromba*, had condescendingly extricated or "exiled" themselves from these practices.

⌇

Writing recently on musical and spiritual practices in northern Malawi, Steven Friedson (1997) has suggested that during divination practices in which ancestors are invoked, though possession itself does not occur, Tumbuka-speaking people undergo a "consciousness doubling" in which the individual becomes "himself and more than himself at the same time."[5] For Tumbuka, this mode of trance purportedly is not a loss of self but "an expansion of self." Although possession is a primary facet of *tromba* ceremony, Friedson's observations might warrant some thought here. Analyses of ritual practices have sometimes zealously sought to comprehend collective experience while overlooking elements of individual interpretation, expression, and history in these practices, the personal meanings and motivations that are likely infused integrally with collective ceremonial experience. Thomas Csordas (1994) has advocated a cultural phenomenology that is concerned with "synthesizing the immediacy of embodied experience with the multiplicity of cultural meaning in which we are always and inevitably immersed" (vii). Michael Jackson (1998) asks, "How is the *lived* experience of individuals connected to the *virtual* realities of tradition, history, culture, and the biology of the species that outrun the life of any one person?" (3). He continues:

The question of the relationship between particular and universal domains thus dissolves into a set of questions about how the give and take of *intersubjective* life in all its modes and mediations—physical and metaphysical, conscious and unconscious, passive and active, kind and unkind, serious and ludic, dyadic and collective, symmetrical and asymmetrical, inclusive and exclusive, empathic and antagonistic—prefigures and configures more discursive and categorical forms of relationship. (Ibid.: 4)

Since Honorine was the only *tromba* medium to become possessed by the unique spirits Klintsky and Hoseny, while many of the other *tromba* spirits could be encountered throughout Honorine's community as well as throughout the island, I gathered that these personalities were in part expressions of Honorine's personal experience. Indeed, they were related to the personal experience of watching French TV broadcasts. *Tromba* mediums proclaim that they have no memory of themselves when possessed, except perhaps for what might be thought of as some body memory from aching joints or limbs that results from sitting long hours in cramped quarters. That Honorine had no recollection of herself possessed afterward does not preclude the role of her own volition, imagination, and creativity in giving life to disembodied spirits that eventually came to her. Such a personal connection with spirits such as Klintsky and Hoseny made more sense when I reflected upon some aspects of Honorine's nonpossessed personality and social life and those of her family. Just before first introducing me to Honorine, Marie Yvonne had said somewhat cautiously, "Tsy mitovy ny sasany izy" (She's not like the others). Marie Yvonne went on to say that Honorine was moody, that she was nice but that sometimes she could be impertinent or otherwise bold in character. Honorine and her family lived not quite of or in the world of experience of other Betsimisaraka.

Honorine was indeed different from many of the members of her *tromba* community. She possessed more material things than many others, such as a bigger house with some Western-style furniture, the TV, tablecloths—all attributable, said Honorine, to the generosity of her *tromba* spirits. A greater number and variety of spirits came to Honorine than to most other mediums, a cause for much esteem, added clientele, and thus social and economic empowerment. Honorine was also quite self-confident and vocally expressive of her sometimes contentious views, and she could be quite persistent or stubborn on some matters. These were qualities not often displayed in this community, and they contrasted with the general communicative aesthetic of indirectness/nonaggressiveness among many east coast Malagasy. The excesses brought into *tromba* ceremony by Klintsky and Hoseny, for instance, were meaningful and powerful in part because they modeled or reflected some of Honorine's own behaviors. Through these two foreigners (and others), Honorine could enact a unique expansion of her own self onto ceremonial consciousness and action.

In addition, Honorine's children were rather unique among Betsimisaraka children. She had twin boys, five years old at the time. To survive the birthing of twins was believed by these *tromba-istes* to be exceptional and empowering. Both boys had haircuts unknown among other Betsimisaraka—shocks of hair sticking straight up in the front with the rest of the head shaved. Another of Honorine's children, a girl then thirteen years old, had some cognitive and speech difficulty that made it quite difficult for her to verbally formulate her thoughts and feelings, though she was quite sensitive and seemed able to look through people and situations. Honorine had several other children, each in their own way distinct from other Betsimisaraka children.

To me and to other Betsimisaraka, Honorine and her family were quite obviously unusual in their capacity for incorporating difference; indeed, for being different (yet similar), they themselves seemed to stand for an intensification of ceremonial as well as everyday *maresaka*. Honorine's ceremonies were always among the largest, longest, most frequent, and most elaborate of any in Tamatave. Yet Honorine's distinctive individualism was contained within parameters acceptable and workable in *tromba* ceremony. The following chapter introduces a Betsimisaraka accordionist, Tsiariagna, whose behavior represented to many other Betsimisaraka an oversaturation, an undesirable amount of the foreign.

The significance of appearances by foreigners such as Sadam Hoseny and Georges Klintsky at Honorine's *tromba* ceremonies implicitly touched upon other encounters with *vazaha* throughout the past in Madagascar. As mentioned, east coast Malagasy have long been involved in struggles with foreigners over control of their ancestral homeland. These foreigners have included early pirates and traders, British missionaries, intruding Merina, French colonials, and development and conservation organizations. Images of the Gulf War on TV represented a struggle between foreign forces over control of resources and territory in a small militarily defenseless nation. What remained off-frame in the exploding Iraqi night was the suffering of local people, who paid for the transgressions of their nation's leader, and the destruction of untold ancient archeological sites and other valued landscapes.[6]

Malagasy themselves had been subject to a particularly deleterious presidency from 1975 through 1993 under Didier Ratsiraka, who purportedly drove Madagascar deeper into poverty with his own corruption and avarice. Ratsiraka, however, as half-Betsimisaraka, has commonly won the allegiance and support of east coast Malagasy even though he has directly contributed to their worsening economic and social problems. Hoseny and Klinstky, while different and foreign, were also in some ways reflective of the familiar, of that already Malagasy, of abuses of power and struggles over land in the Malagasy past and present, and perhaps even of the absolution that some east coast Malagasy had allowed for their own despotic ruler from the past; in fact, Ratsiraka was recently reelected president of Madagascar. Interestingly, it has also been suggested that Ratsiraka was receiving campaign financing from Libya and *Iraq* in the early 1990s (Allen 1995: 112).

I was later privileged to sit in on several TV viewings with Honorine and her family. Their responses to these viewings ranged from good-natured mimicry of the gestures and speech they saw and heard to comments on the apparent aggressiveness, meanness, or general strangeness of *vazaha* behavior. Oddly (I mused then), neither Honorine, her family, nor anyone else in this *tromba* community ever asked me about life in America or for that matter for any details of events outside Madagascar. Regular appearances by Hoseny and Klintsky in Honorine's *tromba* ceremonies served in part as pacification and critique of these sometimes vague, sometimes very specific outside worlds. Segmented mannerisms and gestures of these foreign powers broadcast over French TV, which meant very brief glimpses and only a flash of English before a voiceover in French interjected, provided Honorine with images for further articulating Betsimisaraka histories, recollections, and ways of interacting already in place. In Honorine's *tromba* ceremonies, though, the potential for enacting any aggressive confrontation between George Bush and Saddam Hussein had been completely forestalled, since Georges Klintsky and Sadam Hoseny, the *tromba* representatives of these foreign personalities, came only to Honorine. They could never appear simultaneously and therefore could not interact with nor confront one another.

Clinton, Bush, and Hussein had appeared auspiciously as familiar enough TV images that Honorine could absorb into her ceremonial practice. The altered Klintsky and Hoseny could echo varied traces of Malagasy events, collective and individual, and act as mediums through which Honorine and her friends could recollect and implicitly interact with and in such events, long past or more recent. Like the TV broadcasts that featured them, Honorine's *tromba* ceremonies transformed George Bush, Bill Clinton, and Saddam Hussein into images that could be effectively mediated and manipulated, though to different ends. Honorine created combinative personalities that came into the present as mediums of sacred *maresaka*, and that allowed her to simultaneously empower herself personally.

Bringing images of foreign leaders into Betsimisaraka *tromba* ceremony also involved other reworkings of power. Such incorporations elevated these particular Others to the status of powerful *tromba* spirits, who were also foreigners from distant places. Thus, clear divisions between foreigner and revered *tromba* spirit could become blurred. Foreign non-Malagasy *tromba* spirits could also implicate the presence and effect in Madagascar of French colonials or other Europeans, another type of powerful Other from elsewhere—recall, for instance, the French woman spirit who demanded six barrettes for her hair, whiskey, and an ashtray with ridges. However, these characters did not arrive simply so that Malagasy could evaluate current or past global excesses. Rather, like bicycle brake cable strings for *valiha* and European-made accordions that had been incorporated as vital elements of *tromba* ceremony, images of foreign personalities were made part of the interactional combinations and composites that comprised sacred *maresaka*. Hoseny and Klintsky contributed elements of difference upon which *maresaka* was predicated, yet because they, like royal ancestral *tromba* spirits, were powerful Others, in this instance from "out there," they were also similar and familiar. Bill Clinton, George Bush, and Saddam Hussein themselves, however, were neither accepted nor useful in *tromba* events until they could be decomposed, refined, and reassembled into compound figures, part *vazaha* and part Malagasy. It was the actual process of enactment and engagement with these foreign personalities that was empowering to Honorine and her friends, not merely an overt discursive critique or response made by Malagasy while in contact with them.

Tromba ceremonies in Tamatave are complex, multimeaningful events of composite images, sounds, and behaviors in which difference and foreign power can be at once absorbed and restated as something uniquely Malagasy. A sense of global linkage has been an embedded and historically present characteristic of Malagasy consciousness on the east coast, though this feeling of connection has often meant internalizing the outside on specifically Malagasy terms rather than seeking to identify with an externally derived significance of, for example, a Saddam Hussein or a musical figure such as Michael Jackson (who is quite well known in some circles throughout Madagascar). Malagasy who perform *tromba* spirit possession ceremonies have not expressed a predominant concern over the truths of outside worlds—indeed, anywhere outside Madagascar is commonly referred to generically as *ampitany* (out there). Rather, *tromba-istes* have concerned themselves with how remnants of the global might be brought together to enhance their own spiritual beliefs and practices and to make sense of their own unique local position in a global ecumene (imagined though it might be). Furthermore, Malagasy truths are interactive, contestable, fluid, storied. Malagasy conceive these truths in part as sets of participatory past-engaging processes, not necessarily as static reiterations nor affirmations of true worlds out there.

CHAPTER NINE

Style as Iconicity of Aesthetics

[S]tyle (as *dulugu ganalan*) is more than the statistical core reflection of the place and time, or patterned choices made within constraints. It is the very human resources that are enacted to constitute the reality of social life in sound. Style is itself the accomplishment, the crystallization of personal and social participation; it is the way performance and engagement endows humanly meaningful shape upon sonic form. Style is an emergence, the means by which newly creative knowledge is developed from playful, rote, or ordinary participatory experience. Style is the way an internalization and naturalization of felt thoughts and thought feelings guides experience. (Feld 1988: 107)

Morondrano ("water's edge") had two halves, run through by the profuse Maningory River. One half of this Betsimisaraka village was the endpoint of a hilly, partially paved road, approximately forty kilometres from Fénérive-Est. On this side of the river, village commerce was conducted. Bananas from across the river were either sold there or taken from there to Fénérive-Est for sale; there was a small *hotely* (restaurant that serves basic Malagasy rice dishes), a *betsabetsa* stand, and a small market. To get to the distant side of Morondrano it was necessary to cross the Maningory by *lakana,* a metal pirogue three or four metres long propelled by a Malagasy youth pushing against the mud-thick river bottom with a long metal pole.[1] This was a factory-made, riveted-together vessel, an old rusting remnant of colonial era productivity. At the docking area on the more residential distant half of Morondrano sat a huge rusting backhoe, long since immobilized and sunk into the mud. Broken down and captured by the very earth it was once meant to dig up and develop, this mechanical remnant of European modernization commemorated some abandoned colonial project. Perhaps it stood as a taunting sign to the people of Morondrano of unrealized colonial plans for their village. The backhoe also elicited a power inherent in Malagasy land, ancestral place of rest, which had swallowed it up and frozen it in place.

The other side of Morondrano was a collage of forested hillsides and ones deforested by slash-and-burn agriculture. The air was thick with the syrupy smell of rotting pressed sugarcane, the residue of *betsabetsa* production. I had come to this half of Morondrano to search for an accordion player named Tsiariagna. Two young Betsimisaraka boys led me through about a kilometre of sparsely wooded area, steeped in mud and cow manure, to Tsiariagna's house. As we trudged barefoot, often up to our calves in thick wet muck, my guides giggled at my silly jokes: "Tsisy vorogna amin'ilay hazo eto Morondrano izegny, fa omby izay magnano elatra fô" (There must not be any birds in the trees in Morondrano, just cows with wings).

I had been hearing stories about Tsiariagna's extraordinary, even legendary accordion playing almost everywhere I went in the Tamatave region. My friend Jaka (Betsimisaraka for "Jacques") in Fénérive-Est, the town's *mécanicien* (there were only a handful of automobiles owned in the town) had once played an old distorted tape he had of Tsiariagna for me. Indeed, Tsiariagna's style of accordion playing struck me as quite unusual in comparison to that of other Betsimisaraka. Melodically, it was extremely ornate and elaborate. Tsiariagna often did not emphasize a regular rhythm or one at all with his left hand (the chordal accompaniment side of the instrument); and he employed much manipulation of performative dynamics, such as crescendo and accelerando. There were also several *valses* on this tape, which were also elaborate and ornate in melody, dynamics, and harmonic structure, in ways distinct from the performative styles of other Betsimisaraka.

Tsiariagna was not in Morondrano on the day I first went to search for him. His wife and son were at home, though, and his wife told me, rather uninterestedly, that he had left for Vavatenina, a village about forty kilometres from Fénérive-Est in another direction, to perform for a *tromba* ceremony. I wrote a note of introduction to leave for him. His teenage son told me that Tsiariagna would come into Fénérive-Est to search for me within the next few days. This encounter was unusual, for it was the first time I had visited Malagasy people who had shown little interest in being visited. In other villages, as well as in Tamatave-ville, I had grown accustomed to being welcomed, invited to eat rice, to stay and chat. The air in Tsiariagna's house was complacent, unresponsive, and perhaps even scornful, all confusing since I had seen other Malagasy be particularly gracious and hospitable to strangers, even *vazaha*.

In this chapter, I want to look into Tsiariagna's style of accordion performance, which resounded with an iconicity of an irregular aesthetics of both everyday and ritual life. Indeed, to many other Betsimisaraka (he was not known among Antandroy in Tamatave-ville), Tsiariagna's style of performing on the accordion was less representative of their familiar combinative aesthetics of *maresaka* than of a distinctly *vazaha* or colonial aesthetics. Other Betsimisaraka had employed incorporative principles to take in elements and recollections of colonialism and other foreign contact in Madagascar, principles by which the (once) foreign could be fragmented and recombined as something distinctly Malagasy. Tsiariagna was consumed by a desire not to fragment and incorporate the colonial but to exactingly sound like and inevitably to *be* it.

Although Tsiariagna did perform for some *tromba* ceremonies, none of the *tromba-istes* represented in this writing ever employed his services at their ceremonies. One reason was that his rate was excessive, and his style was commonly thought to be too divergent, too *vazaha*-like. Tsiariagna represented to many an overflow of difference, by and for itself rather than combined.

In a move iconic of Malagasy propensities for reorienting things, for finding new or different value in them, I have reordered Steve Feld's "aesthetics as iconicity of style" (1988), which refers to a Kaluli sound sense in Bosavi, Papua New Guinea.[2] I have done so to address some specific qualities that other Betsimisaraka and I as well noticed in the performative style of this particular Betsimisaraka accordionist. I am suggesting that Tsiariagna's musical style and his style of conducting himself in everyday life had co-evolved (also Feld 1988) as an intentional iconicity of an aesthetics of a colonial past. I reiterate the distinction between a colonial-like aesthetics and a Betsimisaraka aesthetics that incorporates only components of the colonial. Tsiariagna's style, both musical and social, exuded forceful signs of individualism, aggressiveness, and class sense. These characteristics contrasted greatly with the aesthetic components prevalent among many other Betsimisaraka. Most found his style peculiar and rejected it; an elite few shared Tsiariagna's aesthetic orientation and adored his musical style.[3]

On Style

Dick Hebdige (1979) has written extensively on historical components of different musical styles in England. Also recognizing a historical significance in regard to style, Susan Sontag has written

[T]he notion of style, generically considered, has a specific, historical meaning. It is not only that styles belong to a time and a place; and that our perception of the style of a given work of art is always charged with an awareness of the work's historicity, its place in a chronology. Further: the visibility of styles is itself a product of historical consciousness . . . the very notion of "style" needs to be approached historically. Awareness of style as a problematic and isolable element in a work of art has emerged in the audience for art only at certain historical moments—as a front behind which other issues, ultimately ethical and political, are being debated. (1990: 18).

In Madagascar and likely in other places throughout Africa (as well as elsewhere), performative styles themselves have created or perhaps have been created from different historical linkages to varied pasts. For many Malagasy on the east coast, style is inextricably connected to beliefs about and sentiments for the past, for one, its nature of *métissage*. Betsimisaraka *basesa* itself is often conceived stylistically as a combination of both *vazaha* and (other) Malagasy traits—recall that Jily and Roger explained *basesa* as having evolved from both the northern *salegy* and the *valse*. Yet different styles are also differentiated by Malagasy and connected to dissimilar pasts. For example, Antandroy style is commonly imagined by non-Antandroy to be connected to a past of savagery from a distant place, Africa itself (chap. 11). Tsiariagna's style at another extreme mimed particular facets of colonialism, sometimes to the exclusion of such familiar feelings for *métissage* in Madagascar.

Charles Keil, for one, has evoked connections between musical style and class forces (1985).[4] Indeed, Tsiariagna's musical style was in part a strategy with which he enunciated his sense of class distinction from other Betsimisaraka. For Merina who expressed an avid fondness for Edith Piaf and colonial era jazz, stylistic preference could also be part of a desire to express class distinction. Thus, wealthier Merina could distance themselves from impoverished Merina as well as from other Malagasy through their taste in music, performed on exclusive musical occasions at the Alliance Française in Tamatave-ville. Tsiariagna also used his musical taste and performative style as public displays of distinction.

On the musical role of individual volition in urban areas of Africa, Chris Waterman agrees with Stephen Blum that musical style "carries *traces* of the processes through which the performer has effected and realized his choices, has established his personal (and social) 'stance' or position" (Blum 1975: 217, quoted in Waterman 1990a: 7). In "The Trace of the Other" (1986), Emmanuel Levinas described the trace as "a presence of that which properly speaking has never been there, of what is always past" (p. 357). Mark C. Taylor elaborates upon Levinas's idea, "The trace marks the lapse of time by remarking the way in which the pre-original *anarchie* comes toward the subject as departure. Never arriving or arriving only as departing, the trace opens everything but is not itself disclosed" (1987: 205). An ungraspable *ouverture,* a difference that never arrives. Applying this image, Tsiariagna, so enamored of the colonial, embodied a trace of colonial aesthetics, social events, and inevitably of Europeans themselves. He had taken on a phantom nostalgia (Emoff n.d.) for something that could never quite be disclosed to or bestowed upon him.

Even though he had occasionally been hired to perform for European social events, Tsiariagna had never been accepted into European social circles. He remained always an Other to his European patrons. His highly individualized accordion style, with its primacy of melodic development, irregular dynamics, and suppression of the driving left-hand rhythmic emphasis, comprised an iconicity of a colonial aesthetics informed in part by elements of materialism, self-interest, and commodification. Ironically, this very European aesthetics was often concomitant with a condescension toward Malagasy people and their expressive forms. Tsiariagna had created for himself a no-man's-land, an *entre-deux* in which only traces of the European could echo through him, in which he had alienated himself from many of his Betsimisaraka compatriots.

Rhythm of Insistence: Commodification and Payback

Several days after receiving the note I had left for him, Tsiariagna showed up in Fénérive-Est with one of his teenage sons, the one I had met in Morondrano. He sent some local children to find me, and they led me to a *hotely* at which Tsiariagna had stopped to eat. He was perhaps in his early fifties. He was shoeless, revealing that he had a severe birth deformity in both feet. Eating rather voraciously, he stopped abruptly upon catching sight of me and led me outside the *hotely*. He dispensed with any of the usual introductory pleasantries and launched into an aggressive interrogation about how much money I would pay him for coming into town to meet with me. All this struck me as very strange behavior—I had not known Malagasy to interrupt a meal, forgo the introductory talk that usually opened an encounter or conversation, or engage in direct aggressive questioning.

I was willing to pay Tsiariagna for his trouble to come into town, though it was not my desire or practice to set up play-for-pay sessions. However, after much dealing we agreed upon a price for such a session—he was already in town and the stories I had heard about his legendary performance skills had made me curious. We agreed to record one side only, on Tsiariagna's insistence, of a ninety-minute cassette tape for an amount equivalent to three months' rent for a house in Fénérive-Est, still much less money than Tsiariagna had initially demanded.[5] Almost everyone in Madagascar was concerned to some degree with money (or the lack of it), but I had not known any musician to be so openly confrontational, persistent, or aggressive about it.

Tsiariagna here and in later encounters revealed himself to be an experienced culture broker. Judging from his demeanor with me and others, he also seemed bitter and driven by some sense of retribution, perhaps for his constraining physical deformity, for his historically undercompensated talent, or perhaps even for eventually being abandoned in Morondrano by his colonial models, an abandonment memorialized by the aged backhoe left behind on the muddy dock of his village.

Tsiariagna and I met the next morning at the Restau-doany, a small hotel and restaurant run as a cooperative by varied Fénérive-Est town officials. Several Fénériviens showed up, including Jaka, as well as Gasy Alfred (a name specifying that the French name Alfred referred here to a Malagasy man), an accordionist from a nearby village. Tsiariagna again dispensed with the common introductions, with me as well as with other Malagasy present. He was accompanied by his son and another man. He demanded coffee, bread, fried eggs, and then rum before they would play. Providing these things, of course, was no problem for me, though Tsiariagna's open demand again was quite unusual. He was rather surly.

Tsiariagna's repertoire consisted largely of non-*basesa* compositions, based, for instance, on duple or 4/4 meter, and included numerous *valses*. In the few *basesa* he played, as well as in the other compositions, he used techniques I had not heard deployed by other Betsimisaraka accordionists. In addition to those qualities already mentioned, Tsiariagna frequently elaborated melodically, for instance, with rapid sixteenth- or thirty-second-note diatonic runs over an extended pitch range, mechanically difficult to perform on the button accordion. He occasionally employed a technique in which each eighth note of a melodic motif was doubled, forming pairs of sixteenth notes, a sort of tremolo; he also used a very fast alternation between two adjacent notes for a vibrato effect. Betsimisaraka Corso accordions come from the factory with sets of reeds wet-tuned—in this case that means there are three reeds per pitch, each tuned only a few cycles per second away from one another. Thus, each button, when depressed, produces its own tremolo effect. With his method of note doubling and rapid alternation, Tsiariagna was effectively quoting and intensifying the tremolo-effect voicing built into his accordion, a voicing, of course, aesthetically pleasing to Europeans, who had developed such accordion tunings in the first place. Antandroy completely retune this tremolo effect *out* of their accordions.

As on the tape Jaka had played for me, Tsiariagna commonly played long linear phrases that might extend in range over two octaves. He used the left-hand chordal accompaniment buttons sporadically, sometimes allowing left-hand parts to drop out all together. Other Betsimisaraka accordionists might vary the left-hand accompaniment in performance, though the left hand rarely, if ever, stopped providing some chordal pattern. Tsiariagna also fully exploited the harmonic potential of the diatonic accordion, adding frequent key changes and sometimes making transitions to keys that were structurally limited by the diatonicism of the instrument. Other Betsimisaraka accordionists also might deploy key changes, though not to the extremes exercised by Tsiariagna.

Tsiariagna's melody-privileged style brought to mind the jazzlike linearity of the improvisational sections of non-*tromba* accordion *basesa*. In contrast, though, he de-privileged left-hand rhythmic/chordal parts, and he generally ignored the more common, restrained style of improvising within replicable phrases in the "head"—his style was more consistently linear and more autonomous in form. In addition, his vocabulary of improvisational phrases was quite distinct from that of other accordionists. Tsiariagna's elaborate melodic excursions and ornamentations, with left-hand rhythmic accompaniment backgrounded or left out, often made it difficult to follow him even on *kaiamba,* an accompaniment usually so vital to most musical performance among Betsimisaraka as well as other Malagasy.

At one point in this recording session, Tsiariagna boasted that in his youth he had often been paid handsomely by Europeans to perform on accordion for their social events and that he had even been paid by Europeans on several occasions to make tape recordings of his music for them, which he claimed then became very popular back in France. A European fondness for Tsiariagna's style of performing on accordion contradicted other European reactions, in which Malagasy ceremonial musics were commonly assessed to be *trop répétitive* or *pas assez intéressante*. Similar distaste for Malagasy musical style(s) had been expressed in earlier colonial accounts. The following was written near the end of the colonial regime in Madagascar:

Tantôt aussi, il n'existe dans les vers (des chansons traditionelles) aucun idée de rime; tantôt on rencontre de assonances qui n'interviennent que pour l'agrément de l'oreille. Très fréquemment enfin, la chanson ne possède pas d'unité dans l'idée qui l'inspire, pas de sens suivi, et les motifs sont indépendants les uns des autres. Le rythme seul en constitue l'unité, c'est le seul lien qui réunit les vers. (Decary and Faublée 1958: 273)[6]

Sometimes as well there is no hint of rhyme in the verses of traditional songs; sometimes one encounters assonances which only interfere with the ear 's capacity for enjoyment. The song frequently as well has no compositional unity, no coherence, and the motifs are independent of one another. Only the rhythm gives the song any unity—it's the only bond that brings the verses together.

Another colonial observation depicted Merina musics at that time as "simple et monotone," of a "pauvreté harmonique" and a "developpement trop court" (Rason 1933: 42, 59). More broadly, Europeans have commonly taken what they perceive as the centrality of rhythm in African musics as a musical sign of primitiveness and underdevelopment.

Tsiariagna's constant and elaborate harmonic and melodic ornamentations, with his use of accelerando and crescendo, lent a certain romanticism and sentimentality to his style, especially juxtaposed with the *basesa* based upon improvisations within a short-duration phrase structure I had more commonly heard elsewhere. I use "romantic" and "sentimental" here as deliberate referents specifically to nineteenth-century European Romanticist aesthetics and conventions of composition, characterized in part by relative subjectivity in the expression of musical emotionality and more formal autonomy in composition. It seems possible that Tsiariagna had some knowledge or experience of such a Romanticist aesthetics, one quite likely expressed among French settlers and overheard in Madagascar during the colonial era, which in its early stages coincided with the Romantic period (approximately 1820 to 1910). Perhaps Europeans reflectively had found Tsiariagna's style all the more Romantic not only because he replicated so well their own musical *sensibilité* but because it was so replicated by this deformed, excluded Other, a hobbling primitive aspiring nobly to mirror back to colonials their own aesthetics.

Noely, a teenage Betsimisaraka boy who worked at Restau-doany, told me that Tsiariagna was *tegna mahay* (an extraordinarily capable player), though his style was *mitovitovy ilay mosika vazaha* (more like that of *vazaha* music). Noely and other workers at Restau-doany told me that they much preferred the playing of other local accordionists, who performed more *basesa* and in a more familiar style. Back in Tamatave-ville, Roger Jean Louis also said that Tsiariagna's style was more reliant on European principles *(karaha ilay mosika vazaha)* than that of other Betsimisaraka accordionists. He played one of the *valses* for me that Tsiariagna was known for playing but in his own more familiar and widely acceptable style.

Jaka the mechanic, on the other hand, expressed an adoration for Tsiariagna's style, indicative perhaps of his own desire and preference for European-like things. Jaka was part of a very small Betsimisaraka elite sometimes found in towns like Fénérive-Est, Betsimisaraka who were usually Christian (i.e., not *tromba-istes*) and who held important civic positions such as that of *fonctionnaire*. It was not uncommon for these Betsimisaraka to emulate European-like styles and aesthetics. For instance, Jaka's house was an old colonial-style two-story, rare in Fénérive-Est, and it was filled with European-style furniture. Jaka also had a large component stereo system (rather than a small magnéto), something I had seen nowhere else in Fénérive-Est. In addition, Jaka preferred to converse with me in French rather than Malagasy. He was one of the few people on the east coast with whom I communicated in French. Jaka seemed to enjoy sharing with me his knowledge of worlds outside Madagascar.

Tsiariagna himself boasted that he did not play like other accordionists, that his style was unique, that it was more expressive: "'Zaho tsy mitovy ny sasany—raha fa midôla akordôgna 'zaho dia moramora, miadana izay. Mipetrapetraka ela sy miteny betsaka ity mosika ity" (I'm not like the others—when I play the accordion, it flows easily, and it slows down in places. In my musical style the notes stay longer and speak more). It was unusual simply to hear Malagasy make such direct stylistic analyses, much less such a vaunting self-evaluative, detailed, and exclusionary one. About her own style of performing on accordion, Jily once told me, "Tsy mpôla mahay mikoragna ny tantarakô" (I'm not yet able to tell my own story). This comment undoubtedly was multilayered, embedded with varied meanings. I took it in part as Jily's humility at speaking analytically about herself.

Tsiariagna also enacted an unusual sense of self-distinctiveness during the recording session when he handed his accordion to Alfred and goaded him to play. Alfred, embarrassed and timid before Tsiariagna (the legend), shyly declined, stating modestly, "Tsy mahay 'zaho," (I'm not good enough). Alfred, however, was quite respected locally as an accordionist. It seemed as though Tsiariagna had anticipated or solicited Alfred's deference to his own playing, which was so proficient on European terms.

Some of the titles of Tsiariagna's compositions were also idiosyncratic and unusual. Titles of other Betsimisaraka compositions often had to do with ancestral spirits or with collective sentiments about land, custom, and family, such as Roger's, "Tanoran'i Dadilahy," (Grandfather's youngest). One of Tsiariagna's *valses* was entitled, "Tsiariagna mizaha raha roa" (Tsiariagna has his eyes on two things). This title is unusual in its pronounced subjective centrality of the musician/composer, Tsiariagna himself. It is also implicit with sexual desire and objectification–the "two things" being women. While women occasionally are objectified in Betsimisaraka songs, it is usually with some proverbial, universal message, such as "It's not good to fight with your wife."

Discussing Style in Tamatave

Some Malagasy musicians on the east coast infrequently made subtle stylistic evaluations, often based upon linguistic difference. Once, when discussing differences between Betsimisaraka and Antandroy musics, Vinelo told me, "Tsy mampitovy azy, dia ilay resaka tsy mitovy. Hafa ny resaka hoe teny frantsay, hafa ny resaka teny anglisy, hafa ny resaka Sakalava, hafa ny resaka Betsimisaraka, hafa ny resaka Antandroy" (Those ways of talking are not the same. French talk, for instance, is different, English talk is different, Sakalava talk is different, Betsimisaraka talk is different, Antandroy talk is different). Vinelo was not referring specifically to linguistic differences in song texts, for instance. He was implicating these varied musics themselves as different forms of *resaka* (talk—resaka is contained nominally in *maresaka*, its meaning virtually interchangeable), as different ways of communicating, especially with the *razana*. In Vinelo's reference to *teny frantsay* and *teny anglisy*, he was also differentiating between Antandroy music and certain foreign musics that he knew were not intended to communicate with ancestral spirits (recall Vinelo's belief that some musics, such as reggae and *zouk*, were based *in* Madagascar even though they were sung in English or French).

Betsimisaraka *valiha* player Tombo Daniel restated Vinelo's subtle linguistic-based differentiation between Antandroy and Betsimisaraka musical styles: "Tsy mampitovy anazy ilay fitenenana" (Those ways of speaking aren't the same). Tombo Daniel also explained to me early in my research, "Dia rehefa tena mahay tsara mihitsy anao izany amin'ilay teny Betsimisaraka izany, amin' ny teny gasy, dia mahay mosika gasy koa anao. Atero voa hay anao ilay 'langue' ilay olona, dia hay anao mitendry ilay hira" (So once you are completely fluent in the Betsimisaraka dialect, with our ways of talking, then you'll also be able to play Malagasy music. Once you know someone's language, then you can play their music). While neither Vinelo nor Tombo Daniel explicitly voiced it exactly this way, I believe they were both getting at two major music/language junctures: one, that each individual Malagasy dialect has its own lyricality, rhythm, timing, and timbres that transfer into similar musical principles of articulation; and two, that each different group of Malagasy speak musically to their *razana* with unique musical styles of expression.

Enacting Style

In my experience, Malagasy generally are loath to criticize or to say unflattering things about other people. There were, however, several harsh stories about Tsiariagna in the Fénérive-Est area (though I had to dig somewhat for them). Several Betsimisaraka told me that Tsiariagna was a habitual drunk who could become quite mean. Two good friends in Fénérive-Est—Jean Freddy, a brilliant and sensitive songwriter and singer, and his wife, Marcelline, a teacher at the local primary school—had a particularly disturbing story to tell. Taking turns narrating in their small (two-room) rented house in Fénérive-Est, Jean Freddy and Marcelline told me that, in the 1970s, Jean Freddy had put together a band that was beginning to have national success performing largely his own original compositions.[7] He had been hired to play for a *bal* in Fénérive-Est, and he was to share the bill with Tsiariagna, who would play traditional accordion *basesa* to complement Jean Freddy's electric guitar band *basesa*. Jean Freddy's band at that time had its own full set of instruments and amplifiers, supplied by Betsimisaraka president Ratsiraka (who tended to support and sponsor Betsimisaraka musicians). During the time I spent in Madagascar, a time much more economically lean than the 1970s, owning or even having access to things such as electric guitars was most often only a broken dream.

Marcelline said that while Jean Freddy and his band were taking a break from playing at the *bal*, Tsiariagna, drunk and brooding over Jean Freddy's musical success, destroyed the band's irreplaceable instruments. This put an end to Jean Freddy's musical career. With his creative outlet destroyed, Jean Freddy sadly stopped writing songs and took to drinking heavily.

There were similar stories about Tsiariagna that made it difficult to remain objective toward him. Yet his style was clearly marked and differentiated by other Betsimisaraka, so I continued to pursue a relationship with him, sometimes rather reluctantly. Our visits were always strained by Tsiariagna's insistence on dwelling upon money and his stark enumerations of things he wanted me to buy for him. Other *tromba-istes* with whom I associated understood that I was conducting research; they acknowledged and appreciated that I was truly interested in their ancestral customs. Tsiariagna seemed concerned only with selling himself and commodifying his talent.[8]

Appadurai evokes instances in which people in distant places create imitations of other worlds although "the rest of their lives is not in complete synchrony with the referential world which first gave birth [to these imitations]" (1996: 29). Of course it is possible that a new referential world of the imitation can replace or operate independently of the referential world of the original. Tsiariagna's own world of experience, though, was not filled with European-derived sentimentality. His was a "sentimentality" driven by the daily exigencies of material poverty, of always coming up short, of disdain at only being able to trace his desires onto situations that could not support them, of an overall resentment of the inequity of his condition.

With his very colonial-like aesthetics, Tsiariagna "looked back to a world he had never lost" (ibid.). Appadurai has discussed a "nostalgia without memory" among Filipinos who appropriate American popular musics. Tsiariagna more likely experienced a memory without a truly knowable or ownable nostalgia.[9] He might have regularly been a paid guest providing simply the musical soundtrack for colonial *bals*, though he had never been an equal participant at these events (reminiscent perhaps of Sammy Maurice's recollections of being at colonial *bals*). He had cultivated his own phantom nostalgia for a mode of expression that would always remain foreign to him, that had commodified and yet excluded him, and that inevitably made him into a peculiar foreigner in his own homeland.

Among most Malagasy, *maresaka* is an aesthetic that affects both musical style and everyday accordant social interaction. While Tsiariagna had distorted this aesthetic by individualizing and attempting to commodify it, he had yet left intact its capacity to infuse musical style and social style into one another. Other Betsimisaraka musicians had created imaginative musical composites that interacted productively with the past; Tsiariagna and his hypercompetent (Appadurai 1990:3) replication of colonial style had become dislocated in a colonial excess of mimetic appropriation.

All of the Betsimisaraka accordionists I knew had a repertoire of *valses*, but most of these musicians seemed to consider this a peripheral genre, for instance, in its unusual disconnection from an accompanying dance form. Other than Tsiariagna, Betsimisaraka accordionists did not often play their *valses* unless specifically asked to do so. Their style of performing these *valses* conformed basically to that of ceremonial *basesa*, for instance, in privileging improvisation within short-duration phrase structures. Tsiariagna's *valses*, on the other hand, were a focal genre to him, and his style of performing them subverted conventional performance parameters—for example, to privilege long linear excursions over a great pitch range, with unusual timbral manipulations. The *valse* itself was recollected differently by Tsiariagna. For other Betsimisaraka, the *valse*, although distinct from *basesa*, was yet a transformational genre, one more Betsimisaraka than European. For Tsiariagna, the *valse* seemed stylistically an expression of European aesthetics and of his own desire for personal distinctiveness.

A Word on Hybridity

Asserting its ambivalence, Homi Bhabha has written:

Hybridity is a problematic of colonial representation and individuation that reverses the effects of the colonialist disavowal, so that other "denied" knowledges enter upon the dominant discourse and estrange the basis of its authority—its rules of recognition. . . . The presence of colonialist authority is no longer immediately visible; its discriminatory identifications no longer have their authoritative reference to this culture's cannibalism or that people's perfidy. (1994: 114)

Hybridity here represents in part the capacities of colonized peoples to subvert colonial dominance into conditions of "intervention." Expanding upon possibilities for hybridity to represent more than simply a counterforce,

Robert Young has found in Bakhtin's notion of "unconscious" or "organic" hybridity ("generative" hybridity that tends toward fusion) a "pregnancy [that] gives birth to new forms of amalgamation rather than contestation" (1995: 21). It has been suggested that Malagasy do not use the composite forms and processes of *tromba* practice simply or primarily to "estrange the basis" of colonial authority. On the east coast of Madagascar, *métissage* is always already a style of being, recollecting, and interacting. "Hybrid"[10] forms have not arisen there as oddities emanating from colonial or postcolonial inequities. Combining has been a natural (historical) process in Tamatave. This is one reason that many Betsimisaraka heard Tsiariagna's style as odd. It was too de-hybridized, too distinctly *vazaha*-like to be effective for them.

Earlier in this book, Tombo Daniel and particularly his wife, Marcelline (not to be confused with the wife of Jean Freddy), are presented somewhat similarly as Betsimisaraka culture brokers. They have performed in France, they charge a much elevated fee to perform for *tromba* ceremonies in Tamatave, and some *tromba-istes* shun and will not hire them. However, there was no aversion among *tromba-istes* to Tombo Daniel and his style of playing *valiha*. Most Betsimisaraka praised him and his musical style, which *was* compatible and congruent with that of other *valiha* players. Rather, it was Marcelline's temperament that many wished to avoid, and she was usually blamed for forcing Daniel to charge inflated fees. While Tombo Daniel's musical integrity was not in question, the *valiha* itself—its structural makeup, its timbral capacities, the repertoires playable on it—perhaps has discouraged excesses of the European or European-like to be expressed upon it. Recall that *valses* are not performed on the *valiha*.

෴

Tsiariagna's style was an unusual sort of "crystallization of personal and social participation," lacking the more common maneuvering through colonial social events to incorporate fragmented images or sounds from them. His style expressed a desire to freeze time, rather than to juxtapose varied times, as is more common among other Betsimisaraka. As iconicity of an aesthetics of colonial individualism, exclusivity, and musical virtuosity, Tsiariagna's ornate style brought him a considerable amount of social displacement in the present, a displacement he did not seem to mind.

CHAPTER TEN

Discourse on Illness, Healing, and Abnormality

ᔐ

In the second half of the eighteenth century, medical science began to rely on a distinction between the normal states of the body and its pathology, that is, its diseases and abnormalities. Disease, abnormality and immorality became linked in a powerful trinity which is still in force today. (Mirzoeff 1995: 45)

[I]f something is said or done that is the open expression of a shared hidden transcript, the collective exhilaration of finally declaring oneself in the face of power will compound the drama of the moment. There is power in numbers, and it is far more significant than the now long-discredited sociology that treated crowds under the rubric of mere hysteria and mass psychopathology. (Scott 1990: 66)

Suffering, its alleviation, and subsequent joyous celebration are all vitally interconnected and intersubjective experiences in *tromba* ceremony. There is the difficulty of the moment of possession itself. The *tromba* spirit enters convulsively into the medium's body. It then might abuse the medium's body by consuming much rum, smoking an excessive number of cigarettes, or drinking a litre or more of purifying water from the Indian Ocean. After possession, though, mediums rarely complain of aftereffects such as hangover or digestive disorder; they are often simply *reraka*, or fatigued. Also hard on the ceremonial body is the illness that *tromba* might inflict upon a medium. Such difficulties, however, inevitably give way to the joyousness of interaction with the *razana* and with other *tromba-istes*.

It is pertinent to note here that *tromba* spirits represent a curative paradox. They can heal illnesses caused by some other source, yet they can also inflict and then release a person from an illness they themselves have imposed. Such infliction is usually a sign of a *tromba*'s desire to possess a particular person, though sometimes it is also an expression of a *tromba*'s displeasure with the behavior of a medium. In the case of *tromba*-imposed illness, the cure consists of ceremonially inviting the inflicting *tromba* into the body and hence entering into a relationship as that *tromba*'s medium. In healing illnesses caused by some other source, the spirit is called into a medium's body so as to heal someone else who has come to the healer/medium for assistance. While Malagasy believe in either instance that possession cures the illness, it has commonly been the colonial or other European interpretation that possession itself is pathologic.

The spirit, not the medium, most often possesses the knowledge and skill to heal difficult illnesses. Sometimes unpossessed *ombiasa* are also able to mix herbal remedies for some ailments, a skill commonly facilitated by *sikidy* divination (which according to some Malagasy in Tamatave is another mode of communication with ancestral spirits). Thus, healing is commonly dependent upon a powerful Other presence, which nevertheless has to speak and act through the Malagasy body. Healing calls for cooperative effort between present and past, everyday and royal, interior and exterior, living and dead. Sound itself is in a particular sense curative, as music and other sound production has the power and indeed is necessary to bring the healing spirit into a medium's body from which it effects its remedies.

In one case, I accompanied Vinelo, both an accomplished Antandroy musician and a powerful spirit medium and healer, over several weeks to cure a woman who was displaying symptoms of severe psychic distress. Her behavior was erratic—one moment she would be sullen, unresponsive, gazing off distantly; the next moment she would be agitated, incoherent, even violent. Vinelo said this was a *viavy minegny,* a woman out of her mind—this would be an extremely difficult illness to cure. This was one of the few healings I witnessed that involved an overt "mental" illness, in contrast to more common occurrences of bodily illness.

In the several healings of this woman I attended with Vinelo, he would become possessed by a powerful Sakalava *tromba,* to music provided by Velontsoa on *valiha* and Nofy Soa on *kaiamba.*[1] Even with all the ministerings from Vinelo's *tromba,* the woman's erratic outbursts countered by periods of disengagement persisted. After four sessions, Vinelo's royal *tromba* himself decided that he would need to inhabit the body of the afflicted woman to affect a cure. After three more ceremonies, in which the patient herself became possessed, her psychosis-like symptoms disappeared, and she became timidly communicative and consistently personable. This was the first time in my experience that a *tromba* had needed to possess a person with an illness not initiated by that particular *tromba* to be able to effect a cure. Vinelo assured me that this was not uncommon. And it was specifically a powerful foreign spirit that had to take control of the body to heal the abnormal psyche. Here the foreign (Sakalava) *tromba* spirit played a crucial role in restoring order where abnormality had prevailed.

As part of a remedy, *fagnafody* (medicinal mixtures of herbs and tree barks) are commonly mixed by the healing *tromba* while in the medium's body (or by the unpossessed *ombiasa*) and given to the afflicted person to be ingested or applied upon the body. Such mixtures are specifically referred to as *fagnafody gasy*, "Malagasy medicine," in contrast to *fagnafody vazaha*, "European medicine" or French-produced pharmaceuticals, which could be purchased in larger towns in a *farmasy*. Sometimes other purifying agents, such as the blood of a rooster, has to be applied directly to a part of the body. There are other types of *fagnafody* that externally applied to the body, effect behavioral control over others, such as in cases of unreciprocated love or children who might not be obeying their parents' wishes.

Antandroy *ombiasa* Tsiately once warned me of the maleficent talents of some northern Betsimisaraka. He admonished me that, if a Betsimisaraka woman from the north ever cooked chicken for me, I should subtly take a piece of the chicken bone, excuse myself, and go out into the courtyard, break the bone, and toss the fragments into the soil. This, he assured me, would protect me from any poisoning motivated by jealousy. Tsiately's preventive remedy indicates that spiritual healing or protective powers, whether *tsara* or *ratsy* (good or bad), did not merely work physiologically, for I would not need to ingest something myself to protect me from poisoning. Instead, by breaking the bone and dispersing it in the courtyard dirt, I would be calling upon the *razana* to intervene spiritually in the space of my own body, to protect me from what might have been a physiologically active chemical agent. Sometimes *fagnafody* itself acts internally in the body, or it is applied topically upon it. It might also be placed in the environment around it.[2]

Jesosy

Recall the evaluation made by the elderly Merina man at the *famadihana* ceremony near Antananarivo, "Christianity for one didn't need to be forced upon us—this spirit, Jesus, sounded familiar to us; he fit well with our preexisting beliefs and practices involving our own ancestors. We *took* Christianity ourselves because it suited us and our own spiritual beliefs." I often heard similar expressions on the east coast, in which stories about Jesus were said to resound with preexisting Malagasy beliefs in their own *razana*.

Christian doctrine, of course, recounts Jesus's capacity to heal the sick. Malagasy have certainly heard these tales. Perhaps *tromba-istes* in particular found similarities between their own curative practices and European discourses on healing (or salvation)—both after all involve a powerful healing

spirit Other. Taking into account as well Malagasy propensities for fragmenting and combining, especially to do so across and through different
time periods, it seems natural (i.e., historical) that colonial and postcolonial
discourses might have become entangled with Malagasy beliefs about possession and healing. In accordance with principles of *maresaka,* and in
mind of the power inherent in the talk of foreigners, perhaps fragments of
colonial beliefs and observations have paralleled and even affirmed Malagasy practices, even to co-evolve into them.

Among *tromba-istes,* anti-Christian behavior or discourse was very
rarely if ever expressed to me. In fact, as previously illustrated, icons from
Christianity often possess incorporative value in *tromba* practice. Several
Betsimisaraka *tromba* mediums even told me that they believed in Jesosy.
Honorine had been married in a Catholic church. The scent of the incense
burned in church is similar enough to that of the *emboka* used in *tromba*
ceremony, and therefore, Honorine's *tromba* had agreed to allow her to
partake in such a Christian-style ceremony.[3] Hanging in her *tromba* house,
Marie Yvonne had a painting of a Bible opened to a page that had simply
"Jesosy" inscribed in red on it. She told me that she had *nangata-dalana
tamin' ilay tromba,"* "asked permission of her *tromba,"* to believe simultaneously in Jesosy, and her *tromba* had consented.

Tatasy confirmed early in my stay in Madagascar: "Il n'y a pas d'effets
même si on croit au *tromba* et au réligion à la même fois. Le *tromba*
n'empêche pas les hommes d'aller à l'église"; as translated from Malagasy
by Kiki: "There's no harm in believing in *tromba* and European Christianity at the same time. *Tromba* don't prevent people from going to church."
Fulgence Fanony, minister of education when I was in Madagascar, has
even described a *tromba-mompera* (from *mon père*), the spirit of a European priest that at one time possessed mediums in Betsimisaraka *tromba*
ceremony (1975: 271).

Malagasy Christians, on the other hand, commonly expressed a belief
that *tromba* detest Christianity and Jesus. These Christians also believed
that bringing the Bible as well as some other signs of Christianity anywhere
near the body of a *tromba* medium angers and drives away *tromba* spirits.

Public Hysteria

Indeed science only emerged as an autonomous set of discursive values after a pro-
longed struggle against ritual and it marked out its own identity by the distance
which it established from "mere superstition"—science's label for, among other
things, a large body of social practices of a therapeutic kind. (Stallybrass and
White 1986: 174)

A graphologist, an expert in writing styles, or a psychoanalyst could interpret a trace's singular signifyingness, and seek in it the sealed and unconscious, but real, intentions of him who delivered the message. But then what remains in the specific sense a trace in the writing and style of the letter does not signal any of these intentions, any of these qualities, reveals and hides nothing. In a trace has passed an absolutely bygone past. In a trace its irreversible lapse is sealed. Disclosure [*dévoilement*], which reinstates the world and leads back to the world, and is proper to a sign or a signification, is suppressed in traces. (Levinas 1986: 357, quoted in Taylor 1987: 205)

Europeans throughout the past have commonly thought possession practices in Madagascar to be outbursts of irrationality, hysteria, or demonic embodiment. *Tromba* practice in many instances confirmed to colonials as well as to later observers the immorality and backwardness of the local "savages." In many cases denigrative discourse among colonials about *tromba* likely filtered "down" to Malagasy. Such colonial disapprobation was certainly transferred more overtly in French prohibitions against *tromba* practice and in widespread Christian sermonizing about the evils of spirit possession. The story of the naming of *basesa* itself attests that Malagasy on the east coast were overhearing colonial era European evaluations and then imaginatively making new sense of them.

In a 1928 Malagasy newspaper article, *tromba* among Betsimisaraka was referred to as an *aretin-demony,* a demon-sickness, and as

tena aretin'tsaina mpanimba ny fanahy sy ny vatana tokoa izy io [ny *tromba*]. No sady mamohehatra ny firenena sy mety hikasika ny fanjakana koa aza, fa manimba ny toetr'olombelona mihitsy ("Ny 'manongay' na 'tromba,'" 1928).

a serious disease of the mind, *tromba* is a destroyer of the soul and the body. Also, it is injurious to the people and will perhaps affect the government as well, but it is definitely destroying our quality of life.

More extensively, in the following colonial medical report, possession practices throughout Madagascar were credited as bouts of hysteria:

Les rapports annuels de 1909 des médecins chargés de Fianarantsoa et de Nossi-be signalent la fréquence relative, nous forme d'allure épidémique, d'une affection nerveuse survenant par crises, appelée en Emyrne "*ramanenjana*," "aretin'bilo," ou "bilom-bara" en pays Betsileo, et "Menabe" chez les Sakalava.

"Aretin-bilo" signifie maladie de la danse et "bilom-bara" danse des Baras. Les principaux symptômes de la crise, qui survient généralement au lever ou bien au coucher du soleil, consistent en effet en mouvements frénétique de danse—à l'approche de l'accès, le malade prétend ressentir à l'épigastre une brûlure qui remonte vers la gorge, accompagné de frissons, de refroidissement des extrémités, puis de tremblements du corps et de la tête qui est projetée dans tous les sens pendant que les membres supérieures tout agités de façon plus ou moins rythmique. A ce moment, spontanément ou poussée par son entourage qui l'y convie, le malade se met à danser, hors de sa case, souvent sur les tombeaux des ancêtres. Les assistants frappent des mains, chantent, tapent sur des objets ou jouent du tambour pendant que la danse s'accélèrer et que des spectateurs plus ou moins nombreux s'y mêlent, atteints à leur tour de la même crise ou parfois, semble-t-il, la simulant. D'ailleurs quelque soient la violence des mouvements et de désordre des gestes, les malades semblent conserver conscience de leurs actes. La vie d'étoffes de couleur vive, rouge en particulier paraît souvent les inciter et entraîner un paroxysme de la crise au cours de laquelle beaucoup déchirent leurs vêtements. Le mal atteint surtout les femmes qui sortent de la crise prostrées, se plaignant de cephalée. L'intervention d'une personne ayant sur les malades quelque autorité; un ordre nettement donné; un coup porté; ou l'immobilisation forcée des individus en periode d'excitation, la compression des globes oculaires, des testicules, des ovaires, les moyens utilisés dans l'hystère produisent l'arrêt de la crise. Des mesures administratives énergiques, la menace de sanctions ont suffi pour enrayer l'extension du mal qui, dans le sud, au cours de l'année 1909, se propageait rapidement. (Archival Document H 298)

The annual reports of 1909 from doctors in charge of Fianarantsoa and Nosy be indicate the relative frequency of a form of epidemic, a nervous affliction that comes in bouts, called in Merina territory "*ramanenjana*," "bilo-illness," or "Bara bilo" in Betsileo territory, and "Menabe" among Sakalava.

"Bilo-illness" indicates a dancing sickness and "Bara bilo" the dance of the Bara. The main symptoms of the attack, which generally occur at sunrise or sunset, consist of frenetic dance movements—as the symptoms advance, the afflicted claims to feel a burning in the abdomen that rises toward the throat, accompanied by shivers and chills in the extremities, then trembling of the body and the head while the limbs move restlessly more or less rhythmically. At this moment, either spontaneously or goaded by the entourage that has assembled there, the afflicted person begins to dance, often on the ancestral tombs. The participants clap their hands, sing, beat on objects or they play drums while the dance heightens and the many onlookers mingle, themselves susceptible to their own bout of the crisis, or sometimes it seems, simulating it. However, in spite of the violent movement and disordered gestures, the afflicted still seem to be aware of their acts. Materials of vivid colors, red in particular, often seem to excite and evoke a bout of the crisis in the course of which many tear at their own clothes. The affliction overtakes particularly the women who come out of the crisis prostrate, complaining of headache. The intervention of an authoritative person; an order distinctly given; a blow; or the forced immobilization of the excited individuals, pressure on the eyeballs, the testicles, the ovaries, these are the means used in hysteria to bring about an end to the crisis. By emphatic administrative action, the threat of sanctions have sufficed to halt the diffusion of the affliction which, in the south during 1909, was spreading rapidly.

Most of the symptoms described in this medical account—"frissons," "refroidissement des extrémités," and "tremblements du corps," for example—are also common symptoms of malaria, a disease historically rampant throughout most of Madagascar, especially in the two regions named above, Fianarantsoa and Nosy be. In their haste to confirm psychic abnormality, colonial medical observers might have in some cases mistaken the common symptoms of malaria-induced fever, *ny tazo*, for instances of hysteria/possession.

And the violent bodily intervention by colonials to disrupt what they determined to be hysterical episodes among Malagasy—swift blows, pressure on the eyeballs, testicles, or ovaries! *Tromba* as well are powerful Others from distant places. Perhaps some of the difficulty of *tromba* practice—punishments inflicted by *tromba* upon mediums, excesses of rum and cigarettes, hyperventilation and other bodily irregularities—signal a sort of imbricated recollection that incorporates colonial assaults upon the Malagasy body. Forced labor, oppressive colonial taxation policies, and the extreme of colonial torture and mutilation were other colonial forces imposed in one way or another upon the body. I shall return to the centrality in the above account of dancing as a pathologic symptom.

In the Malagasy Lutheran church, weekly exorcisms are commonly held to expel unwanted *tromba* supposedly plaguing Christian Malagasy.[4] Sedy Roger was the pastor of the Lutheran FLM church in Tamatave-ville. Each Monday evening there he conducted such a *tromba* exorcism service. Five or six pastors dressed in long white robes with Bibles in hand served as the exorcists. The afflicted people in the congregation would come to the front of the church to kneel and be "treated" by the pastors. This usually consisted of placing the Bible, often rather forcefully, upon the head of the afflicted person (the head is often the point of entry of *tromba*) while shouting vociferous threats at the *tromba*, such as "Mivoaka amin'ny anaran' i Jesosy!" (By the name of Jesus, get out!). Usually an hour or so of this aggressive treatment was enough to symbolically drive away *tromba* (for most of these people were not actually possessed by *tromba* during these services but had experienced some outside indication that *tromba* were interested in them).

There was one particularly difficult case involving a ten-year-old girl. Her deceased father had been a Betsimisaraka *ombiasa*, and the spirit of the father had for some time been trying to possess his daughter. The girl was usually tied up in restraints, for her body would tense and convulse violently when approached by Sedy Roger and the other pastors. She would require focused ministering from all the pastors at once, sometimes over several consecutive hours. The ministers would scream insults at the *tromba*, slap at the girl's head with their *bibles*, as well as at her head and abdomen with their open hands. This was a dramatized contestation between *tromba* and Lutheran pastor over control of the young girl, her body as field of contestation. In a sense these exorcisms, especially this difficult one, trace a historicized struggle for control over the minds and bodies of Malagasy people, waged in part by Protestant missionaries and of course by French colonials in Madagascar. The techniques used by the pastors to offend and expel *tromba* also resemble in form the "therapeutic" assaults upon the "hysterical" body described in the colonial medical account above. Upon my last communication with Sedy Roger, the young girl had not yet been "cured."[5]

Kiki, who usually accompanied me to see Sedy Roger, was skeptical of these exorcisms (though she was not at all skeptical anymore of *tromba* practice). She suggested that these services might have been dramatizations, a hoax intended to strengthen the congregation's Christian beliefs by contraposing them against an evil, abnormal, and immoral Malagasy alternative. The young girl herself told me that she really wanted to accept the spirit of her father, but her mother was forcing her to go through this exorcism process.[6] Some amount of religious ambivalence was not uncommon among Christian Malagasy, who often found it difficult or undesirable to fully ignore or vilify spiritual and ancestral links to their pasts.

Lutheran hymns were sung by the youth in the congregation at Sedy Roger's exorcisms. Interestingly, these hymns were sung in the Merina dialect, the dialect into which Lutheran doctrine had originally been translated by European missionaries in the Haut Plateau region, rather than in Betsimisaraka spoken by most of the congregation. These musical church events actually relied upon some of the combinative components of *maresaka,* as in the ceremonial mix of hymn singing and a chorus of out-of-phase shouting from the pastors co-occuring with much physical commotion. This density of aural, visual, and corporeal activity was also being employed to affect *tromba* spirits, though negatively. Interestingly, as in *tromba* ceremony, a hierarchy was espoused, Jesus, of course, being a supreme spirit. About the hymns themselves, Sedy Roger told me that they were *ilay teny Andriamagnitra* (the words of God). Sedy Roger went on: "Manatanjaka ilay fagnahy 'pasteur' raha mbola miasa izy, fa mampatohatra ilay tromba ireo hira ireo. Ilay hira manome herim-pô amin'ny 'pasteur' raha mbola miasa izy," (The songs strengthen the pastor's soul while he's working, but *tromba* are afraid of these songs. The hymns give courage to the pastor while he's working). Thus, the hymns in a sense are doubly curative: they can be internalized beneficially by the Christian body while simultaneously expelling evil from the abnormal spirit-inflicted one.

These musical events actually relied upon some of the combinative components of *maresaka,* as in the ceremonial mix of hymn singing and a chorus of out-of-phase shouting from the pastors occurring with much physical commotion. This density of aural, visual, and corporeal activity was also being employed to affect *tromba* spirits, though negatively. Interestingly, and in *tromba* ceremony, a hierarchy was espoused, Jesus, of course, being a supreme spirit.

Dancing Sickness

A widely publicized spirit possession event in Madagascar was the *ramanenjana* phenomenon of 1863.[7] Lesley Sharp, in her book on migration and *tromba* practice in northwestern Madagascar, writes:

The *ramanenjana* or "dancing mania," which occurred in the Merina capital of Antananarivo in 1863, is perhaps the most large-scale resistance movement against foreigners involving religious forces. At this time, the streets were crowded with hundreds of people possessed by the dead Queen Ranavalona. The possessed often disturbed and even attacked Europeans, many of whom were Protestant missionaries. (1993: 48)

Maurice Bloch describes *ramanenjana* as "a popular reaction to the apparent disintegration of traditional culture" under the reign of Radama II (1986: 145), who had sought to widen connections with Europe while generally abandoning Malagasy customs. Bloch writes that people in the central Haut Plateau region became possessed to act as messengers calling for the return of Queen Ranavalona, rather than as embodiments of the queen herself, as Sharp suggests. According to Bloch, this wave of possession was specifically an attempt to force Radama II to restore the circumcision ritual from which he had disassociated himself by decree in 1862 (ibid.). Bloch also refers to *ramanenjana* as "dance mania" and "spontaneous possession"[8] (p. 27) and as "mass hysteria" (p. 145). "Mania" and "hysteria" clearly echo colonial pathologizing of Malagasy ritual practices.

In 1889 the London Missionary Society published a detailed account of the *ramanenjana* in the Haut Plateau region, compiled by missionary Andrew Davidson. He described a "choreomania" of "dancing and singing carried to an extraordinary and abnormal extent" (p. 19). Davidson elaborated:

[O]ne could not go outside without meeting bands of these dancers. . . . We found even in the remote hamlets, and, more wonderful still, near solitary cottages, the sound of music, indicating that the mania spread even there. . . . The native Christians had no difficulty in recognizing it as a true demonical possession. . . . The patients usually complained of a weight or pain in the praecordia, and great uneasiness, sometimes as a stiffness, about the nape of the neck. Others, in addition, had pains in the back and limbs, and in most cases there seems to have been an excited state of the circulation and occasionally even mild febrile symptoms. . . . If they happened to hear the sound of music or singing, they got perfectly uncontrollable and, bursting away from all restraint, escaped from their pursuer and joined the music, when they danced sometimes four hours at a stretch with amazing rapidity. (Pp. 21–22)

The most intellectual of all the senses, that of hearing, is always affected to a remarkable degree, as evidenced not only by the morbid desire for music, but by the illusions connected with this special sense. . . . The music served to regulate and control the wild muscular movements that might otherwise have proved injurious. (Pp. 24–25)

Davidson also wrote that many dancers "professed to have intercourse with the departed, and more particularly with the late Queen" (p. 23).

Davidson's narrative portrays Malagasy as primitive though sometimes wonderful savages who are controlled in this case by their "morbid" taste for music, reflected as well in their morbid sexual desires. Music, which usually affects "the most intellectual of all senses," in this narrative reaches down corporeally to regulate the otherwise uncontrolled bodily movements of the possessed. While Davidson diagnoses music here to be abnormally sentient and corporeal, in opposition to its more cerebral "natural" character, he also suggests that Malagasy music and dance could be *curative*. In the cases of Malagasy possession he observed, dance apparently regulated movement and thus was a preventive as it controlled "the wild muscular movements that otherwise might have proven injurious." It appears overall that Davidson was not certain whether he felt Malagasy music and dance to be beneficial or symptomatic. His narrative also reflects a common European-conceived separation between mind, representative of control and propriety, and body, which stands here for primitiveness and immorality.

Antonio Scarpa, an Italian doctor who visited Madagascar in 1962, made this observation about Malagasy ritual performance: "Le rythme qui dure des heures et des heures, est absolument obsédant et même le système nerveux le plus équilibré ne peut éviter à la fin d'en ressentir les conséquences" (cited in Blot 1964); (The rhythm which continues for hours is absolutely haunting and even the most balanced nervous system cannot in the long run avoid experiencing its consequences). This evaluation fails to conceal Scarpa's own obsession—it is *his système nerveux le plus équilibré* about which he writes. Indeed, Davidson also expresses his own fascination with the "more wonderful still" sound of music in the remote villages. While both of these Europeans associated Malagasy expressive practices with disorder and abnormality (Davidson somewhat paradoxically), they also might have been implicating their own perverse attraction. Both imply a longing or compulsion to participate in the abnormality and immorality of these events, to abandon mindful control, and to become immersed in local corporeal pleasures. These two writers seem to have felt the affective, immersive powers of Malagasy music and dance themselves.

In these accounts, *ramanenjena* is portrayed as the act of an agitated hysterical mob, subject particularly and often focally to bouts of hysterical dancing.[9] On pages 305–6 of the colonial medical report quoted above, dancing is also focused upon as pathology. The following appears in another colonial era account:

[*Tromba*] n'attaque pas les gens intelligents et instruits. . . . Le traitement institué par les habitants est le suivant: chant avec applaudissement, bouteille à verre blanc moitié pleine d'eau froide . . . si le malade danse, la guerison est rapide, par contre le malade ne danse pas, la guerison est lente. (Archival Document D112, no. 5)

[*Tromba*] does not afflict intelligent, educated people. . . . The following is the treatment used by the locals: song with clapping, a bottle of plain glass half full with cold water [possibly placed on the head while dancing—a sign of the bodily control exercised by the *tromba*] . . . if the afflicted dances, the healing is quick, but if the afflicted does not dance, the healing takes much longer.

In this observation the curative dimensions of dancing are again suggested.

It is possible that the possessed in 1863 *were* publicly embodying resistant sentiments shared with Queen Ranavalona, whose policies had been staunchly anti-European.[10] Recall James Scott's observation, which opens this chapter: "if something is said or done that is the open expression of a shared hidden transcript, the collective exhilaration of finally declaring oneself in the face of power will compound the drama of the moment. There is power in numbers, and it is far more significant than the now long-discredited sociology that treated crowds under the rubric of mere hysteria and mass psychopathology." Yet dancing, as in many other practices throughout the world, can be a vital facet of healing in Madagascar. Could *ramanenjana* have been more than an outward expression of public resistance, to encompass something internally empowering? Perhaps *ramanenjana* was also an attempt, en masse, to heal the afflicted Malagasy body, of the dis-ease of European presence and pressure.

Tromba-istes in Tamatave have been adept at cleverly reordering the intent and timbre of often contemptuous colonial discourse. Once overheard in Madagascar, European condemnations of Malagasy dancing and musical expression, as pathologic, abnormal, even immoral, have likely been taken in and revalued by Malagasy, to become even complementary reflections back upon their practices. Ceremonial dancing has perhaps become more empowering to Malagasy through European discourse about it. As with the sometimes strange, condescending, or even incomprehensible talk of Georges Klintsky or Sadam Hoseny, for instance, foreign discourse can create empowering *maresaka,* fuel for further creative articulation.

Foreign Illness

Several times when I was chatting with Sammy Maurice in Betampona he turned to the topic of disease. He once told me:

Ary ny olona indraiky tamin'ny andron'ny vazaha tegna ravô indraiky satria afaka ny nendra, ny nendra tamin'ny andro talôha afak'i vazaha. Afaka ny bôka, afak'i vazaha. Ny vazaha ihany nagnala ireo farasisa taketô Madagasikara. Atao ny olona ohabo-lana: "Lelahibe tsy mpôla lany ketsa, tsy mpôla afaka haretina.' Tonga frantsay ni-foagnany ny ketsa io. Tsisy farasisa fa ny ketsa.

And during the colonial era people were extremely happy that *vazaha* could cure smallpox. They could also cure leprosy. Only *vazaha* could cure cases of syphilis here in Madagascar. We have a proverb: 'It is a great man whose rice plants are not all gone, he will not become sick.' When the French came, rice crops flourished. There was no syphilis; there was rice.

Sammy Maurice synthesized images of the abilities of French colonials to cure local diseases with the prosperity and health implicit in an abundant rice crop. Some of the diseases that colonials could cure, however, had actually been introduced and spread *by* these very foreigners in Madagascar. Rice itself was not indigenous to Madagascar but had been brought, likely by Southeast Asians. As with *tromba,* foreigners could both introduce and alleviate illness, bring and take away prosperity (colonials, for instance, took charge of the natural resources in the Tamatave region).

As mentioned, the first Europeans in Madagascar were quickly driven away by their susceptibility to local disease; by 1895 nearly six thousand French colonials in Madagascar had been killed by disease; and in the anticolonial insurgence of 1947, *tromba* spirits were said to have mystically left emptied uniforms of French and Senegalese soldiers strewn across battle sites. As with Vinelo's difficult patient, *tromba* spirits have sometimes taken an intrusive role in restoring order, in correcting abnormality. Illness itself has been a varying text in which power has been inscribed upon the body in Madagascar, a text in which colonial order (or colonial discourses of disorder) could be mirrored, transformed, or integrated back into Malagasy practices. Boundaries between *vazaha* and ancestor are commonly complicated or blurred by and in the ceremonial body, which can incorporate and express both Malagasy and European characteristics.

Malagasy have certainly revalued and internalized some colonial concepts, materials, and criticisms. Colonial evaluations that foreground the significance, albeit abnormal, of Malagasy dance and musical expression have perhaps actually fed back into and empowered Malagasy modes of healing. Europeans share with *tromba* spirits an aura as powerful Other, capable of greatly affecting daily life among Malagasy. With *tromba*-imposed illnesses in particular, inviting the afflicting *tromba* into the body is essential to curing the illness. This specific facet of possession perhaps encodes in part a reconciliation with foreign presence. While healing the body, such possession can in part signal some healing of a grievous colonial past. In *tromba* ceremony, fragments of ancestors and *vazaha* combine, inevitably joyously. The ceremonial body and the past work reciprocally upon each other, each ameliorating the condition of the other.

꿍

I used to imagine the magazine cutout models on Betsimisaraka *tromba* house walls, their gaze set fixedly out upon Malagasy ritual, to be traces of adjudicating colonial gazes that had overseen similar Malagasy practices. These initial colonial gazes commonly led to diagnoses of the pathology of Malagasy ritual action, based in part upon Christian beliefs that separate Spirit and body. To *tromba-istes,* spirits and body are intimately connected. Such a separation would itself be abnormal on Malagasy terms. And perhaps Betsimisaraka *tromba-istes* have returned this Other curious gaze fixed in the magazine photos, internalizing some of its foreign power, absorbing and revaluing the traces of its evaluative yet desirous glance. Malagasy have certainly displayed other varied capacities to retune and refine foreign voices so that they echo back favorably upon their own practices.

CHAPTER ELEVEN

Imagining Antandroy in Tamatave-ville

〜

Narratives based upon difference and exclusion sometimes circulate among Malagasy in the Tamatave region (as well as elsewhere in Madagascar). Merina are often said to have better access to positions of political, social, educational, and economic privilege than other people in Madagascar, and they are frequently suspected of being *fetsifetsy,* deceptive and untrustworthy. Merina are commonly said to be most closely and purely connected to Southeast Asian ancestry, which can be a factor in imagining an elevated Merina class and group distinctiveness. This particular connection might reflect another distinction, sometimes made among Europeans between "high art" cultures of Asia and "underdeveloped" African cultures.[1] Coastal peoples in Madagascar are generally believed to be more closely connected to Africa.

Sakalava are supposed to be particularly receptive to Europeans, to seek out interaction with them, and are sometimes said to be somewhat arrogant to other Malagasy. Betsimisaraka are often deemed to be lazy, apathetic *côtiers,* a perception that echoes some early European evaluations of local people in Tamatave. Northern Betsimisaraka in particular are more often rumored to be *mpamôsavy,* or evil spell-casters.

Myth of the Antandroy Savage

There is a particular essentializing narrative commonly expressed in Tamatave, in which Antandroy are quite often portrayed and feared as primitive wild men and women, as dangerous foreigners.[2] Antandroy are also believed and feared to possess extraordinary spiritual powers. Similar sentiments about Antandroy are also expressed outside the Tamatave region. Once, at a *tromba* ceremony in Diégo in the north, the presiding *tromba* (a male spirit in a woman's body) told me that I ought to marry a

Malagasy woman but that I should absolutely avoid Antandroy women who, he said, are savage *(masiaka),* unclean *(maloto),* and bad-spirited *(ratsy fagnahy).* I also commonly heard discriminatory remarks toward Antandroy made with some frequency in the capital, Antananarivo.

Stories about Antandroy from other Malagasy were always extreme, almost panicked: "Antandroy are fiercely argumentative, confrontational, violent," "An Antandroy will kill you just to get one thousand Malagasy francs (the equivalent of about twenty-five cents) from you," "Don't ever go into an Antandroy *quartier*—Antandroy will cut off the head of a stranger who goes foolishly onto their turf." And then gendered dehumanizing slurs: "Antandroy women don't cleanse themselves; they are rough, even violent sexual partners; they like to bite; they carry disease." Antandroy are also commonly said to dance too wildly or to argue among themselves as well as others too aggressively. With some frequency other Malagasy would describe Antandroy as sub- or pre-human primitives, driven by aggressive instinct rather than by reason.

Dida once told me quite melodramatically that an Antandroy would cut off a person's head simply over pocket change.[3] It is possible that Dida was simply trying to joke with and agitate me, though in spite of his avid passion for music, he absolutely would not venture into Antandroy territory in Tamatave-ville with me. Dida's wife warned vehemently that Antandroy are obstinate and aggressive and that no one in Tamatave-ville would pass through their local neighborhoods for fear of being murdered. Dida and his wife were both wealthy Protestant Merina and undoubtedly were projecting and improvising upon the disdain and fear perpetuated in Protestant as well as some elitist class discourses in Madagascar.[4] Indeed, if Merina were not the ones telling tales of Antandroy terror, it was usually other Christian Malagasy (among non-*tromba*-practicing Betsimisaraka in Tamatave, Catholicism tends to be more prevalent than Protestantism). Excesses of Antandroy spiritual and ancestral prowess are and have been an abnormality and immorality particularly heinous to many Christians in Madagascar. While most Malagasy believe in one way or another in the *razana,* the collective of ancestral spirits, it seems that too much spirit power in the wrong hands is often feared to be a bad thing, even a manifestation of evil.

෴

Colonial impressions of Antandroy savageness and backwardness were commonly recorded. One colonial era observer wrote, "Les Antandroy, qui habitent à l'extrême-sud de Madagascar entre les Antanosy et les Mahafaly, forment la population la moins évoluée de l'île" (Grandidier 1959: 191; The

Antandroy, who live in the extreme south of Madagascar between the Antanosy and the Mahafaly, constitute the least evolved group of the island). In another colonial account, Antandroy were depicted as irreverent and even cruel: "L'antandroy est extrêmement moqueur, riant de tout et de rien, d'une femme qu'il rencontre, d'un chien qui se sauve dans la brousse, d'un faux-pas qu'il fait en marchant, riant aussi à l'occasion du blanc, malgré le respect qu'il professe pour lui" (Decary 1933: 35; The Antandroy embodies ultimate mockery, laughing at everything and nothing, at a woman he meets, at a dog that scurries into the bush, at a stumble he takes while walking, laughing also at the white person notwithstanding the respect he professes for him).

Antandroy in Tamatave-ville tend to live and work segregated from other Malagasy. By their very distancing they are more readily a mystery to others. Most Antandroy convey a general aura of disinterest in the goings-on of other Malagasy (except in regard to music) or Europeans, preferring intense immersion in their own ancestral customs. In a town with a long history of contact with foreigners and much familiarity with modernizing influences, Antandroy self-seclusion seems to be taken as a sort of recalcitrance by some Malagasy (though anti-Antandroy sentiment in Tamatave-ville itself undoubtedly plays back into such a desire for seclusion). There is also a style of being Antandroy that visually sets them apart, a style that includes carrying spears, largely for herding cattle in the south but often transformed into a guardian's symbol of power and fear in Tamatave-ville; sporting blue-painted straw hats and silver bracelets; wearing clear plastic sandals rather than some other kind; and sometimes bearing blue-green tattoos on their foreheads, which identify an Antandroy's ancestral village (these tattoos are said to be emblazoned on with a knife dipped in battery acid).

Some non-Antandroy Malagasy recall a particular Antandroy connection to Africa, not only a spatial displacement but a temporal one as well, in which Antandroy become associated with a premodern world of African "savagery." Imagining Antandroy in this light can take on a moral quality— Africa as place of unrestrained wildness perhaps reflects colonial and missionary discourses depicting it as "the dark continent." Yet Africa can be recollected in a positive light as well among Malagasy. For instance it is a place to which *vazimba*, the first inhabitants of Madagascar, are ancestrally connected.

Dancing Savages

A few times I heard an association made specifically between Antandroy and Zulu people from South Africa. Zulus have commonly been represented in the media dancing wildly, carrying spears, wearing loincloths—all things potential signs of being Antandroy as well. A specific history of Zulu anti-apartheid struggle in South Africa is sometimes familiar to some Tamatavi-ens. Here Antandroy might serve as sign of foreign wild man *as well as* sub-tle evocation of nearby struggles against oppression and injustice, conditions that feel familiar to many Malagasy.[5]

On occasion I heard non-Antandroy Malagasy even draw a connection between Antandroy and *peaux rouges*. *Peaux rouges*, "red skins," refers of course to Native Americans. Some Malagasy had learned about "Indians" in primary or secondary school, though the term is often picked up from viewing American Westerns, dubbed into French and shown frequently at video houses and at the one cinema in Tamatave-ville. Upon discovering that I was from Texas, some Malagasy would grin and say, "Téxas Cité!" (French orthography here), apparently a reference to a particular Western (with which I was not familiar). Antandroy are associated not only with the wildness of Native Americans, whooping and dancing as portrayed cine-matically, but perhaps as well with mediated images of their subjugation and suffering, often at the hands of others. In support of this, Antandroy are sometimes implicitly admired by other Malagasy for withstanding fre-quent long droughts and other extreme hardships in the south of Madagas-car. Antandroy also are admired in recollections of their pronounced, sometimes legendary resistance to French colonization. There are numer-ous stories about Antandroy tenacity against French colonial attempts to intrude into their ancestral homeland in the south—Antandroy are recalled to have effectively fought off French rifles with just their spears.

Antandroy dancing, vigorous and unrestrained, is often conceived by them as another mode of communication to and with ancestral spirits. In-deed, such dancing is often met with a combination of fascination and re-pugnance by other Malagasy. Antandroy could more broadly be an ambiv-alent force in Tamatave-ville, implicitly admired as people most powerfully connected to revered ancestral spirits and most capable of surviving adver-sity. Antandroy are at the same time seen as dangerous foreigners to be feared and for the most part avoided. Yet signs and images of Antandroy music and dance are commonly incorporated into popular or commercial musics in Madagascar.

⁊

I walked through one of the Antandroy sections of the bazary be in Tamatave-ville this evening—had not yet met any of these vendors. At each stall I was invited in by strangers to eat rice out of a communal bowl on a mat on the floor. All of these Antandroy had large families and seemed to have few material resources. After stopping and partaking in the evening meal with five different families, all very gracious and friendly, I went to find Vinelo, who was already settled in front of Dida's quincaillerie to guard it for the night. I relayed the story of the vendors' generosity at the market and of my dismay that strangers with barely enough food for themselves would share it with me, a *vazaha* obviously capable of supplying myself with nourishment. Vinelo said, "Havana Antandroy amin'izao 'anao, ka tsy maintsy mihinambary amin'ilay Antandroy hafa" (You are Antandroy kin now, so you have to eat rice with other Antandroy).

I later recalled Dida's nervous admonition about Antandroy beheadings and widespread aggressiveness—indeed, I had never seen any indication that Antandroy felt any animosity for other Malagasy or that they were subject to bouts of senseless violence. In fact, Vinelo himself *protected* Dida and his business interests, as Antandroy guardians did for other wealthy Merina throughout Tamatave-ville. Antandroy are so needed in Tamatave, yet they are widely (and unjustly) disdained.

(From my notes, January 13, 1994)

∽

The extremely fast tempo and unusually intricate rhythmic, melodic, formal, and processual dimensions of Antandroy musics are often incomprehensible to some Malagasy.[6] Betsimisaraka *tromba* performance, for example, relies on what might be described as medleys, of perhaps two or three musical compositions strung together into one musical segment. There is usually a sense of one composition beginning and ending before it then gives way to another. Among Antandroy, formal structuration is looser. A musician might return numerous times throughout a performance to a specific motif, varying it differently each time and sequencing it in different combinations with other motives. Antandroy performance thus creates an improvised and autonomous flow rather than a more rigid process of passage from one explicit composition to the next.

Such processual freedom among Antandroy *tromba* musicians could contribute to the aural iconicity of Antandroy wildness construed by some other Malagasy. Antandroy were seen to possess excessive abilities to improvise, to step beyond other limitations upon form, articulation, and sheer musical speed, to possess a musical acuity that translates directly into ancestral communicative power. Especially to many non-*tromba-istes* in Tamatave, Antandroy were thought to produce an overflow of *maresaka*.[7] Detty and several other Betsimisaraka *tromba-istes* told me they were actually fond of the intensity of Antandroy music. Detty specifically said that she admired Antandroy because "tegna mahay fombandrazana 'zareo (Antandroy are extremely strong in ancestral ways).

Antandroy on Radio

The radio/cassette magnéto is a device that commonly evokes desire among Antandroy. When requesting that I take formal photographs of them, Antandroy (and sometimes Betsimisaraka) commonly insisted on holding in plain view a magnéto, even if one borrowed solely for the taking of the photograph. This machine could be a medium through which varying, and sometimes elusive signs of power passed.

Antandroy *tromba* music is virtually never broadcast over the Radio Nationale in Madagascar. Yet denatured sound bits from Antandroy musics are quite popular when segmented, filtered, and reined in through the recordings or performances of popular musicians such as Rossy, Poopy, or Tarika.[8] Images of Antandroy are sometimes used by these musicians to invoke a poetics of loss, one represented by the particular hardships of Antandroy. In Tarika's song "Haintany" ("Drought"), for instance, the narrator, who is implicitly Antandroy, laments the extreme conditions in southern Antandroy territory through images of starving children and widespread sadness (this song appears on *Bibiango*, Green Linnet CD 4028). Antandroy *lokanga* (three-stringed bowed instrument) or *ndrimotra* breath singing are also frequently copied and incorporated by Tarika and other pop stars, in part to instill among others a sympathetic nostalgia for Antandroy.

Upon first entering Antandroy *tromba-iste* Nofy Soa's one-room house in an Antandroy *quartier* on the outskirts of Tamatave-ville, I noticed etched in the rusting *tôle* roof the single word, *mampalahelo*. This term expresses a collective and pervasive sadness. Indeed, sadness, dislocation, loss, and yet perseverance are prominent intersubjective components of Antandroy experience in Tamatave-ville. Sound bits of Antandroy musical practices could evoke images of suffering, disconnection from ancestral homeland, and survival, experiences able to arouse anguish even among Malagasy who are not Antandroy.

Tarika and Rossy's bands also commonly enacted imitations of unique Antandroy dance and dress. This often included (un)dressing in loincloths and carrying spears (ironically, in front of an audience itself exclusively in European-like style of dress, an audience in Tamatave-ville usually with no Antandroy members). In such exclusive auditorium or stadium performance spaces, these musicians fragmented Antandroy savageness into purified images, disconnected from the peril these musical signs, when produced by Antandroy themselves, could arouse in the streets of Tamatave-ville.

While other Malagasy musically encoded and marketed a sentimentality drawing upon images of Antandroy poverty, suffering, and wildness, such expropriating processes themselves could rebound negatively upon Antandroy, effectively augmenting their suffering. For instance, Velontsoa and Vinelo sometimes expressed consternation over hearing sound bits of their own musics broadcast over the radio, for it is mostly Merina musicians who profit from popular hits reliant upon Antandroy-like musical signs and principles. Velontsoa and Vinelo had to struggle constantly to feed their families, while their own musical skills went unrecognized and uncompensated.[9]

The expensive magnéto radio-cassette player (or images of it) gave Antandroy some room to imagine a capacity to amplify, disseminate, and profit nationally from their own musics, a capacity itself beyond their grasp in Tamatave-ville. Obtaining the machine itself could in some sense represent a way of capturing and recycling some of the (copied) *maresaka* rightfully due them. Indeed, many Antandroy persistently expressed a strong desire to purchase a magnéto. Perhaps some Antandroy musicians had constructed their *mandôlina* to replicate in form this sound-producing machine (chap. 5) so as to reappropriate, symbolically though in other ways as well, musical ideals over which they had a just claim.

⁋

Certain Betsimisaraka and Merina lead an existence *entre-deux* in a particular fashion—they often practice Christianity while at the same time performing ancestral customs. A cause for anxiety among these other Malagasy, Antandroy can exist perhaps more effectively *entre-deux* in a different sense, between the world of the living and the world of the dead, without feeling inherent obstacles to their beliefs and practices imposed by Christian doctrine. Antandroy bring into the present a past from which some Merina, for instance, have disconnected themselves. *Tromba* spirit possession itself, for example, is often shunned by Merina, especially those more economically privileged. The past with which Antandroy connect so effectively is a past Merina must filter through ever-present reservation (to put it mildly) emanating in part from their experience as Protestants. While Antandroy might evoke fear and apprehension, other Malagasy can simultaneously be fascinated with Antandroy expressive culture, evident in the compulsion to tell tales of Antandroy savagery and terror and in the desire to creatively copy Antandroy performance practices.

Qualities of sound production can play into such an ambivalence. Merina and other Christian Malagasy commonly complain fervently that they find Antandroy music to be distasteful, that it is incomprehensible to them, even demonic. This last evaluation perhaps brings to mind more widespread tales of musical virtuosity so pronounced that it is feared to have been acquired only by making some pact with the devil. Through their expertise in improvising musically, in manipulating (what might be thought of as) a somewhat constraining diatonically tuned instrument, in composing and remembering such intricate music, Antandroy are able to create what others often hear as an excess of sound, which then signifies in part a dangerous excess of spirit connection and power.

Some Malagasy were clearly expressing a desire to have a say in constructing a particular ethnographic self, an imagined Antandroy savage. Christian Merina and Betsimisaraka wanted to influence the path of my (really their) ethnography, castigating Antandroy *as even more* Other and placing themselves, in even another sense, somewhere *entre-deux*. Having made a long, arduous trek from Ambovombe, someplace distant and often unfamiliar to other Tamataviens, Antandroy immigrants in Tamtave-ville play a role in a broader infusion of distant powers into the region, itself already imbued with reverence for varied spirit powers from the past and from distant places. Antandroy immigrants, "wild savages" or not, evoke good talk among other Malagasy in Tamatave. Such everyday *maresaka,* in this case as narrative, is also enhanced by a wealth of "foreign" sounds that Antandroy produce, just audible from the corners of Tamatave-ville's public spaces. In a sense, the ambivalence they evoke, the foreignness they bring in, the stories they fuel all make Antandroy into mediums that empower, if dangerously, the Tamatave region.

CHAPTER TWELVE

Retour

の

The longer I was in Madagascar, the less I could picture returning to the excess, velocity, ambition of the United States. There were many people to see throughout Tamatave before leaving, people who had taken me into their sacred practices, their families, their personal lives. Mendoe and Tompezolo were tearful and seemed even upset with me for leaving, as though I could have stayed if I wanted to. Full of perplexing details, this "option" still plagues me. Indeed, leaving felt in varied ways a betrayal, for one, as though I had got what I needed and was now abandoning my friends to ever-worsening economic conditions among other severe hardships in Madagascar.

Velontsoa was calm, yet reflexive of his own being away from home. He said "Tsara andeha hody ka mahita ilay papanao sy mamanao" (It's good to get to go home, to see your mother and father). Roger Jean Louis made me promise to write to him and to try to make a commercial release of the recordings I had made of him and to send him the profits (a CD with UNESCO is in the works — UNESCO allocates a sum of money for the musicians). Magnampy Soa and Very Soa reminded me to bring them *two* Vienna-style accordions. They gathered their large families on the sidewalk of the main street of Tamatave-ville, where they lived and worked, and together they chanted *tsodrano* and danced, a blessing for the voyage home. Vinelo, the friend with whom I had spent so many evenings sipping wine and chatting, insisted on meeting at 5 A.M. the next morning to go with me to the taxi-*brousse* station. We both joked nervously as we hauled my numerous bags and musical instruments, including the *valiha* Velontsoa had made and given to me, to the station. As the small truck was pulling away toward Antananarivo, I barely heard Vinelo say from a cloud of dust, "Aza adino!" (Don't forget!).

Musing upon his relationship with his Kuranko research assistant in Sierra Leone, Michael Jackson has recently written:

> As for me, I needed Noah to bolster my sense of humanity in a situation that constantly threatened to undermine it. For as long as I remained socially inept and linguistically incompetent, Noah was indispensable to me. I drew strength from him. This explains, no doubt, why I thought of him as a close friend. It was consistent with the way anthropologists have always extolled the virtues of "their" people, played up the emotional significance of their adoption into local families, and referred to individual informants as personal friends. But there is often a world of difference between these bonds of kinship and friendship in the field, and nominally identical bonds back home. The intimate and incorporative bonds of fictive kinship and friendship that belong to the fieldwork situation are frequently opportunistic and transitory; what they often connote is a deep sense of gratitude that the ethnographer feels toward his host community for having saved his or her sense of dignity in a culturally disorientating and debilitating environment. It is an overcompensatory gesture to the other for having recognized one's humanity, rescued one's ego, saved one's face. (1998: 104)

I hope that Jackson's generalizations upon his encounters arise from just a moment of skepticism, especially in consideration of his usual abilities to offer sensitive appraisals of ethnographic experience. And if relationships in the field are informed in part by opportunism and transitory-ness, whether "theirs" or "ours," is it perhaps unfair to suggest that such relational hindrances will emerge only when "we" interact with or among "them," out there somewhere? Back in the United States, for instance, some might recognize opportunism and transitory-ness as quite familiar styles of interacting there. Relationships between people in distant places and researchers who come to live among them cannot be reduced to a dependence of one upon the other for survival or profit. Certainly, these relationships vary with differing circumstances in different places.

Our very difference in part enabled and substantiated a closeness between many Malagasy and myself. Selectively incorporating otherness was in varied ways familiar, desirable, and indeed part of a complex Malagasy aesthetic that extended back through the past as well as outward across group, regional, and national boundaries. Reciprocally, I found Malagasy as well to be desirable others. Before ever going to Madagascar, I had long been attracted musically to difference, whether, for instance, in the unique timbral and compositional qualities of Leroy Jenkins' violin playing, the elegant twists and turns coaxed from Cajun (diatonic) accordions, the unusual chromatic capacities of North Umbrian small pipes, or the speed, complexity, and unique beauty of West African *kora* performance, to list only a few.

This writing is in part an attempt not only to represent but to step into Malagasy ways of performatively recollecting (from) varied pasts and of piecing things from these pasts together into aesthetically pleasing and meaningful wholes. I do not presume to have somehow captured a Malagasy aesthetic essence, which I can now transfer to the reader. Certainly, this book is only a bare replication or translation of some structural and procedural elements of *maresaka*. As Vinelo and others were constantly reminding me, it is best to sing, dance, clap hands, play accordion or *valiha* with *kaiamba* accompaniment, engage in much talking, among other actions—all in combination to *miresaka amindrazana,* to communicate with ancestral spirits. To adequately convey *maresaka* to people outside Madagascar would require that they also become immersed in such feelingful performative diversity and interaction. This book stands as fragmented image, as recollectful connection back to a more complete world of sounds, interaction, and other recollecting.

⁊

Twenty months later, the renovations of the terminal at the Ivato airport had been completed. No longer the barnlike structure I recalled, the building was now designed much like any other airport terminal. A Merina man dressed in suit and tie sat down next to me as I was waiting for my flight to Paris. He pulled out a photocopied pamphlet describing tours he would organize throughout Madagascar for *vazaha,* trying to interest me in one. I felt a moment of anguish, imagining touristic excess in Madagascar.

Upon entering Madagascar so long ago, a Merina customs agent had asked me in French if I had any French francs and if I'd like to make a "contribution"—to his family I supposed. This time a different customs agent joked with me in Malagasy, telling me that I'd likely be taking *tromba* back with me to the United States, and that Americans hence would become *tromba* mediums. He asked for a *cadeau vazaha,* a gift from outside, on my next return to Madagascar. Then his parting words strangely echoed Vinelo's own: "Aza adino!" (Don't forget!).

Notes

༂

Introductions (pages 1–24)

1. There has been very little literature written on musical practices in Madagascar and no previous work, to my knowledge, on music specifically in *tromba* practice. The following documents housed in the Aristivim-Pirenena (National Archives) in Antananarivo do contain some observations on music: Aujas 1927, Grandidier 1910 and 1917, Rakotomalala 1986a and 1986b, Rason 1933, Razakandraina 1962, and Shaw 1896. Outside the holdings of the Arisivim-Pirenena, the following documents involve Malagasy musics to varying degrees: Edkvist 1997, McLeod 1964, 1966, 1977, Norborg, 1981, Rakotomalala 1998 (although none of these documents specifically addresses musical practices in the Tamatave region). Charles Duvelle and Bernard Koechlin have written liner notes on several Ocora recordings of Malagasy musics. The recent CD series on Shanachie compiled in the capital of Madagascar, Antananarivo, by David Lindley and Henry Kaiser provides some useful information.

Estrade 1985 and Sharpe 1993 are concerned primarily with *tromba* practice. These are two very different interpretations of *tromba*, the first psychological/religious (Estrade was a priest), the latter predominantly functionalist.

2. I of course implicate myself here, as a Western academic, as part of the problem. But is not the point of reflexive ethnography to be somewhat self-critical?

3. Specifically on musical performance, see Béhague 1984, Coplan 1985 and 1994, Erlmann 1991 and 1996, Friedson 1996, Halbwachs 1939, Kapferer 1986, McLeod and Herndon 1980, Qureshi 1987, Stone 1982. For some other theoretical frameworks on performance, see also Bakhtin 1981, Barthes 1957, Bauman 1977, Bauman and Briggs 1990, Bauman and Sherzer 1989, Briggs 1988, Cantwell 1993, Cosentino 1982, Fabian 1990, Sherzer 1987, and Urban 1991.

4. Some Madagascar scholars might dispute the mutual unintelligibility of northern and southern Betsimisaraka dialects. Yet this difference was commonly, even vociferously voiced by many people in Tamatave. Such strong perceptions of difference and divisiveness among Betsimisaraka seemed important, even if such essentializing traits could not actually be substantiated.

5. This literature included the doctoral *thèse* of Eugène Mangalaza (1990); Fulgence Fanony's work on *fasigna* and other aspects of Betsimisaraka cosmology (1975); and Pascal Lahady's analysis of symbolic structures in Betsimisaraka practices (1979).

6. The Comaroffs have asserted that "all local worlds have their own *intrinsic* historicity, an internal dialectic of structure and practice that shapes, reproduces, and transforms the character of everyday life within them" (1992: 97). Local commuities are then also dialectically engaged with the historicity of external social worlds with which they have been in contact; each world "works to transform the other" (ibid.).

7. See Althabe 1969 and 1983 and Estrade 1985 on correlations between Christianity and *tromba* on the east coast of Madagascar. A discussion of religious discourse in Tamatave follows in chap. 10.

8. Jily usually charged from 7,000 to 15,000 FMg (Malagasy francs) per performance, which might have lasted all day and/or all evening. These sums converted then to about $1.60 and $3.50, respectively, in American dollars. A typical rent payment for a small one-room house in Tamatave-ville was about 15,000 FMg per month, so Jily actually earned a relatively large income, although in material terms she lived no differently from other Betsimisaraka. The usual income for an Antandroy who was hired as a shop guardian was 35,000 FMg (about $8.30) per month.

9. Musically, *hira gasy* performance among Merina is one form of expression through which their adeptness with verbal articulation is publicly displayed. These often day long events distinctively combine musical ensemble with elaborate sung orations, known for their layered and improvised political, social, and sexual meanings. These performances are also known for much discursive interation between various performers and audience members (Mcleod 1964 briefly mentions *hira gasy;* see also Edkvist 1997).

10. Gillian Feeley-Harnik's ethnography of western and northwestern Sakalava people, *The Green Estate* (1991b) is one of the more extensive ethnographic works on Madagascar to date. Although she is not primarily concerned with musical practices, Feeley-Harnik does discuss Sakalava *tromba.*

Chapter 2 (pages 25–36)

1. Anthropologist Michael Taussig offers some valuable thoughts on assembling histories in "History as Commodity in Some Recent American (Anthropological) Literature" (1989). After opening with Nietzsche, "There are no facts *as such*. We must always begin by introducing a meaning in order for there to be a fact," Taussig elaborates upon "the challenge and implications that the commodity-principle, understood historically, delivers to writing and rewriting the real" (23). Both writing histories as texts and enacting them in *tromba* ceremony involve laying claim to particular versions of the past. I would point out here that history in *tromba* practice is not without its own political "nature."

2. Mervyn Brown (1979: 111) gives 1823 as the date of Radama's arrival on the east coast. I rely upon Grandidier, the earlier source, although Brown's history is also usually respected. The Grandidiers (1910) also wrote nine extensive ethnographic volumes on Madagascar.

3. Malagasy (and I as well) were still sometimes baffled by the behavior of *vazaha* (White outsiders). For example, in 1993 the U.S. Peace Corps began sending volunteers to Madagascar, a country that has for some time been one of the world's most economically impoverished. But the Peace Corps arrived only after the fall of Malagasy president Ratsiraka's socialist "deuxième république." Ratsiraka had kept political and economic ties with what was then the Soviet Union, likely causing a rupture in the complicated web of U.S. foreign aid policy. Astonishingly, this first wave of Peace Corps volunteers was sent, not to address the crushing poverty, the alarming rate of environmental destruction, nor rampant disease—all prevalent in

Madagascar—but to train Malagasy elementary school teachers to teach the English language! This was most often a futile and frustrating mission, since almost none of these elementary school teachers themselves spoke English (personal communications from several of the Peace Corps volunteers). In Antananarivo the Peace Corps director, living behind barbed-wire security in blinding opulence yet surrounded by slums of dirt-poor Malagasy in rusting sheet metal huts, was hesitant to discuss Peace Corps priorities. These were obviously marked by some incomprehensible diplomatic agenda over the actual needs of Malagasy people.

4. Ratsiraka is supposedly half Betsimisaraka, half Merina. Although Ratsiraka has been accused of corruption and massive misappropriation of Madagascar's resources, he was recently reelected president of Madagascar, following the downfall of Zafy Albert's "troisième république."

Chapter 3 (pages 37–59)

1. *Tromba* ceremonies in the Betsimisaraka villages of the northern Tamatave region most often closely resembled Velomaro's Tamatave-ville practice in form and dénouement.

2. Of some relevance on Malagasy speech modes, Maurice Bloch (1975) has suggested that oratorical style among Merina in the central Haut Plateau region greatly constrains linguistic form and creativity (a view that has been contested; see Bauman and Briggs 1990: 62).

3. Most of the Malagasy whom I knew did not celebrate birthdays, so ages given were often approximate and even variable.

4. Michael Lambek has told me that *emboka* in the northwest of Madagascar is actually a resinous firlike cone (personal communication, 1999). It seems that semantic and other meanings do not necessarily hold universally throughout the various regions of Madagascar.

5. Interestingly, Michael Taussig has asked, "Is not this same electroshocked man mimicking mimicking?" (ibid.: 243). I should add here that Malagasy mediums with whom I worked generally were shyly amused to see themselves later through the videorecorder's lens.

6. Michael Lambek (1981) has written that, among Malagasy speakers of Mayotte (Comores), possession is thought to be *asa*, or work, and is contrasted with *soma*, or play. Gillian Feeley-Harnik (1991b) has stressed that possession among Sakalava is *sarotra*, or difficult. Among both Antandroy and Betsimisaraka in the Tamatave region, elements of *tromba* possession were also considered to be work or difficult, though *tromba-istes* there consistently emphasized the joyousness of *tromba*. As I've suggested, the particular signs, procedures, and significance of *tromba* practice could vary throughout the island.

7. A distinction in types of altered states might be in order here: trance often refers to a condition in which one's own spirit primarily becomes disjoined from its body; thus, one is no longer in this world or in control of one's actions, psyche, emotional state, etc. Possession usually means inhabitation by some other spirit, so some specific Other is in control of the body. The spirits of Malagasy mediums left their bodies, which were then taken over by ancestral spirits; while inhabited by *tromba*, mediums (the spirits that were inhabiting them) were usually quite coherent, interactive, and aware of their present surroundings. Thus, some qualifications inherent in "trance state" might be complicated in *tromba* possession.

8. I emphasize again that Antandroy customs, as practiced in Tamatave-ville, could be distinct in form and process from those practiced by Antandroy in their southern homeland of Ambovombe.

1. Among Cajuns in southwestern Louisiana (with whom I have also performed ethnographic fieldwork), conditions of material poverty have also been pervasive throughout the past. The term "gumbo," derived from cooking, is sometimes used to speak about other cultural practices (including music) in which varied ingredients are imbricated together in precise combinations to form meaningful and unique wholes. Among Cajuns, "bricolage" does not simply reflect histories of poverty—it can be aesthetically pleasing.

2. Jennifer Cole asserts that Betsimisaraka in Ambodiharina (in the southern Tamatave region) have "incorporated, and thus subordinated, the French colonial period to their own historical narrative" (1998:621). While I agree that "incorporation" is an integrative component in the creation of *maresaka,* Betsimisaraka with whom I worked in the northern Tamatave area did not necessarily see this as a mode of "subordination" of colonial things. I will take up issues of dominance, subordination, and resistance in chap. 7. Remarking on the absence of certain memories of colonialism among Betsimisaraka in Ambodiharina, Cole continues, "Their (Betsimisaraka's) successful incorporation of colonial events into local narratives in such a way as to foreground local experience partially explains the 'absence' of colonialism that initially confronted me" (ibid.).

3. The French term *métissage* is sometimes used on the east coast by Betsimisaraka, though not by Antandroy.

4. I have been hesitant simply to call this combinative rhythm hemiola, because it signifies and embodies distinct modes of history and power to different *tromba-istes.* This rhythm itself can stand for uniquely contexted significance that goes beyond the structural implications of hemiola.

5. For other views on tradition, identity, and musical practices in Africa, see also Alaja-Browne 1989, Barber 1987, Bemba 1984, Berliner 1981, Blacking 1986, Coplan 1985, Erlmann 1983, 1990, and 1991, Euba 1970 and 1973, Irvine and Sapir 1976, Koetting 1975, Kubik 1986 and 1988, Mapoma 1969, Merriam 1982, Nketia 1971, Ranger 1975, Rouget 1971, Sowande 1965, and Waterman 1990a. These offer varied interpretations of tradition as unfixed and adaptive.

6. Indeed, some Tamatave *tromba-istes* held Andriamarofaly to be such a child spirit, although an adult spirit with the same name can appear in other parts of the island.

7. I have written elsewhere about extrasemantic capacities of song texts, specifically among Cajuns in southwestern Louisiana (Emoff 1998).

8. Though often evoked, R. Murray Schafer's concept of soundscape (1977), the density of sounds that fill in an environment, might be useful here. Some other examples of soundscapes: Steve Feld (1991) has recorded and produced a soundscape of a Papua New Guinea rainforest; Kofi Agawu (1995) has recently used the concept of soundscape to discuss rhythms of societal interaction among Northern Ewe in Ghana.

9. The replicative nature of Malagasy musics itself is often viewed by Europeans in Madagascar as antithetical to their own ideals of proper musical form and practice. Thus, the common French evaluation that Malagasy music is *trop répétitive* or *pas assez intéressante.* These European evaluations overlook, of course, subtleties in timbre, rhythm, endurance, articulation, and improvisation, among many other qualities that make these musics spiritually effective and aesthetically pleasing to Malagasy.

10. On poetics, see, for example, de Certeau 1984, Clifford and Marcus 1986, Coplan 1994, Feld 1990, Herzfeld 1985, Hymes 1981, Jakobson 1960 and 1968, Kee-

nan 1973, Sherzer and Woodbury 1987, Stallybrass and White 1986, K. Stewart 1988 and 1996.

11. This title refers in part to the act of offering cattle to the *razana*. Antandroy in particular slaughter cattle upon the death of a family member in part as an enactment of transference from the world of the living into the spirit world. In another sense, these offerings bring the spirit world and the world of the living into another form of contact, since eating *aomby* (beef) is sometimes believed to nourish not only the living body but at the same moment the *razana* as well.

12. Antandroy small-duration phrase structures differ significantly in melodic, modal, rhythmic, and harmonic character from those of Betsimisaraka musical practice.

13. Anderson (1968: 19) writes on musical genres that evoke different histories in Uganda.

14. That *broken* wristwatches are occasionally worn throughout the east coast of Madagascar in towns and in rainforest villages signals, whether deliberately or not, an out-of-timeness, a Malagasy perception of temporality that extends beyond Western confines upon the organization of space and time. This is an idea played with in the title of a CD of Malagasy musics compiled by American musicians David Lindley and Henry Kaiser, *A World out of Time*. The notes that accompany this CD suggest that Madagascar is not only out of time, in the sense that it somehow operates beyond regular or conventional temporal bounds, but that it is also out of time to resolve its environmental and economic problems.

15. Recordings of musics from outside Madagascar generally were rare. Only a very limited body of recordings was circulated in Tamatave (Michael Jackson, Michael Bolton, etc.), through a pirate tape trade. There actually were copyright laws in Madagascar, though they were not enforced or policed. Pirate tape merchants sold their tapes in plain view at the *bazary be*, the large market in Tamatave-ville.

A small privately run radio station in Tamatave-ville called Radio Voanio (coconut) featured available "Western" pop musics. The recently formed local Tamatave branch of the Radio Nationale was striving to feature Malagasy popular artists, in part as reaction to the Western format of Radio Voanio.

16. Other performances at the Alliance Française almost exclusively featured early jazz standards performed by European musicians brought in by Dida. The body of jazz represented in these performances usually spanned the 1930s through the 1950s, perhaps the "height" of the colonial era?

17. Bourdieu has written, "The denial of lower, course, vulgar, venal, servile—in a word, natural—enjoyment, which constitutes the sacred sphere of culture, implies an affirmation of the superiority of those who can be satisfied with sublimated, refined, disinterested, gratuitous, distinguished pleasures forever close to the profane. That is why art and cultural consumption are predisposed, consciously and deliberately or not, to fulfill a social function of legitimating social differences" (1984: 7).

Kiki and I often remarked upon Dida's enthusiasm for French musics, especially from the colonial era. With this image of him in mind, we used to joke about the acoustic similarity yet semantic difference of the French phrases *c'est pareil, ses pareils,* and *séparé*.

18. It would perhaps be interesting to juxtapose Edith Piaf with Josephine Baker's "exotique" stage performances, which were also popular in France during the 1930s (along with Le Revue Nègre, one accompanying group with which she performed). These performances commonly touted Baker, barely clothed, as a somewhat tamed savage. Indeed, she was well known for performing a particular number entitled, "La danse de sauvage." Baker seems to have portrayed the exotic savage caged on and by a theater stage.

Yet, Josephine Baker was never simply a manipulable object of colonial desire. In an autobiographical book she recalled her own sense of control and power while performing:

> Whenever I was introduced to a playwright in Paris or Deauville, I asked, "With all your African colonies, why are there so few Negro actors on the French stage?" After a startled silence, my listener would smile and admit that it *was* curious . . . But no one offered me a part. After my film experience, I was anxious to perform before a flesh-and-blood public, to hear their laughter and provoke an occasional tear. I was possessed by the need to make an audience react. After a year and a half on the road, I wanted to conquer Paris. (Baker and Bouillon 1977: 95)

Josephine Baker was not merely the focus of colonial panoptic lust. She gazed back upon her audiences with her own desire for power, one that "possessed" her. And it is curious that she speaks of "flesh-and-blood public," as though it is the (French) public itself that is primal, visceral, exposed.

Edith Piaf, beginning to perform during the same period in which Josephine Baker was popular in Paris, often sang of loss, sometimes for a soldier who had departed for the colonies. *Outre-mer,* as represented by Piaf, was a place of loss, nostalgia, and even despair.

Chapter 5 (pages 89–104)

1. An actual evolutionary connection between *valiha* and instruments of similar form in Indonesia, as suggested by some early cultural diffusionists, has not been convincingly supported. Clearly, apparent similarities in instrumental form across great gaps do not necessarily correlate with similarities in uniquely contexted interpretations, meanings, uses, etc.

2. The Grandidiers recorded an observation dated 1632 made by traveler Augustin de Beaulieu, who described a bowed instrument he saw while in Madagascar (and which he referred to as a violin):

> 1 corde bandée avec une cheville par le dessus; la corde passait par (sur) une boîte de trois pouces de rondeur (de tour) couverte des deux côtés d'une peau bien tendue, et, sur celle-ci, un chevalet de demi pouce de hauteur qui soutenait la corde attachée à l'autre bout à une cheville, qui se tournait comme l'autre qui était au-dessus pour bander (raidir) ou relâcher la corde quand il plaisait au ménétrier, qui avait un archet en main duquel il la touchait par le milieu pendant qui'il remuait les doigts sur les touches du manche, qui était d'un très beau bois. La corde du violon était de mahaut at celle de l'archer d'une herbe que nous nommons 'pitte' (espèce d'aluès) et que ceux de cette île de Madagascar appelent 'ahitsa'; elle est blanche est ressemble au crin de cheval (1910: 81) .

> 1 string wound around a peg above; the string passed over a sound box three inches in width covered from side to side with a taut skin, and, over this, a bridge half an inch in height that sustained the string attached at the other end by a peg which turned like the one above to tighten or loosen the string when desired by the player, who had a bow in hand with which he touched the string in the middle while he shifted his fingers on the neck of the instrument, which was made from a very beautiful wood. The string of the violin was of mahaut and that of the bow was of a plant called 'pitte' (a type of aloe) which Malagasy call 'ahitsa'; it is white and resembles horsehair.

3. Ben Mandelson has included two tracks of Tombo Daniel's music on a 1986 recording on Globe Style Records entitled *Madagasikara I*. Although these recordings were made in a local disco frequented by sailors, tourists, and other *vazaha*, a venue in which Tombo Daniel would never be found, Mandelson writes in the liner notes that the tapes of this session represent "authentic field recordings." Certainly these recordings represent a distant and unfamiliar "field" of musical experience. This use of the term "authentic" intones an enthusiastic though misconceived notion that differs from Malagasy ideas of proper contextualization, etc.

4. One colonial era observer reported the use of European instruments and the playing of "La Marseillaise" in Merina territory prior to 1884 (Shaw 1896).

5. Jennifer Cole has written of southern Betsimisaraka, "Villagers accepted items that they considered to be quintessentially European. Incorporating them through rituals like house entering (*idiran trano*), which essentially required begging permission from ancestors, meant that rather than creating new dependence on the French, these commodities symbolically reaffirmed people's prior links to their ancestors (1998: 622). Cole is referring to Malagasy houses specifically constructed with *tôle* roofs, the same material from which Tombo Daniel's and other Betsimisaraka *valiha* were made.

6. In my experience, Merina used their bamboo *valiha* most often to perform for leisure or profit, usually not for ceremonial practice.

7. Average rainfall in the Tamatave region is regularly over 350 centimetres (889 inches) per year. On the coast itself the humidity is particularly corrosive. The temperature averages in the ninety-degree Fahrenheit range. Tamatave is in the Indian Ocean cyclone belt—in 1994, over twenty different cyclones of varying degrees were reported. The lesser of these consisted of a day or two of moderate wind and rain; the most severe, named "Geralda," after thirty-six hours of near-200-kilometre-per-hour winds, wiped out the east coast, destroying every structure but the most solid colonial ones and damaging even these.

8. I thank my friend Ralph White, a multitalented Austin, Texas, musician, for giving me this accordion years ago.

9. Some larger accordions have what is called a free bass system. On these accordions the left hand, rather than being restricted to just chording buttons, has access to a full range of pitches, as on the right-hand side. Thus, counterpoint between right and left hands is possible. The Russian Bayan, a large chromatic button accordion, is an example of such a free bass instrument.

10. For recorded examples of Very Soa and Magnampy Soa, listen to Emoff 2001.

Chapter 6 *(pages 105–120)*

1. Only elder *tromba-istes* in Tamatave actually experienced any of the colonial era. Many younger ones, though, recall the decade and a half just after independence in 1960 as a time of much French economic and political manipulation. *Tromba-istes* old enough to have lived through colonization might have different experiences and perceptions of *tromba* ceremony than younger ones who were born into a postcolonial state. Sentiments toward and select recall of colonialism (and its vestiges), however, are sometimes expressed by younger *tromba-istes*. There can be a shared consciousness in Tamatave of *having been* dominated. Mannoni (1990) discusses (albeit arguably in many places) a colonial mentality in Madagascar.

2. Feeley-Harnik (1991b) writes of the difficult effects of *tromba* upon Sakalava mediums as a defining tenet of this spirit practice.

3. There are several important works on memory that are useful and pertinent here, for example, Connerton 1989, Fentress and Wickham 1992 (includes some discussion of social memory in sub-Saharan Africa), Johnson, McLennan, Schwarz, and Sutton 1982, Wright 1988, and Yates 1978.

I am attempting in this writing not to subordinate *the experience of enacting* histories in *tromba* ceremony to specifically European models or perceptions of the mechanisms of memory.

4. It was not uncommon in some non-*tromba* circles, especially among wealthier Merina and some Betsimisaraka, to hear some anti-French sentiment voiced. I never heard such sentiment from *tromba-istes*.

5. Recall that east coast Malagasy commonly refer to the outside world as *ampitany,* "out there."

6. The behavior of American conservationists in the Tamatave region was often embarrassing (to me at least). They commonly reoccupied the most lavish colonial mansions; they freely and unreflexively rampaged through small towns in large 4×4 Land Rovers, etc. They also usually hired educated Merina from the capital to work for them in Tamatave rather than hiring local Betsimisaraka, a cause for resentment among some local people in Tamatave.

7. Both Velomaro and Sammy were quite old for Malagasy—the average life expectancy is closer to perhaps fifty years.

8. In Thomas Csordas's *Embodiment and Experience* (1994) it is suggested that "the interactive and relational aspects of emotion are, in fact, as etiologically crucial and constitutive as the psychological and cultural. The supra-individual and social-relational bases of emotion are unavoidable" (Lyon and Barbalet 1994: 62).

Chapter 7 *(pages 121–152)*

1. Zafy Albert, president of Madagascar's *troisième république* (he has since been deposed) was sometimes criticized for refusing to deal with the IMF and World Bank. He wanted in part to deter a particular wave of economic and political *re*-colonization of Madagascar by foreigners.

2. *Famadihana* ceremonies are performed primarily in the Haut Plateau region of Madagascar. The remains of deceased relatives are unearthed, rewrapped in new *lamba,* then reburied in the family tomb. Before the remains are placed in the tomb, the living participants spend the better part of a day embracing, addressing, and dancing with these enshrouded fragments of their deceased family members or friends. It is interesting to note that in Betsimisaraka *tromba* ceremony the spirit form as living medium is redressed, while in Merina *famadihana* it is the fragmented remains of the dead that are rewrapped.

Rakoto Frah, a Merina *sodina* (six-hole flute) performer, with his flute and drum ensemble, performed the music for this particular *famadihana*. Rakoto Frah's music is stylistically related to the large *hira gasy* performance troupes particularly popular in the Haut Plateau region. In the liner notes to David Lindley and Henry Kaiser's recent recordings in Antananarivo (Shanachie 64041—*A World Out of Time*), Rakoto Frah is compared to "John Coltrane, Ornette Coleman, Billy Pig or Miles Davis." These evaluations are interesting, perhaps inadvertently, in light of some of the connections between Malagasy musics and jazz proposed earlier here.

3. As a note, on colonial strategies for educating Africans, see Stoller 1995.

4. The following recordings made by Jaojoby are available in the United States and Europe: *Salegy!* Danbury CT: Xenophile CD 4040 (1996); *E Tiako.* Paris: Indigo Label Bleu CD LBLC 2533 (1997).

5. Prostitution in Tamatave-ville was not policed as a criminal activity, nor did it seem particularly frowned upon by Malagasy (except perhaps among Christians). It was often viewed simply as the Malagasy supply for a *vazaha* or wealthier Merina demand and thus as a means of obtaining difficult to find capital.

Paulla Ebron (1997) suggests that Gambian men who sexually entertain European women tourists see themselves as capitalizing on an opportunity rather than as acting immorally.

6. Betsimisaraka *tromba* did not place their borrowed bodies in physical contact with the instrument itself. Rather, it was the instrumentalist who would approach the medium, usually to induce possession or to compound the *maresaka* produced as spirit entered medium's body. Betsimisaraka *tromba* would commonly dance vigorously, evoking another musical embodiment of power. This heavy-footed, house-rattling dancing added to the visual, aural, and bodily felt dimensions of *maresaka*.

7. Other worlds of significance, such as fragmented Antandroy recollections of an Islamic past in the south of Madagascar informed these en-genderings. For instance, some Antandroy men in Tamatave-ville proclaimed that they would be permitted by Antandroy custom to take four wives (though I knew none who actually did so). I am not denying that certain en-gendered imbalances existed among Antandroy. I also knew a few younger Antandroy men and women in Tamatave-ville who had not yet married. I will more thoroughly take up the complexities of en-gendered practices among Antandroy and Betsimisaraka in future writings.

8. Famboara, Vinelo, Velontsoa, and other Antandroy told me, "Raha fa maty ilay olona kristiana, dia mivavaka 'zareo. Raha fa maty ilay Antandroy, dia mitsinjaka 'zahay" (When a Christian dies, the rest of them pray. When an Antandroy dies, we dance). In other words, among Antandroy, dancing is a mode of communicating to and with ancestral spirits, as Christian prayer is a mode of communicating with a single Spirit. Antandroy group dancing is also a matter of much vocal sounding, stomping, and general commotion, meant in part to be overheard by the lamenting family as reminder that their Antandroy friends, extended family, and *razana* are nearby. Neither the accordion nor the *valiha* (both associated with *fifaliagna*, or joyousness) is used at *fahavoazana,* a time predominantly of sorrow and loss for the immediate family.

9. Interestingly, a triple pulse was *not* called upon in instances, which arise only infrequently, in which an obstinate *tromba* was refusing to depart from the body.

10. For his more recent articles on Madagascar see Althabe 1983 and 1980. In another postcolonial account, the *tromba* medium was purported to

> vit une sorte d'esclavage atroce et bienheureux à la fois, dans la mésure où il ne tient pas compte du tout du principe de réalité. On observe en lui un sentiment d'abandon à un soi-distant fatalité, une faiblesse souvent lucide, des résolutions inutiles de libération. Un entraînement vers des actes extrêmes qui le conduisent au-delà de lui-même. Le *tromba* apparaît contagieux. Il exalte pour son entourage le prestige de l'arrachement à la misère quotidienne; il représente pour beaucoup le seul espoir de béatitude liée à la sortie de la prison intérieure. (Raseta-Ravelo Manatsoa 1964: 172)

Similar discourses from the colonial era itself are taken up in chap. 10.

11. I am reminded here of the film *The Shawshank Redemption,* in which an older long-term inmate in a Maine prison expresses the ease with which he has come to accept his own institutionalization and his fear of being on the unfamiliar outside that receiving parole instills in him.

In his book on *tromba* practice, Estrade, who conducted his research in Madagascar in the early 1970s, criticized Althabe "d'avoir fait une étude rapide, pêchant par excès de géneralisation et peut-être de systématisation" (1985: 19) (to have made a hasty study, with an excess of generalization and perhaps systematization). Estrade's criticism refers in part to Althabe's tendency to write as though he had uncovered the general essence of *tromba* practice throughout Madagascar, although Althabe's ethnographic experience had been limited to one small village in the Tamatave region.

12. On narrativizing the body in Northern Ireland, Allen Feldman has written: "In a colonized culture, secrecy is an assertion of identity and of symbolic capital. Pushed to the margins, subaltern groups construct their own margins as fragile insulations from the 'center.' Secrecy is the creation of centers in peripheries deprived of stable anchorages" (1991: 11). While I greatly admire Feldman's work, I might contend on more general grounds with the propriety, in Madagascar at least, of a center/margin orientation that extends spatial delimitations into ideologic ones. I would contend as well as with the idea that Betsimisaraka are actually deprived of stable anchorages—indeed, *tromba* practice has been one of these anchoring events in which Malagasy power ("symbolic" power one might argue) could find expression even under conditions of foreign domination.

13. During the colonial era, Rason (1933) noted as well a fondness among Malagasy for the "imitation et assimilation" of European musical forms.

14. Chambers's thoughts on opposition and resistance are elaborate and in particular are often focused upon written narrative and readings of it. I have fragmented and borrowed some useful concepts from Chambers's invaluable book rather than fully engaging with his theory of opposition in narrative.

15. Ranger does not distinguish between opposition and resistance in Chambers's terms.

Chapter 8 (pages 153–165)

1. Some Malagasy friends, vendors at the large market in Tamatave-ville, and I once made a very playful yet critical video of Europeans shopping at the market. We entitled this video, "Mahidy *vazaha!*," or "White People are Stingy." The video included much joking voiceover as we watched other *vazaha* shopping. The joke, of course, was also on me, since I am also a *vazaha*.

2. Toward the end of my stay, public rallies were being staged in Tamatave-ville to voice dissent against Ravony, who was still insistent on maintaining the monetary devaluations. Tombo Daniel and Roger, along with their families, were usually hired to perform at these rallies, likely in an attempt to instill some unified nationalist sentiment among Tamataviens. Such attempts at unification, though, did not seem to be too effective. People in Tamatave commonly expressed the sentiment that nationalist politics were too abstracted from and negligent of the immediacy of their own daily difficulties on the east coast.

3. However, Karana were purported by some other Malagasy to be involved in shady dealings to buy rice from villagers at very low prices.

4. Most of my Malagasy friends distinguished me as *vazaha tsara fagnahy*—in other words, an okay *vazaha*, one unlike, for instance, the common impressions of Americans taken from video house viewings. I was even sometimes referred to as *vazaha gasy*, or Malagasy white guy, which made me feel quite honored and which I believe evolved in part from my participation in *tromba* performance, my ability to speak Malagasy, and likely from the amount of time (nearly all of it) that I spent with Malagasy (rather than with the local *vazaha*).

5. Friedson is perhaps evoking Paul Gilroy's explication of a "double consciousness" (reworking W. E. B. DuBois's concept) expressed in *The Black Atlantic?*

6. While mediums themselves directly profess little current awareness of events outside Madagascar, some *tromba* are able to transcend temporal and spatial as well as communicative bounds to attain such awareness.

George Lakoff (1991) points to some linguistic metaphors deployed during the Gulf War, which in part masked Kuwait's actual stance in the Middle East, for instance, its representation as "victim" of Sadam Hussein's tyranny. Lakoff writes that, because of Kuwait's inequitable economic and social policies toward Iraqi and Saudi laborers brought there to work the oilfields, it was not perceived in that region as being victimized. Rather, Kuwait itself was viewed by many Iraqis as being the victimizer.

Chapter 9 (pages 166–178)

1. *Lakana* also refers to smaller dugout canoes used by Betsimisaraka.

2. Briefly, *dulugu ganalan* (lift-up-over-sounding) refers to a Kaluli performative style of aural, visual, choreographic, ecological, historical, spatial, spiritual, and interactional dimensions. Kaluli aesthetics draw upon sounds, motions, and experiences of their forest home. Performance among Kaluli iconically incorporates sights and sounds of the rainforest environment—birds (e.g., in ceremonial dress), bird songs, and waterfalls, for instance—in part to embody recollections of varied people and places. *Dulugu ganalan* involves communication to, with, and about voices of the forest.

3. I have suggested that, in comparison to Antandroy in Tamatave, Betsimisaraka are generally more conditioned to European methods of exchange. Signs of European influence in the practices of other Betsimisaraka, though, usually show up more incorporatively, not to the extremes expressed in Tsiariagna's individualism (for which many other Betsimisaraka marginalized him).

4. Keil goes on to say, "Style may or may not be said to exist in non-class societies, where one broad view of music making tends to prevail and everyone is an innovator within it; the culture is the style and all members are stylists" (1985: 122). Is Keil suggesting that individual stylization is largely class-dependent here, except perhaps as what he calls "participatory discrepancies," or performative inflection," "articulation," "creative tensions," "relaxed dynamisms," "semiconscious or unconscious slightly out of syncnesses" (1987)? In Betsimisaraka villages, which seemed to be "non-class" societies, there could be much variance in performative styles between villagers, who might be Christians, Muslims, or *tromba-istes*, among others, yet of the same "class" economically and socially.

5. Monetary issues were complicated and difficult in Madagascar. Certainly everyone was in dire need of things. Yet one cannot establish relationships of much integrity if they are based upon payments of money for each encounter with people. Play-for-pay sessions might only mean contrived performance settings. I was apprehensive that such sessions would likely impede the establishment of more personal relationships with Malagasy people—I didn't want to become known as some culture broker who would simply pay to obtain a good video or audio recording. My work also depended upon experiencing things as best I could as they usually occur in Madagascar (my own presence at most ceremonial events, of course, was quite unusual and unnatural).

Stories commonly circulated on the east coast of missionaries who had come to Madagascar doling out gifts as part of a ploy to lure people to Christianity. How to reconcile one's own colonial-like presence and demands made on local people, in the midst of their own great hardships, which one cannot alleviate?

6. Decary and Faublée went on: "la poésie populaire est une affaire moins de mémoire ou de tradition que de verve et d'improvisation" (ibid.).

7. In the 1970s, Jean Freddy had had several national hit recordings in Madagascar on the Kaiamba label, produced in Antananarivo by Discomad. Often the music

recorded and released by Kaiamba from this era became known as *tapany maintso* (half green), because the Kaiamba record label itself was half green. Many of these record releases on Kaiamba featured *salegy* music from the north.

8. I hope not to make condemnations of Tsiariagna and the choices he made here. I mean only to remark upon his uniqueness and how his behavior diverged from other Betsimisaraka.

9. Appadurai, on creating musical imitations, mentions the popularity of Kenny Rogers and the Lennon Sisters among Filipinos. Once I was riding through the Malagasy countryside in a taxi-*brousse* while a Kenny Rogers song was blaring through mid-range heavy speakers dangling by speaker wire from the back window of the truck's cab. Tapes of Rogers's music were astonishingly abundant in Madagascar though Malagasy musicians did not, to my knowledge, sing versions or copies of his songs. Here Rogers was singing about a gunfighter from outer space and an ensuing big gun battle showdown, all to a country instrumental background. Pressed into what back in the United States would have been considered a dangerous overload—of adults, children and infants, live fowl, thirty-kilogram sacks of rice, plastic satchels of necessities, and various parcels—it was evident to me that what Malagasy found likable about this song had nothing to do with its narrative content, for none of these Malagasy understood the English text (though ironically, Rogers was singing about an "out there," outer space, evocative to me of *ampitany,* the "out there" that much of the rest of the world represents to many Malagasy). Nor was this song's meaningfulness or feelingfulness among Malagasy connected to an association with an American working class (among whom Rogers's music is most popular in the United States) or even an association specifically with the United States. In fact, one passenger in this taxi-*brousse* remarked to me about the lyrics of Rogers's song, "Teny *vazaha* izegny!," which means literally "That's white outsider talk." This woman's observation referred nonspecifically to non-Malagasy talk, for *teny vazaha* could refer to French, English, or any other foreign language. Rather than as an evocation of a specific foreign world, this Kenny Rogers song was likable because it engendered and exuded *maresaka.* This very taxi-*brousse* event, with loud music playing, much talk occurring between passengers, the compacting of many and varied things and people into close contact, as at *tromba* spirit possession events, was itself *maresaka.* So Kenny Rogers's song was enjoyable in several ways for participants in this particular taxi-*brousse* ride—as contribution to the *maresaka* of the moment, as a medium for electronic amplification of *maresaka* through the Peugeot's radio/cassette player, and for the empowering difference, represented in part by the *teny vazaha* of this song, which could be incorporated into the feelingful experience of the moment among the passengers. Indeed, in *tromba* ceremony, ancestral spirits commonly speak in dialects or languages that other participants do not understand.

10. Hybrids have sometimes been thought of scientifically as the result of anomalous combinations. The term *hybrid* might convey other denigrative implications as well. For one, hybrids sometimes possess genetic frailties not possessed by either parent donor. Hybrid generations commonly are also reproductively sterile, incapable of reproducing themselves and thus replicable only through some external intervention and manipulation (see Young 1995 on hybridity, culture, and desire). And in general, being hybrid usually means standing out against a purer, more historically contiguous nonhybrid form.

Deborah Kapchan (1996) has focused on a *space* of hybridity among women at the marketplace in Morocco. She suggests that rather than attempting to categorize hybrid forms, focus should be shifted to "the *instrumentality* of hybrid genres— what do these inherently ambiguous and self-reflexive forms accomplish? And how are they generated?" (p. 6).

1. I have avoided an authoritative characterization or naming of spirits, partly because there is often potential for variability in characteristics of spirits with like names, especially between Antandroy or Betsimisaraka, but among either as well. I've wanted to emphasize the recollected (imagined, reconstructed, revalued, altered) nature of these spirits rather than to imply that each spirit is an exacting or universally felt reflection of a specific royal personage from the past. Royal Malagasy *tromba* can be differently recalled and interpreted, sometimes as composites.

2. While there were stories of poisonings, usually motivated by envy, I knew of no such cases. Antandroy commonly made protective *aoly* to be placed in the house of someone with a particular problem. Dominique, a young Betsimisaraka woman and friend in Fénérive-Est, had lost her job keeping books for Ko-fi-fen, a taxi-*brousse* line that ran daily excursions between Fénérive-Est and Tamatave-ville. Aware that Antandroy were often purported by other Malagasy to be the strongest and most skilled in spiritual matters and that I had connections with Antandroy healers in Tamatave-ville, Dominique asked me to help her. She was Christian, skeptical, and frightened of Antandroy prowess communicating with the *razana*, though she was desperate because her job had been the sole source of income for her large family. In Tamatave-ville, Famboara (Tompezolo's husband) determined with his *sikidy* divination seeds that Dominique's house contained harmful spirit forces brought in by *fagnafody ratsy*, implanted in the house by someone with a score to settle with Dominique. He then made a particular protective *aoly* to be placed in Dominique's house. Three days later, Dominique told me ecstatically that she had been offered an opportunity to join a small, though relatively lucrative cooperative business that transported bananas from the villages into Tamatave-ville for sale.

3. The family of Patrice, Honorine's husband, had wanted this type of ceremony. In spite of his family's religious preferences, Patrice was a vital assistant in Honorine's *tromba* ceremonies.

4. There are two separate churches in the Tamatave area that perform these exorcisms. One is the FLM (Fiangonana Loterana Malagasy, the Malagasy Lutheran Church); the other is called Jesosy Mamonjy (literally, Jesus Saves). Interestingly, the Jesosy Mamonjy church in Fénérive-Est had converted an Antaimoro man (Antaimoro are from the southeast of Madagascar), named Edmund Justin, who had previously been a *valiha* player for *tromba* ceremony. I recorded his repertoire of Christian hymns which he sang while accompanying himself on a Betsimisaraka *tôle valiha*. He shyly refused my request that he play a sample of his old *tromba* repertoire.

5. When asked about how he had become an exorcist, Sedy Roger told me that his wife had had a *tromba* tormenting her in her dreams, and he had wanted to help her. Sedy Roger said that he had developed his technique for driving away *tromba*, not through any instruction from a mentor but by improvising until he found a method that seemed to be consistently effective.

6. In passing, if I were to describe anything that I witnessed in Madagascar as demonic, it would be the physically and psychically assaultive exorcisms practiced upon this young, physically frail girl.

7. Estrade gives examples of dancing mania in 1958 in Vohemar in the north, in which the spirits of Malagasy soldiers who had died overseas fighting for the French army returned with the intent to overthrow the colonial government. Young men and women apparently became possessed by these spirits and began to dance publicly and wildly. Gendarmes were sent by the colonial government, but

purportedly they also began to dance. About eighty people were finally arrested. Estrade gives another account of dance mania in Masoala, in northern Betsimisaraka territory, in 1971 (1985: 48).

8. By this account, *ramanenjana* contrasts with *tromba* practices as I knew them on the east coast; as mentioned, spontaneous possession did not occur among the *tromba-istes* with whom I worked there.

9. Again, the story of the naming of *basesa*, also a dance mode, is exemplary. Europeans widely found Malagasy dancing to be abnormal or even repugnant.

10. One account suggests that in the Haut Plateau region during the latter half of the nineteenth century, Ranavalona had so persecuted her subjects with her anti-European edicts that they felt terrorized, to such an extent that they altogether lost the inspiration to perform music (Rason 1933: 59–60). Under Radama II musical performance supposedly began to flourish again, though as a new "musique métisse" heavily influenced by European musical principles (ibid.).

Chapter 11 (pages 192–199)

1. Witness the historical prevalence of gamelan or sitar ensembles in Western university music departments. While African drumming ensembles might be on the rise more recently, there is still an inherent bias here, that percussion dominates Africans' musical sensibilités. There are, of course, widespread African performance traditions on complex stringed instruments, accordions, lamellophones such as mbira, marimbas, and a host of varied wind instruments, to only begin to scratch the surface of musical diversity throughout Africa.

2. I use the term essentialism with some caution. In Omi and Winant's definition, essentialism is a "belief in real, true human essences, existing outside of and impervious to social and historical context" (1994: 181n.6). Although this might be splitting hairs, Malagasy beliefs are almost always on the *inside* of social intersubjectivity and historical contingence. Context, beyond a space and time frame, is as well something socially constructed, enacted, interactive.

As a note, Michael Jackson has suggested that "judging others gives a spurious moral legitimacy to an estrangement whose cause has neither been fully explored or accepted" (1998: 108).

3. Although he had set up my introductory meeting with Velontsoa, in my experience the only public musical (or other) interaction that Dida had with Antandroy musicians was a show he put on at the Alliance Française in Tamatave-ville billed Vinelo, Velontsoa, a young Betsimisaraka trap set drummer, and myself together. Dida wanted Vinelo and Velontsoa to perform on *valiha* and *kaiamba*, respectively, while the drummer and I (on an electric bass loaned by Dida) jammed along. The result was discoordinated and acoustically imbalanced. The Betsimisaraka drummer overpowered us all with what resulted in very antagonistic rhythms, for he did not understand Antandroy musical principles or performance practices.

Not clear on the reason for any of this, Vinelo, Velontsoa, and the drummer had still gone along good-naturedly. I knew that Dida had hoped to profit by drawing a paying crowd of local French and wealthier Merina, but only approximately fifteen people bought tickets and showed up for this collaborative performance.

4. There were, however, some Antandroy converts to Protestantism or Catholicism in Madagascar. The pastor of the Jesosy Mamonjy church in Fénérive-Est, who had converted Edmund Justin, the Antaimoro *tromba* musician, seemed very proud of this particular convert. It seemed that southern Malagasy—Antandroy, Antaimoro, Bara, as well as a few other groups—were perceived as particularly hard cases for conversion to Christianity; and if this transformation could be accom-

plished, it was not uncommon for these Malagasy to become exemplary or "prize" converts in the church.

5. There was not much familiarity with Zulu modes of musical expression in Tamatave, except perhaps as represented in Johnny Clegg's song *Asimbonanga,* which was infrequently played over the radio. Yet I wondered if Malagasy might not have imagined musical likenesses. The Antandroy *lokanga* and the Zulu mouth-bow for instance, both instruments played by drawing a bow across a string of some kind; also Zulu township music, played on violin and accordion.

6. I have witnessed numerous friends back in the United States, especially musicians, respond with awe upon listening to tapes of Antandroy musics, particularly the accordion playing of Magnampy Soa and Very Soa. One friend recently said that such accordion playing is so remarkably intricate and fast paced that it is "disturbing." This friend even reiterated several days later that he was still recollecting and feeling this intensity.

7. Interestingly, recall that some east coast Malagasy can feel disdain toward Merina based largely upon their supposed discursive power and prowess (chap. 1).

8. Rossy told me that he is Betsimisaraka (from Tamatave), though he moved long ago to Antananarivo. He had a modest recording studio in his home, provided by President Ratsiraka in the 1980s. Most commercial artists in Madagascar recorded in Rossy's studio, the only one there capable of producing professional-quality tapes. There was no CD production in Madagascar at that time; recordings were released only on cassette tape.

Poopy is from a wealthier Merina background. Tarika, a group of Merina musicians, some of whom had once been part of the group Tarika Sammy, are more popular outside Madagascar than within. They have recorded on Western labels such as Shanachie, and Hanitra Rasoanaivo, the group's leader, spends much of her time in London. Tarika in particular thrives on a performative amalgamation of varied musical styles from around the island.

A Tamatave branch of the RNM (Radio Nationale Malagasy) station was formed in mid-1994. Antandroy musics as they were performed in the streets and neighborhoods of Tamatave-ville were only then heard, though infrequently, over the local radio, as I either brought Antandroy friends into the studio to perform live on the air or as I occasionally broadcast my field recordings of Antandroy musicians living in Tamatave-ville (I would put together and broadcast a radio show or two a week when I was in Tamatave-ville).

9. Tsimihole, a university student in Antananarivo, was one Antandroy who had been able to profit to some degree from Antandroy musical practices. He had a popular band that performed Antandroy-like songs arranged with electric guitar, keyboard, bass, and trap set.

Glossary

∽

akoho	chicken
akoholahy	rooster
akondro	bananas
akordôgna	Betsimisaraka accordion
akory?	how?
ambanivolo	in the villages or countryside
ampìtany	"out there"—anyplace outside Madagascar
anao	you
Andriamagnitra	a name for the Malagasy supreme being
any	there
aody	Betsimisaraka curing amulet
aoly	Antandroy curing amulet
aoly aby	herbal mixture inside an *aoly*
arabe	paved road
aretina	illness
atsimo	south
aty	here
avaratra	north
avia!	come!
baolina	an organized dance (from the French *bal*)
basesa	Betsimisaraka music/dance genre
bazary	market
be	big
betsabetsa	alcoholic drink made from fermented sugarcane juice
bilo	often dangerous spirit among Antandroy
divay	wine
emboka	hardwood incense for *tromba* ceremony
fady	usually a spiritually ordained prohibition upon the living
fagnahy	spirit, soul, or personality
fahavoazana	Antandroy funerary ceremony
faliagna	joyousness
faly	happy
famadihana	Merina re-burial practice
fagnafody	medicine; remedy
fanompoana	royal service
feo	voice

fetsifetsy	sly, manipulative, deceptive
fiangonana	church
fifaliagna	a reciprocal or interactive action of making joyous
filoha	"chef" of a village
fomba	custom
fombandrazana	ancestral customs
foza	crab
gasy	Malagasy
gorodora	Antandroy accordion
havana	kin
hira	song
hira gasy	music/dance/oratory genre, largely in Haut Plateau area
hotely	small Malagasy restaurant
inona?	what?
itsika	us, we (inclusive)
izahay	us, we (exclusive)
izaho	I, me
izany	that
izay	that, which
jiaby	all or everyone
kabary	ritual or everyday form of oratory
kabôsy	stringed instrument
kaiamba	percussive shaker
kambana	twins
karana	Indian
kokolampy	often dangerous, disease-causing spirit among Antandroy
koronta	a fight (Antandroy)
labiera	beer
làlana	path, road
lalàna	law
lamba hoany	decorative cloth wrap worn by both men and women
lambo	pork, pig
lavitra	distant
lehilahy	man
lokanga	Antandroy (also Bara) three-stringed bowed instrument
mafy	hard
mahatavy resaka	produce "thick conversation"
mahay	competent, capable, possible
maloto	soiled, unclean
mandôlina	Antandroy stringed instrument similar to *kabôsy*
manontolo	Antandroy *maro tady* tuning
maresaka	multidimensioned music/sound/performative aesthetic
maro	many
maro tady	literally, "many strings"—Antandroy term for *valiha*
maro vany	see *maro tady*
masiaka	mean-spirited
matanjaka	strong
Menalamba	Red Shawl, Malagasy colonial resistance movement
mety	possible, acceptable
miady	to fight or quarrel
miantso	to call
midegana	Antandroy musical section for *maro tady*
midôla	to play

mikoragna	to speak or converse (Betsimisaraka)
milalao	to play
minegny	emotionally disturbed, crazy (Antandroy)
mira feo	Antandroy *maro tady* "mode"
miresadresaka	small talk
miresaka	to speak with
miresaka amindrazana	to converse with ancestral spirits
misôma	to dance or party
mitady	to search
mitovitovy	similar
mitovy	same
mitsangatsangana	to walk about, stroll
mitsinjaka	to dance (Antandroy)
mivavaka	to pray
mosika	music
mpamôsavy	one who is skilled in causing others harm
mpisikidy	one who practices *sikidy*
nanto	hardwood similar to rosewood
ndrimotra	Antandroy breath-song/chant
nofy	dream
olona	person
ombiasa	healer, seer, advisor, sometimes spirit medium as well
omby	zébu
osika	Betsimisaraka traditional songs
ramanenjana	mass possession phenomenon of nineteenth century
rano	water
rano magnitra	perfume
ranomasina	sea water, holy water
ratsy	bad
ravinala	leaf of the traveler's palm
razana	collective body of ancestral spirits
reraka	tired
resaka	talk, speech
salegy	music/dance genre from the Diégo region
sapay	pine (Antandroy)
sarotra	difficult
sikidy	divination system
silamo	Muslim
sinoy	Chinese
soa	good, well
taloha	the past
tànana	hand
tanàna	town, city
tandremo!	caution!
tanindrazana	ancestral homeland
tantara	story
tanty	sisal basket
tany	soil, land
tany malandy	white purifying mineral used in *tromba* ceremony
teny	speech or words
toaka gasy	alcoholic drink made from distilled sugarcane juice
tromba	ancestral spirit; spirit poessession ceremony
tsaboraha	sacrificial ceremony

tsara	good
tsikatrehana	Betsimisaraka *kaiamba*
tsodrano	benediction
tsy	a negation (example: *tsy mety, not* possible)
vakondrazana	traditional music or song
valiha	family of Malagasy stringed instruments
vangovango	Antandroy silver bracelet
vazaha	White outsider
viavy	woman
viavy makorely	prostitute
voafagne	*sikidy* seeds (Antandroy)
Zagnahary	another name for the Malagasy supreme being
zana-malata	"mulatto" child
zandry	younger brother or sister
'zareo	them
zoky	older brother or sister
zoma	Friday, or the large market in Antananarivo

References

〜

Documents from the Arisivim-Pirenena (National Archives) in Antananarivo

Archival Document D112, #5 n.d. "Tromba-bilo-salamanga: Les trois maladies." (Written by Mbazaha Samuel, "écrivain-interprète principal").

Archival Document H298 n.d. "Menabe-bilombara."

Aujas, L. 1905–6. "L'histoire des Betsimisaraka." *Bulletin de l'Academie Malgache* 4: 87–96. Tananarive: Imprimerie Officielle.

———. 1927. "Les rites du sacrifice à Madagascar." *Memoires de l'Academie Malgache*, fasc. 2. Tanananrive: Imprimerie Moderne de l'Emyrne.

Blot, Bernard. 1964. "Le tromba vu par un spécialiste." *Lumière*, no. 1483 (6 September): 5.

Cabannes, R. 1972. "Le plain de Tananarive." *Cahiers du Centre d'Etudes des Coutomes*, vol. 9.

Davidson, Andrew. 1889. "The Ramanenjana or Dancing Mania of Madagascar." *Antananarivo Annual* 4:19–27. Antananarivo: London Missionary Society Press.

Decary, Raymond. 1933. *L'androy (extrême sud de Madagascar), Histoire, civilisation, colonisation*, vol. 2. Paris: Société d'Éditions Géographiques, Maritimes, et Coloniales.

Decary, R., and J. Faublée. 1958. "Contribution au folklore des populations côtière." *Bulletin de l'Academie Malgache* 273–300. Tananarive: Imprimerie Officielle.

Fanony, Fulgence. 1975. *Fasina: Dynamisme social et recours à la tradition*. Antananarivo: Musée d'Art et d'Archéologie de l'Université de Madagascar.

Galliéni, J. S. 1896–1905. *Madagascar de 1896 à 1905: Annexes au rapport du Général Galliéni, Gouverneur Général, au Ministre des Colonies*. Tananarive: Imprimerie Officielle.

Gip, Yugen. 1913. "La legende du songomby et de kalanoro." *La tribune de Madagascar*, no. 577 (7 January): 1–2.

Grandidier, A., and G. Grandidier. 1910. *Collections des ouvrages ancien conçernant Madagascar*. Paris: Comité de Madagascar.

———. 1917. *Ethnographie de Madagascar*, vol. 4, no. 3. Paris: Imprimerie Nationale.

———. 1959. "Histoire des populations autres que les merina," in *Histoire physique, naturelle, et politique de Madagascar*, vol. 3, fasc. 1 of *Histoire politique et coloniale de Madagascar*. Tananarive: Imprimerie Officielle.

Monographie Provinciale de Tamatave 1958 Nos. 428, 439 (chap. 3), and 430.

"Ny 'manongay' na 'tromba' (any amin'ny Betsimisaraka)." 1928. *Ny gazetintsika*, no. 65 (30 September): 2. Andohalo, Antananarivo: Ecoles des Frères.

Pali, A. 1913. "Le psychisme à Madagascar." *La tribune de Madagascar*, no. 580 (17 January):2.

Rakotomalala, Mireille. 1986a. *Bibliographie critique d'interêt ethnomusicologique sur la musique malagasy*. Antananarivo: Musée d'Art et d'Archéologie de l'Université de Madagascar, travaux et documents xxiii.

———. 1986b. "Musique à Madagascar: son évolution selon les divers courants d'influence." *Bulletin de l'Academie Malgache* 64 (1–2):69–79. Tananarive: Imprimerie Officielle.

Randrianiraina, Anselme J. 1928. "Ny 'manongay' na 'tromba' (any amin'ny Betsimisaraka)" *Ny gazetintsika*, no. 66 (7 October):2. Andohalo, Antananarivo: Ecoles des Frères.

Raseta-Ravelo Manantsoa, Aimée. 1964. "Le tromba et la vie traditionelle des betsimisaraka." In *Civilisation Malgache, pp.* 167–79. Antananarivo: Faculté des Lettres et Sciences Humaines.

Rason, Marie-Robert. 1933. "Etude sur la musique malgache." *Revue de Madagascar*, no. 1:41–91. Tananarive: Imprimerie Officielle.

Razakandraina, Michel, 1962. "Le folkore musical malgache." *Bulletin de l'Academie Malgache* 40:70–74. Tananarive: Imprimerie Officielle.

Shaw, G. A. 1896. "Notes on the National Musical Instruments of the Malagasy (1881–1884)." *Antananarivo Annual*, vol. 2, no. 7. Tananarive: London Missionary Society.

Articles and Books Other Than from the Arisivim-Pirenena

Abu-Lughod, Lila. 1990. "The Romance of Resistance: Tracing Transformations of Power through Bedouin Women." *American Ethnologist* 17:41–55.

Agawu, Kofi. 1995. *African Rhythm* . Cambridge: Cambridge University Press.

Alaja-Browne, Afolabi. 1989, "A Diachronic Study of Change in Jùjú Music." *Popular Music* 8(3):231–42.

Alatas, S. H. 1977. *The Myth of the Lazy Native: A Study of the Image of the Malays, Filipinos, and Javanese from the Sixteenth to the Twentieth Century and Its Function in the Ideology of Colonial Capitalism*. London: Frank Cass.

Allen, Philip M. 1995. *Madagascar: Conflicts of Authority in the Great Island*. Boulder, Colo.: Westview Press.

Althabe, Gerard. 1969. *Oppression et libération dans l'imaginaire: Les communautés villageoises de la côte orientale de Madagascar*. Paris: Maspéro.

———. 1980 "Les Luttes sociales à Tananarive en 1972." *Cahiers d'Etudes Africaines* 20(4):407–47.

———. 1983. "L'Utilisation de dépendances du passé dans la résistance villageoise à la domination étatique." In *Les souverains de Madagascar: l'histoire royale et ses résurgences contemporaines,* edited by Françoise Raison-Jourde, pp. 427–48. Paris: Karthala.

Anderson, Lois Ann. 1968. "The Miko Modal System of Kiganda Xylophone Music." Unpublished Ph.D. diss., University of California, Los Angeles.

Appadurai, Arjun. 1996. *Modernity at Large*. Minneapolis: University of Minnesota Press.

Apter, Andrew. 1992. *Black Critics and Kings: The Hermeneutics of Power in Yoruba Society*. Chicago: University of Chicago Press.

Arens, W., and Ivan Karp, eds. 1989. *Creativity of Power*. Washington, D.C.: Smithsonian Institution Press.

Astuti, Rita. 1993. "Food for Pregnancy: Procreation, Marriage, and Images of Gender among the Vezo of Western Madagascar." *Social Anthropology: The Journal of the European Association of Social Anthropologists* 1(3):1–14.

———. 1995. *People of the Sea: Identity and Descent among the Vezo of Madagascar*. Cambridge: Cambridge University Press.

Baker, Josephine, and Jo Bouillon. 1977. *Josephine*. New York: Harper and Row.

Bakhtin, Mikhail. 1981. *The Dialogic Imagination*. Translated by Caryl Emerson and Michael Holquist. Austin: University of Texas Press.

Banks, Marcus. 1996. *Ethnicity: Anthropological Constructions*. London and New York: Routledge.

Barber, Karin. 1987. "Popular Arts in Africa." *African Studies Review* 30(3):1–78.

Barthes, Roland. 1957. *Mythologies*. New York: Hill and Wang.

Baudrillard, Jean. 1990. *Fatal Strategies*. New York: Semiotext(e).

Bauman, Richard. 1977. *Verbal Art as Performance*. Prospect Heights, Ill.: Waveland.

———. 1986. *Story, Performance, and Event*. New York: Cambridge University Press.

Bauman, Richard, and Charles Briggs. 1990. "Poetics and Performance as Critical Perspectives on Language and Social Life." *Annual Review of Anthropology* 19:59–88.

Bauman, Richard, and Joel Sherzer, eds. 1989 *Explorations in the Ethnography of Speaking*. New York: Cambridge University Press.

Béhague, Gerard, ed. 1984. *Performance Practice*. New York: Greenwood.

Bemba, Sylvain. 1984. *Cinquante ans de musique du Congo-Zaïre (1920–1970)*. Paris: Éditions Présence Africaine.

Benjamin, Walter. 1968. "The Task of the Translator." In *Illuminations*, pp. 69–82. New York: Schocken Books.

———. 1978 "On the Mimetic Faculty." In *Reflections*, pp. 333–36. New York: Schocken Books.

Berliner, Paul F. 1981. *The Soul of Mbira* . Berkeley: University of California Press.

Bhabha, Homi K. 1994. *The Location of Culture*. London and New York: Routledge.

Blacking, John. 1986. "Identifying Processes of Musical Change." *The World of Music* 28(1):3–12.

Bloch, Maurice. 1971. *Placing the Dead*. London: Seminar Press.

———, ed. 1975a. "Property and the End of Affinity." In *Marxist Analyses and Social Anthropology*, pp. 203–28. London: Malaby Press.

———, ed. 1975b. *Political Language and Oratory in Traditional Society*. New York: Academic.

———. 1977. "The Disconnection between Power and Rank as a Process: An Outline of the Development of Kingdoms in Central Madagascar." *European Journal of Sociology* 18(1):303–9.

Blum, Stephen. 1975. "Towards a Social History of Musicological Technique." *Ethnomusicology* 19(2):207–31.

———. 1992. "Analysis of Musical Style." In *Ethnomusicology: An Introduction*, ed. Helen Myers, ed., pp. 165–218. New York: W. W. Norton and Co.

Bourdieu, Pierre. 1977. *Outline of a Theory of Practice*. Cambridge: Cambridge University Press.

———. 1984. *Distinction: A Social Critique of the Judgment of Taste*. Cambridge, Mass.: Harvard University Press.

Bourguignon, Erika. 1976. *Possession*. San Francisco: Chandler and Sharp.

Briggs, Charles. 1988. *Competence in Performance: The Creativity of Tradition in Mexicano Verbal Art*. Philadelphia: University of Pennsylvania Press.

Brown, Mervyn. 1979. *Madagascar Rediscovered*. Hamden, Conn.: Archon Books.

Campbell, Gwen. 1988. "Slavery and Fanompoana: The Structure of Forced Labour in Imerina (Madagascar), 1790–1861." *The Journal of African History* 29(3):463–86.

Cannell, Fenella. 1999. *Power and Intimacy in the Christian Philippines*. Cambridge: Cambridge University Press.

Cantwell, Robert. 1993. *Ethnomimesis: Folklore and the Representation of Culture*. Chapel Hill: University of North Carolina Press.

Casey, Edward S. 1987. *Remembering*. Bloomington: University of Indiana Press.

Chambers, Ross. 1991. *Room for Maneuver: Reading (the) Oppositional (in) Narrative*. Chicago: University of Chicago Press.

Chernoff, John Miller. 1979. *African Rhythm and African Sensibility*. Chicago: University of Chicago Press.

Chittick, N. 1977. "The East Coast, Madagascar, and the Indian Ocean." In *The Cambridge History of Africa*, vol. 3 (from c1050 to c1600), pp. 183–231. Cambridge: Cambridge University Press.

Clifford, James. 1988. *The Predicament of Culture: Twentieth-Century Ethnography, Literature, and Art*. Cambridge, Mass.: Harvard University Press.

———. 1997. *Routes: Travel and Translation in the Late Twentieth Century*. Cambridge, Mass.: Harvard University Press.

Clifford, James, and George Marcus, eds. 1986. *Writing Culture: The Politics and Poetics of Ethnography*. Berkeley: University of California Press.

Cole, Jennifer. 1996. *The Necessity of Forgetting: Ancestral and Colonial Memories in East Madagascar*. Ph.D. diss., University of California, Berkeley.

———. 1998. "The Work of Memory in Madagascar." *American Ethnologist* 25(4):610–33.

Comaroff, Jean. 1985. *Body of Power, Spirit of Resistance*. Chicago: University of Chicago Press.

Comaroff, John, and Jean Comaroff. 1992. *Ethnography and the Historical Imagination*. Boulder, Colo.: Westview Press.

Connerton, Paul. 1989. *How Societies Remember*. Cambridge: Cambridge University Press.

Coplan, David B. 1985. *In Township Tonight!: South Africa's Black City Music and Theatre*. New York: Longman Inc.

———. 1994. *In the Time of Cannibals: The Word Music of South Africa's Basotho Migrants*. Chicago: University of Chicago Press.

Cosentino, Donald. 1982. *Defiant Maids and Stubborn Farmers: Tradition and Invention in Mende Story Performance*. Cambridge: Cambridge University Press.

Csordas, Thomas, ed. 1994a. *Embodiment and Experience: The Existential Ground of Culture and Self*. Cambridge: Cambridge University Press.

———. 1994b. *The Sacred Self*. Berkeley:University of California Press.

de Certeau, Michel. 1984. *The Practice of Every Day Life*. Berkeley: University of California Press.

———. 1986. *Heterologies: Discourse on the Other*. Minneapolis: University of Minnesota Press.

DesChamps, H. 1976. "Tradition and Change in Madagascar, 1790–1870." In *The Cambridge History of Africa*. vol. 4, pp. 393–417. Cambridge: Cambridge University Press.

de St. André, H. Pouget. 1886. *La colonisation de Madagascar sous Louis XV (d'après la correspondance inédite du Comte Maudave)*. Paris: Librairie Coloniale.

Dirks, Nicholas B. 1994. "Ritual and Resistance: Subversion as Social Fact." In *Culture/Power/History*, ed. Nicholas B. Dirks, Geoff Eley, and Sherry B. Ortner, pp. 483–503. Princeton, N.J.: Princeton University Press.

Dirks, Nicholas B., Geoff Eley, and Sherry B. Ortner. 1994. Introduction to *Culture/Power/History*. Princeton, N.J.: Princeton University Press.

Drewal, Margaret Thompson. 1992. *Yoruba Ritual: Performers, Play, Agency*. Bloomington: Indiana University Press.

Ebron, Paulla. 1997. "Traffic in Men." In *Gendered Encounters: Challenging Cultural Boundaries and Social Hierarchies in Africa*. ed. Maria Grosz-Ngate and Omari H. Kokole, pp. 223–44. New York: Routledge Press.

Edkvist, Ingela. 1997. *The Performance of Tradition: An Ethnography of Hira Gasy Popular Theater in Madagascar*. Stockholm: Uppsala University Press.

Eggert, Karl. 1981. "Who Are the Mahafaly? Cultural and Social Misidentifications in Southwestern Madagascar." *Omaly sy Anio*, nos. 13–14, pp. 149–73. Antananarivo: Université de Madagascar.

Ellis, Stephen. 1985. *The Rising of the Red Shawls: A Revolt in Madagascar, 1895–1899*. Cambridge: Cambridge University Press.

Emoff, Ron. 1996. "Musical Transformation and Constructions of History in the Tamatave Region of Madagascar." Ph.D. diss., University of Texas at Austin.

——. 1998. "A Cajun Poetics of Loss and Longing." *Ethnomusicology* 42(2):283–301.

——. 2001. *Accordions and Ancestral Spirits*. Sound recording, with booklet of notes and photographs (compact disc). Geneva: VDE Gallo

——. 2001. "Phantom Nostalgia and Recollecting (from) the Colonial Past in Madagascar." Unpublished manuscript.

Erlmann, Veit. 1983. "Marginal Men, Strangers and Wayfarers: Professional Musicians and Change among the Fulani of Diamaré (North Cameroon)." *Ethnomusicology* 27(1):186–226.

——. 1990. "Migration and Performance: Zulu Migrant Worker's *Isicathamiya* Performance in South Africa, 1890–1950." *Ethnomusicology* 34(2):199–220.

——. 1991. *African Stars: Studies in Black South African Performance*. Chicago: University of Chicago Press.

——. 1996. *Nightsong: Performance, Power, and Practice in South Africa*. Chicago: University of Chicago Press.

Esoavelomandroso, Manassé. 1978. "Réligion et politique: l'évangélisation du pays betsimisaraka à la fin du XIXiéme siécle." *Omaly sy Anio* 7–8:7–36. Antananarivo: Université de Madagascar.

Estrade, Jean–Marie. 1985. *Un culte de possession à Madagascar: Le tromba*. Paris: L'Harmattan.

Euba, Akin. 1970. "New Idioms of Music-Drama among the Yoruba: An Introductory Study." *Yearbook for the International Folk Music Council* 2:92–107.

——. 1973 "Evaluation and Propagation of African Traditional Music." *The World of Music* 15(3):34–51.

Fabian, Johannes. 1983. *Time and the Other: How Anthropology Makes Its Object*. New York: Columbia University Press.

——. 1990. *Power and Performance*. Madison: University of Wisconsin Press.

Fales, Cornelia. 1998. "Issues of Timbre: The *Inanga Chuchotée*. In *The Garland Encyclopedia of World Music: Vol. 1. Africa*, ed. Ruth Stone, pp. 164–207. New York and London: Garland Publishing.

Fanony, Fulgence. 1978. "Etudes de littérature orale betsimisaraka." Doctorat (III) d'Etat, Université de Paris.

Feeley-Harnik, Gillian. 1978. "Divine Kingship and the Meaning of History among the Sakalava of Madagascar." *Man* 13(3):402–17.

——. 1988. "Sakalava Dancing Battles: Representations of Conflict in Sakalava Royal Service." *Anthropos* 83(1/3): 65–85.

——. 1989. "Cloth and the Creation of Ancestors in Madagascar." In *Cloth and*

Human Experience, ed. Annette B. Weiner and Jane Schneider. Washington, D.C.: Smithsonian Institution Press.

———. 1991a. "Finding Memories in Madagascar." In *Images of Memory: On Remembering and Representation,* ed. Susanne Küchler and Walter Melion, pp. 121–40. Washington, D.C.: Smithsonian Institution Press.

———. 1991b. *A Green Estate: Restoring Independence in Madagascar.* Washington, D.C.: Smithsonian Institution Press.

Feld, Steven. 1988 "Aesthetics as Iconicity of Style, or 'Lift-Up-Over-Sounding': Getting into the Kaluli Groove." *Yearbook for Traditional Music* 20:74–113.

———. 1990. *Sound and Sentiment: Birds, Weeping, Poetics, and Song in Kaluli Expression,* 2nd ed. Philadelphia: University of Pennsylvania Press.

———. 1991. *Voices of the Rainforest.* Rykodisc (compact disc).

Feldman, Allen. 1991. *Formations of Violence: The Narrative of the Body and Political Terror in Northern Ireland.* Chicago: University of Chicago Press.

Fentress, James, and Chris Wickham. 1992. *Social Memory.* Oxford: Blackwell.

Fox, James J. 1977. "Roman Jakobson and the Comparative Study of Parallelism." In *Roman Jakobson: Echoes of His Scholarship,* ed. J. D. Armstrong and C. H. van Schoonweld, pp. 59–90. Lisse: Peter de Ridder.

Friedson, Steven M. 1996. *Dancing Prophets: Musical Experience in Tumbuka Healing.* Chicago: University of Chicago Press.

Giannattasio, Francesco. 1979 *L'Organetto: Uno strumento musicale contadino dell'era industriale.* Rome: Bulzoni Editore.

Gueunier, N. J. 1994. *Les chemins d'Islam à Madagascar.* Paris: Editions L'Harmattan.

Halbwachs, Maurice. 1939. "La mémoire collective chez les musiciens." *Revue philosophique de la France et de l'etranger* 127(3 & 4):136–65.

Handler, Richard, and Jocelyn Linnekin. 1984. "Tradition, Genuine or Spurious." *Journal of American Folklore* 97(385): 273–90.

Hanks, W. F. 1989. "Text and Textuality."*Annual Review of Anthropology* 18: 95–127.

Hannerz, Ulf. 1987 "The World in Creolisation." *Africa* 57(4):546–59.

———. 1992. *Cultural Complexity: Studies in the Social Organization of Meaning.* New York: Columbia University Press.

Hansen, Karen Tranberg. 1994. "Dealing with Used Clothing: *Salaula* and the Construction of Identity in Zambia's Third Republic." *Public Culture* 6(3):503–23.

Hebdige, Dick. 1979. *Subculture: The Meaning of Style.* London and New York: Routledge.

Herzfeld, Michael. 1985. *The Poetics of Manhood: Contest and Identity in a Cretan Mountain Village.* Princeton, N.J.: Princeton University Press.

———. 1987. *Anthropology through the Looking-Glass: Critical Ethnography in the Margins of Europe.* Cambridge: Cambridge University Press.

———. 1997. *Cultural Intimacy: Social Poetics in the Nation-State.* New York and London: Routledge.

Hymes, Dell H. 1981. *"In Vain I Tried To Tell You": Essays in Native American Ethnopoetics.* Philadelphia: University of Pennsylvania Press.

Irvine, Judith T., and David J. Sapir. 1976. "Musical Style and Social Change among the Kujamaat Diola." *Ethnomusicology* 20(1):67–86.

Jackson, Michael. 1998. Minima *Ethnographica.* Chicago: University of Chicago Press.

Jakobson, Roman. 1960. "Closing Statement: Linguistics and Poetics." In *Style in Language,* ed. T. E. Sebeok, pp. 350–77. Cambridge, Mass.: MIT Press.

———. 1968. "Poetry of Grammar and Grammar of Poetry." *Lingua* 21: 597–609.

Jameson, Frederic. 1988. "Postmodernism and Consumer Society." In *Postmodernism and Its Discontents*. ed. E. Ann Kaplan, pp. 13–29. London: Verso.

Jaojoby, Eusèbe. 1996. *Salegy!* Danbury, Conn.: Xenophile 4040 (compact disc).

———. 1997. *E Tiako*. Paris: Indigo Label Bleu LBLC 2533 (compact disc).

Johnson, Richard, Gregor McLennan, Bill Schwarz, and David Sutton, eds. 1982. *Making Histories: Studies in History-Writing and Politics*. London: Hutchinson and Co.

Kapferer, Bruce. 1986. "Performance and the Structuring of Meaning and Experience." In *The Anthropology of Experience,* ed. Victor Turner and Edward Bruner, pp. 188–203. Urbana: University of Illinois Press.

Keenan , Elinor O. 1973. "A Sliding Sense of Obligatoriness: The Polystructure of Malagasy Oratory." *Language and Society* 2(2):225–43.

———. 1974. "Norm-Makers, Norm-Breakers: Uses of Speech by Men and Women in a Malagasy Community." In *Explorations in the Ethnography of Speaking,* ed. Richard Bauman and Joel Sherzer, pp. 125–43. Cambridge: Cambridge University Press.

Keil, Charles. 1985. "People's Music Comparatively: Style and Stereotype, Class and Hegemony." *Dialectical Anthropology* 10:119–30.

———. 1987. "Participatory Discrepancies and the Power of Music." *Cultural Anthropology* 2(3):257–83.

Knauft, Bruce. 1998. "Creative Possessions: Spirit Mediumship and Millennial Economy among Gebusi of Papua New Guinea." In *Bodies and Persons: Comparative Perspectives from Africa and Melanesia,* ed. Michael Lambek and Andrew Strathern. Cambridge: Cambridge University Press.

Knight, Roderic C. 1973. *Mandinka Jaliya: Professional Musician of the Gambia.* Ph. .D. diss. University of California, Los Angeles.

Koerner, F. 1974. "Le front populaire et la question coloniale à Madagascar: l'année 1936." *Revue français d'histoire d'outre mer* (224):463–54.

Koetting, James T. 1975. "The Effects of Urbanization: The Music of the Kasena People of Ghana." *The World of Music* 17(4):23–35.

Kottak, Conrad Phillip. 1980. *The Past in the Present: History, Ecology, and Cultural Variation in Highland Madagascar.* Ann Arbor: University of Michigan Press.

Kubik, Gerhard. 1986. "Stability and Change in African Musical Traditions." *The World of Music* 28(1):44–68.

———. 1988. "Nsenga/Shona Harmonic Patterns and the San Heritage in Southern Africa." *Ethnomusicology* 32(2):39–76.

Lacan, Jacques. 1966. *Ecrits.* Paris: Seuil.

Lahady, Pascal. 1979. *Le culte betsimisaraka et son système symbolique.* Fianarantsoa, Madagascar: Library Ambozontany.

Lakoff, George. 1991. "Metaphor and War: The Metaphor System Used to Justify War in the Gulf." In *Engulfed in War: Just War and the Persian Gulf,* ed. Brien Hallet. Honolulu: University of Hawaii, Spark M. Matsunaga Institute for Peace.

Lambek, Michael. 1998 "The Sakalava Poiesis of History: Realizing the Past through Spirit Possession in Madagascar." *American Ethnologist* 25(2):106–27.

———. 1981. *Human Spirits: A Cultural Account of Trance in Mayotte.* Cambridge: Cambridge University Press.

Levinas, Emmanuel. 1986. "The Trace of the Other." In *Deconstruction in Context: Literature and Philosophy,* ed. M. C. Taylor. Chicago: University of Chicago Press.

Levi-Strauss, Claude. 1966. *The Savage Mind.* Chicago: University of Chicago Press.

Little, Henry W. 1970 (1884). *Madagascar: Its History and People.* Westport, Conn.: Negro Universities Press.

List, George. 1963. "The Boundaries of Speech and Song." *Ethnomusicology* 7(1):1–16.

Lomax, Alan. 1968. *Folk Song Style and Culture*. Washington, D.C.: American Society for the Advancement of Science.

Low, Setha. 1994. "Embodied Metaphors: Nerves as Lived Experience." *Embodiment and Experience: The Existential Ground of Culture and Self,* ed. Thomas Csordas, pp. 139–62 Cambridge: Cambridge University Press.

Lyon, M. L., and J. M. Barbalet. 1994. "Society's Body: Emotion and the 'Somatization' of Social Theory." In *Embodiment and Experience: The Existential Ground of Culture and Self,* ed. Thomas Csordas, pp. 48–66. Cambridge: Cambridge University Press.

Macerollo, Joseph. 1980. *Accordion Resource Manual*. Canada: Avondale Press.

Madagascar: Musique du sud (l'art du lokanga). 1984 Ocora Record OCR 558630. Notes and photographs by Xavier Bellinger.

Madagasikara One: Current Traditional Music of Madagascar—Various Artists. 1986 Globe Style Records ORBD 012.

Mangalaza, Eugène. 1992. "La Poule de Dieu: Essai d'anthropologie philosophique chez les Betsimisaraka (Madagascar)." Thèse du doctorat, Lyons.

Mannoni, O. 1990. *Prospero and Caliban: The Psychology of Colonization*. Ann Arbor: University of Michigan Press.

Mapoma, Isaiah Mwesa. 1969. "The Use of Folk Music among Some Bemba Church Congregations in Zambia." *Yearbook of the International Folk Music Council* 1: 72–88.

Marcus, George. 1998. *Ethnography through Thick and Thin*. Princeton, N.J.: Princeton University Press.

Marcus, George, and Michael M. J. Fischer. 1986. *Anthropology as Cultural Critique: An Experimental Moment in the Human Sciences*. Chicago: University of Chicago Press.

Maurer, Walter. 1983. *Accordion: Handbuch eines Instruments, seiner historischen Entwicklung un seiner Literatur.* Vienna: Edition Harmonia.

Mbembe, Achille. 1992. "The Banality of Power and the Aesthetics of Vulgarity in the Postcolony." *Public Culture* 4(2):1–30.

McLeod, Norma. 1964. "The Status of Musical Specialists in Madagascar." *Ethnomusicology* 8(3):278–89.

——. 1966. "Some Techniques of Analysis for Non-Western Music." Ph.D. diss., Northwestern University.

——. 1977. "Musical Instruments and History in Madagascar." In *Essays for a Humanist: An Offering to Klaus Wachsmann,* pp. 189–215. New York: The Townhouse Press.

McLeod Norma, and Marcia Herndon, eds. 1980. *The Ethnography of Musical Performance*. Norwood, Penna.: Norwood.

Merriam, Alan P. 1982 "Music Change in a Basongye Village." In *African Music in Perspective,* pp. 389–442. New York: Garland Press.

Meyer, Leonard. 1967. *Music, the Arts, and Ideas*. Chicago: University of Chicago Press.

Mirzoeff, Nicholas. 1995. *Bodyscape: Art, Modernity and the Ideal Figure*. London and New York: Routledge.

Mitchell, Tony. 1996. *Popular Music and Local Identity: Rock, Pop and Rap in Europe and Oceania*. London: Leicester University Press.

Musique Malgache. 1964 Ocora Record OCR 24. Notes by Charles Duvelle.

Nettl, Bruno. 1985. *The Western Impact on World Music*. New York: Schirmer Books.

Nketia, J. H. Kwabena. 1971. "History and Organization of Music in West Africa." In *Essays on Music and History in Africa,* ed. Klaus P. Wachsmann, pp. 3–25. Evanston, Ill.: Northwestern University Press.

Norborg, Ake. 1981 "Some Preliminary Notes on Malagasy Musical Styles." *Folk: Dansk Etnografisk Tiddsskrift* 23:81–90.

Omi, Michael, and Howard Winant. 1994. *Racial Formation in the United States.* London and New York: Routledge.

Ortner, Sherry. 1995. "Resistance and the Problem of Ethnographic Refusal." *Comparative Studies in Society and History* 37:173–93.

Piot, Charles. 1999 *Remotely Global: Village Modernity in West Africa.* Chicago: University of Chicago Press.

Possession et poèsie à Madagascar (sud-ouest): Vezo, Mahafaly, Masikoro-Mikea (Recorded 1967–1969) Ocora Record OCR 83. Notes and photographs by Bernard Koechlin.

Qureshi, Regula. 1987. "Musical Sound and Contextual Input: A Performance Model for Musical Analysis." *Ethnomusicology* 31(1):56–86.

Rabinow, Paul. 1989. *French Modern.* Cambridge, Mass.: MIT Press.

Rakotomalala, Mireille. 1998. "Performance in Madagascar." In *The Garland Encyclopedia of World Music Volume 1, Africa,* ed. Ruth Stone, pp. 781–92. New York and London: Garland Publishing.

Ranger, T. (Terence) O. 1975 *Dance and Society in Eastern Africa, 1890–1970: The Beni Ingoma.* Heinemann: London.

Roseman, Marina. 1991. *Healing Sounds from the Malaysian Rainforest: Temiar Music and Medicine.* Berkeley: University of California Press.

Rouch, Jean. 1954 *Les maîtres fous.* Contemporary Films (McGraw-Hill Films).

———. 1988 "Our Totemic Ancestors and Crazed Masters." *Senri Ethnological Studies* 24:225–38.

Rouget, Gilbert. 1971. "Court Songs and Traditional History in the Ancient Kingdoms of Porto–Novo and Abomey." In *Essays on Music and History in Africa,* ed. Klaus P. Wachsmann, pp. 27–64. Evanston, Ill.: Northwestern University Press.

———. 1980 *Music and Trance.* Chicago: University of Chicago Press.

Said, Edward W. 1994. *Culture and Imperialism.* New York: Vintage Books.

Schafer, R. Murray. 1977. *The Tuning of the World.* New York: Knopf.

Schieffelin, Edward L. 1985. "Performance and the Cultural Construction of Reality." *American Ethnologist* 12(4):707–24.

Scott, James C. 1985. *Weapons of the Weak: Everyday Forms of Peasant Resistance.* New Haven, Conn.: Yale University Press.

———. 1990. *Domination and the Arts of Resistance.* New Haven, Conn.: Yale University Press.

Sharp, Lesley. 1993. *The Possessed and the Dispossessed: Spirits, Identity, and Power in a Madagascar Migrant Town.* Berkeley: University of California Press.

Sherzer, Joel. 1987. "A Discourse-Centered Approach to Language and Culture." *American Anthropologist* 89(2):295–309.

Sherzer, Joel, and Anthony Woodbury, eds. 1987. *Native American Discourse: Poetics and Rhetoric.* Cambridge: Cambridge University Press.

Sontag, Susan. 1990 (1966). *Against Interpretation.* New York: Anchor Books.

Southall, Aidan. 1971. "Kinship, Descent, and Residence in Madagascar." *American Anthropologist* 73(1):144–64.

Sowande, Fela. 1965. "Language in African Music." *Music in Nigeria: Proceedings of the Second African Music Seminar* 1(2):4–36.

Stallybrass, Peter, and Allon White. 1986. *The Politics and Poetics of Transgression.* Ithaca, N.Y.: Cornell University Press.

Stewart, Kathleen. 1988. "Nostalgia A Polemic." *Cultural Anthropology* 3:227–41.

———. 1991. "On the Politics of Cultural Theory: A Case for "Contaminated Cultural Critique." *Social Research* 58(2):395–412.

———. 1996. *A Space on the Side of the Road: Cultural Poetics in an "Other" America*. Princeton, N.J.: Princeton University Press.

Stewart, Susan. 1991 "Notes on Distressed Genres." *Journal of American Folklore* 104(411):5–31.

Stoller, Paul. 1989. *The Taste of Ethnographic Things: The Senses in Anthropology*. Philadelphia: University of Pennsylvania Press.

———. 1995. *Embodying Colonial Memories: Spirit Possession, Power, and the Hauka in West Africa*. London and New York: Routledge.

Stone, Ruth M. 1982. *Let the Inside Be Sweet: The Interpretation of Music Event among the Kpelle of Liberia*. Bloomington: Indiana University Press.

Tarika. 1994. *Bibiango*. Green Linnet 4028 (compact disc).

Taussig, Michael. 1987 *Shamanism, Colonialism, and the Wild Man: A Study in Terror and Healing*. Chicago: University of Chicago Press.

———. 1989. "History as Commodity in Some Recent American (Anthropological) Literature." *Critique of Anthropology* 9(1):7–23.

———. 1992. "Culture of Terror—Space of Death: Roger Casement's Putumayo Report and the Explanation of Torture." In *Colonialism and Culture*, ed. Nicholas Dirks, pp. 135–73. Ann Arbor: University of Michigan Press.

———. 1992. *The Nervous System*. London and New York: Routledge.

———. 1993. *Mimesis and Alterity*. London and New York: Routledge.

Taylor, Mark C. 1987. *Alterity*. Chicago: University of Chicago Press.

———. 1993 *nOts*. Chicago: University of Chicago Press.

Thomas, Nicholas. 1991. *Entangled Objects: Exchange, Material Culture, and Colonialism in the Pacific*. Cambridge, Mass.: Harvard University Press.

———. 1994. *Colonialism's Culture: Anthropology, Travel and Government*. Princeton, N.J.: Princeton University Press.

Tronchon, Jacques. 1982. *L'insurrection malgache de 1947*. Fianarantsoa, Madagascar: Editions Ambozontany Fianarantsoa.

Tsing, Anna Lowenhaupt. 1993. *In the Realm of the Diamond Queen: Marginality in an Out-of-the-Way Place*. Princeton, N.J.: Princeton University Press.

Urban, Greg. 1991. *A Discourse-Centered Approach to Culture*. Austin: University of Texas Press.

Valiha Madagascar. 1964. Ocora Record OCR 18. Notes by Charles Duvelle.

Waterman, Christopher Alan. 1990 a *Jùjú: A Social History and Ethnography of an African Popular Music*. Chicago: University of Chicago Press.

———. 1990b. "'Our Tradition Is a Very Modern Tradition': Popular Music and the Construction of Pan-Yoruba Identity." *Ethnomusicology* 34(3):367–79.

Williams, Raymond. 1989. *Raymond Williams on Television*. New York: Routledge.

Wiora, Walter. 1965. *The Four Ages of Music*. New York: Norton.

Wright, Patrick. 1988. *On Living in an Older Country: The National Past in Contemporary Britain*. London: Verso.

Yates, Frances. 1966. *The Art of Memory*. Chicago: University of Chicago Press.

Young, Robert J. C. 1995. *Colonial Desire: Hybridity in Theory, Culture and Race*. London and New York: Routledge.

Index